Praise for *The Four Global Truths*

"In a brilliantly appropriate application of the Buddha's Four Noble Truths, Darrin Drda provides a conceptual structure for perceiving the unique challenges and opportunities of this planetary moment. He also shows us how to play with this structure, climbing around on it with uninhibited curiosity, and exploring ways to integrate the darkness and the light, the failures and the hopes that taunt and lure this evolving human animal. The book brings such a rich cargo of companionable inquiry and inspiration, I want to see it in every book bag and backpack. I love to think of the hands it will fall into, the minds it will ignite, the hearts it will embolden, so that this great adventure may continue!"

— Joanna Macy, PhD, author of *World As Lover, World As Self*

"With a warm and open writing style, and drawing from his extensive knowledge of Buddhism and the ecological state of the planet, Darrin Drda gives expression to some of the noble possibilities of human consciousness. *The Four Global Truths* is destined to become an essential part of the ongoing illumination of this wild, groping, confused, but ultimately beautiful human species."

— Brian Swimme, Professor of Cosmology, California Institute of Integral Studies

"Darrin Drda potently examines the challenging situation that humanity has created for itself at this time in history, a perspective that is greatly enriched by his accessible understanding of cosmology, ecology, philosophy, and cultural history. This book allows us to see that humanity's current condition is in fact, a larger-scale manifestation of the Buddha's Four Noble Truths—the Buddha knew that we are in a dream of attachment and that we need to wake up and free ourselves from this dream that is robbing us of our true capacity as human beings. Fortunately, the Buddha offered a path to liberation, one that is now possible for humanity as well. This magnificent book powerfully invites us to choose that path."

— Lynne Twist, author of *The Soul of Money: Reclaiming the Wealth of Our Inner Resources* and cofounder of The Pachamama Alliance

"Informed by leading-edge consciousness studies and new paradigm thinking, *The Four Global Truths* is a creative re-visioning of dharma for the planetary era. Packing the pages with fascinating details, Drda nevertheless keeps his eye (and heart) on the Big Picture. He helps us see the grand lines of our collective evolution, uncovering the path that has led to our troubled present, and illuminating a possible, but by no means certain, way forward."

— Sean Kelly, author of *Coming Home: The Birth and Transformation of the Planetary Era*

"In a style at once urgent, witty, and poignant, *The Four Global Truths* gives us a fresh, insightful, and nuanced polemic on global turmoil and its transformation. Darrin Drda has done us a great service by bringing together the best in consciousness studies and fresh perspectives on ancient Buddhist insights. This is a treasure mine of information and resources for changing the status quo."

— Steven Goodman, Professor of Asian and Comparative Studies, California Institute of Integral Studies

"*The Four Global Truths* is a unique take on the central questions that face humanity at this moment. Fusing ancient Buddhist teaching and contemporary ecology, Drda uses the Buddha's Four Noble Truths as a model for addressing the crisis of modernity.

"Working from the assumption that the solution to myriad problems, particularly the ecological crisis, requires a new worldview, Drda uses Buddhist teaching to work toward a new way of relating to the world. The genius of his work is that he takes teachings largely understood in terms of individual process and applies them to the entire planet. Drda's creative process is revelatory: the solution is found in the integration of the personal and the global, the removal of barriers between our isolated, individualistic selves and the planet as a whole.

"Perhaps most impressive is Drda's ability to discuss extraordinarily complex subject matter in an accessible, clear, and inviting tone. Whether one is interested in learning a modern take on Buddhist practice or addressing some of the world's most severe crises, *The Four Global Truths* is highly recommended."

— Theodore Richards, founder of the Chicago Wisdom Project and author of *Cosmosophia: Cosmology, Mysticism, and the Birth of a New Myth*

THE FOUR GLOBAL TRUTHS

*Awakening to the **Peril** and **Promise** of Our Times*

Darrin Drda

Berkeley, California

Published by Evolver Editions

Evolver Editions' publications are distributed by
North Atlantic Books
P.O. Box 12327
Berkeley, California 94712

Art direction, cover design, and cover illustration by michaelrobinsonnyc.com
Interior design by Brad Greene
Printed in the United States of America on 100% post-consumer-waste paper

The Four Global Truths: Awakening to the Peril and Promise of Our Times is sponsored by the Society for the Study of Native Arts and Sciences, a nonprofit educational corporation whose goals are to develop an educational and cross-cultural perspective linking various scientific, social, and artistic fields; to nurture a holistic view of arts, sciences, humanities, and healing; and to publish and distribute literature on the relationship of mind, body, and nature.

North Atlantic Books' publications are available through most bookstores. For further information, visit our website at www.northatlanticbooks.com or call 800-733-3000.

Library of Congress Cataloging-in-Publication Data

Drda, Darrin, 1968–
    The four global truths ; awakening to the peril and promise of our times / Darrin Drda.
        p. cm.
    Includes bibliographical references and index.
    ISBN 978-1-58394-321-2
    1. Human ecology—Religious aspects—Buddhism. I. Title.
    BQ4570.E23D74 2011
    294.3'377—dc22

                                                                2011012829

1 2 3 4 5 6 7 8 9 UNITED 16 15 14 13 12 11

For my mother and family

CONTENTS

TWO
THE ROOTS OF GLOBAL SUFFERING . . . 65

Four Global Truths Word Cloud (from www.wordle.net)

IMAGES AND ILLUSTRATIONS

Page 57: Ten Leading Causes of Death. Table by author, data from World Health Organization.

Page 63: Flammarion Engraving. Artist unknown. Wikimedia Commons (Public Domain).

Page 71: The Great Chain of Being and Great Nest of Being. Images by author.

Page 73: The World Card, Rider-Waite. Image from www.tarotexperts.com.

Page 76: Cosmic Calendar. Image by author, info. from http://en.wikipedia.org/wiki/Cosmic_Calendar.

Page 80: Ken Wilber's AQAL Model. Image by author, data from Wilber's *Integral Psychology* (see Sources).

Page 83: Gebser's Structures of Consciousness, Two Depictions. Image by author.

Page 85: Structures of Consciousness Chart. Image by author, information from Gebser's *The Ever-Present Origin* (see Sources).

Page 85: Symbol of Mars. Image by author.

Page 91: Statue of Pallas Athena. By Antiochos (copy of Phidias). Wikimedia Commons (Public Domain).

Page 92: Tai Chi (Yin-Yang) Symbol. Image by author.

Page 97: Plato and Aristotle. Painting by Raphael. Wikimedia Commons (Public Domain).

Page 100: Constantine's Conversion. Painting by Raphael. Wikimedia Commons (Public Domain).

Page 104: Renaissance Perspective. Painting by Leonardo da Vinci. Wikimedia commons (Public Domain).

Page 109: Ptolemaic Model of the Universe. Image by author.

Page 110: Copernicus, Galileo, Kepler, and Newton. Paintings from Wikimedia Commons (Public Domain).

Page 113: Descartes. Painting by Frans Hals. Wikimedia Commons (Public Domain).

Page 120: Locke, Berkeley, Hume, Kant. Paintings from Wikimedia Commons (Public Domain).

Page 123: De Gouges, Wollstonecraft, Shelley. Paintings from Wikimedia Commons (Public Domain).

Page 125: Einstein and the Curvature of Spacetime. Wikimedia Commons (PD); second image by author.

Page 127: Nietzsche, Heidegger, Kirkegaard. Images from Wikimedia Commons (Public Domain).

Page 132: Top Ten Wealthiest Corporations. Table by author, info. from http://money.cnn.com/magazines/fortune/global500/2009/index.html.

Page 133: Top Ten Defense Contractors. Table by author, info. from http://news.bbc.co.uk/2/hi/business/8086117.stm.

Page 135: The Three Poisons. First Image from http://www.thubtenchodron.org; second image by author.

Page 153: Current Eschatons. Table by author, based on lecture by Sean Kelly.

Page 155: The Great Turning: Three Arenas of Change. Image by author, based on lecture by Joanna Macy.

Page 160: Stan Grof's Model of the Psyche. Image by author, based on a lecture by Stan Grof.

Page 175: The Expansion of the Universe. Image by author.

Page 177: Eating an Apple in Eden. Painting by Lucas Cranach the Elder. Wikimedia Commons (Public Domain).

Page 187: Rooftop Garden. Image by sookie. Wikimedia Commons (Creative Commons License).

Page 208: Wheel of Dharma. Image by author.

Page 212: Gandhi, Tenzin Gyatso, Martin Luther King, Jr. Wikimedia commons (Public Domain).

Page 215: The Chakras. Wikimedia Commons (Public Domain).

Page 229: The Four Immeasurables. Chart by author.

Page 237: Symbol of Jainism. Wikimedia Commons (Public Domain).

Page 239: Battery Chickens. Wikimedia Commons (Public Domain).

Page 247: The Twelve Signs and Ten Planets. Image by author.

Page 248: Major Astrological Aspects. Table by author, based on a lecture by Richard Tarnas.

Page 251: Current and Upcoming World Transits. Table by author, info. from *Cosmos and Psyche* by Richard Tarnas (see Sources).

Page 252: Mayan Divisions of Time. Info. from http://en.wikipedia.org/wiki/Maya_calendar.

Page 254: Dark Rift in the Milky Way. Wikimedia Commons (Public Domain).

Page 257: Joan of Arc. Painting by Eugene Thirion. Wikimedia Commons (Public Domain).

Page 260: Psyche and Cupid. Painting by Anthony Van Dyck. Wikimedia Commons (Public Domain).

Page 268: The Wheel of Existence. Image from www.thubtenchodron.org.

Page 271: Vajra. Wikimedia, under GNU Free Documentation License.

Page 275: Ouroboros. Image from Wikimedia Commons (Public Domain).

Page 278: Spiral. Image by author.

Page 283: The 72 Names of God. Diagram by Athanasius Kircher. Wikimedia Commons (Public Domain).

PREFACE

Buddhism has the characteristics of what would be expected in a cosmic religion for the future: It transcends a personal God, avoids dogmas and theology; it covers both the natural and the spiritual, and it is based on a religious sense aspiring from the experience of all things, natural and spiritual, as a meaningful unity.

As a longtime practitioner and occasional instructor of meditation, I am inclined to agree with the above quotation, questionably attributed to Albert Einstein. I hasten to say, however, that while this book derives its structure and draws its inspiration from Buddhist philosophy, its orientation is by no means strictly Buddhist, nor traditionally religious. It is intended for a general audience, albeit one that might well identify as "spiritual." Seemingly, more and more people are coming to appreciate the richness and fluidity of that word, to the degree that it is frequently used as a welcome alternative to "religious." In fact, an increasing emphasis on a broad and inclusive spirituality over both religious and secular dogmatism could be seen as a defining characteristic of our times, one that I believe offers great hope for a brighter and more peaceful future.

Those readers who do identify as Buddhist will certainly encounter familiar themes, as well as notable departures from the usual offerings of those venerable Eastern traditions, as certain chapters contain

a fair amount of Western philosophy, psychology, and cosmology.*
Ideally, the ideas presented in this book will resonate with many readers, regardless of their previous exposure to either Buddhist or Western philosophy. My aim is not to bedazzle with esoteric concepts or
impress with scholastic rigor, but to put forth as straightforwardly as
possible a set of ideas that I hope will contribute in some way to the
healing of our ailing world and to the repairing of the psychological
rifts felt within each of us as modern humans.

More than anything this book is an offering of the heart, and
my sincere wish is that it will be read and accepted as such. While
I do make an attempt to present the outline of an emerging worldview, the vitality and promise of this philosophical framework lie
in its receptivity to diverse perspectives and modes of perception
that include the imaginative, intuitive, and emotional aspects of the
psyche—a word once used to refer not to the mind but to the soul.
More to the point, I recognize that what is deeply desired in our
world more than a new set of beliefs is a profound reconnection to
the beauty and preciousness of life, to the sacredness of the Cosmos,
and to the sublime mystery of existence—an awakening that can
only be described as spiritual.

Buddhism speaks of the necessity of both wisdom and compassion
in the process of spiritual transformation. These are conceived of as
two wings of a bird, both of which are clearly essential to flight. In
a similar spirit, Einstein once opined that science without religion is
lame, while religion without science is blind. Thus however heady

---

*Cosmology is an account of the origin, structure and/or dynamics of the universe, or
better yet the cosmos, understood by the ancient Greeks as possessing not only order
(the meaning of the Greek word *kosmos*) but an intelligent, spiritual essence. In the hope
of reviving this original spirit, I capitalize the word "Cosmos" throughout the book
and, for similar reasons, the word "Nature" (unless referring to an inherent quality).

this book may be in its approach, the food for thought that it offers is intended to be nourishing to the heart and spirit as well. Significantly, in Buddhist thought, the heart and mind are not conceived of as separate entities; both are designated by the word *citta*, with spiritual practice geared towards developing *bodhicitta*—the wise, compassionate, and spacious heart-mind of the Buddha.

In discussing and advocating a worldview that is more inclusive, holistic, and indeed more spiritual, it might at first seem incongruous to use the emphatic-sounding (and decidedly un-postmodern) term "global truths." As will be elucidated, this is a variation on the title of the Buddha's first sermon, usually translated as "The Four Noble Truths." Although perhaps more palatable in its plural form, the noun in question lacks the subtle flavor of the Sanskrit word *satya*, which can mean not only truthful but honest, beneficial, or effectual. At heart, the Buddha was a pragmatist, more concerned with alleviating suffering than making heavy-handed assertions about the nature of reality, which tend instead to strengthen attachment and anxiety. Likewise, my intention is to present ideas—not proclamations—that I hope might be of some value to the Earth community. As Buddhist teachers often say: Please take what is useful and set the rest aside.

Along with heartfelt wishes for global transformation and healing, I would like to express my gratitude to those who have provided me with guidance, support, encouragement, and inspiration in this ongoing process of growth and discovery: my teachers, family, and friends, including spiritual allies and kindred spirits. In particular I would like to acknowledge my former professors and peers at the California Institute of Integral Studies, especially those in the Philosophy, Cosmology, and Consciousness department—brilliant beings who with their curious minds and open hearts embody the kind of balance and integration so dearly needed in the world during this unique moment in history. Special thanks go to those who have contributed their wisdom to this book, namely Sean Kelly, Joanna Macy, Daniel Pinchbeck, and Brian Swimme. Finally, love and gratitude go to my wife Annabelle for her steadfast support and patience.

INTRODUCTION

Before I flew I was already aware of how small and vulnerable our planet is; but only when I saw it from space, in all its ineffable beauty and fragility, did I realize that humankind's most urgent task is to cherish and preserve it for future generations.

— German astronaut Sigmund Jähn[1]

A NOVEL PERSPECTIVE

On the winter solstice of December 21, 1968, NASA launched *Apollo 8*, the first manned voyage to another celestial body. This successful mission marked the first time in history that any human being had escaped from the Earth's gravitational field to orbit the Moon. As crew members Borman, Lovell, and Anders ventured beyond the stratosphere into space, they were treated to a spectacle that no earthly eyes had ever beheld: their home planet in all its spherical glory, wrapped in wisps of white, glowing deep blue, olive green, and rusty yellow against a backdrop of infinite black space and twinkling stars.

During the ninth of ten lunar orbits, the *Apollo 8* crew made a short Christmas Eve television broadcast—the most widely watched program ever—during which they took turns reading from the Book of Genesis. It was a major symbolic milestone marking the beginning of the global ecology movement, as the first Earth Day would dawn two years later.

Although the photos taken during the *Apollo 8* space flight were not the first images of our globe in its entirety, they were, significantly, the first ones taken by humans. The most iconic of these, shot as the astronauts first rounded the dark side of the Moon, shows the Earth appearing to rise majestically above the cold, gray, and lifeless lunar surface. From this unique and far-out perspective, our planet appears particularly vibrant, disarmingly small, and heartbreakingly precious.

Shimmering like a pearl in the vast silence of space, with no political boundaries, the Earth seems like an immeasurably peaceful oasis. It would have been easy for the *Apollo 8* astronauts to forget about the trouble stirring back home on the beautiful blue orb, particularly in their own country. It had been a dramatic year, marked by the assassinations of Dr. Martin Luther King, Jr., and Robert F. Kennedy, the violent clashes between police and Vietnam War protestors at the Democratic National Convention in Chicago, and the subsequent election of Richard Nixon. It was also the year that Stanley Kubrick released *2001: A Space Odyssey*, bringing millions of starry-eyed viewers back to their simian roots and introducing them to a convincing future of international space stations, interplanetary travel, extraterrestrial life, and artificial intelligence.

This author was born during that same definitive year, almost exactly one solar cycle before Neil Armstrong took his infamous "giant leap" onto the surface of the Moon and planted an American flag in the dust, asserting with colonial fervor that the U.S. had won the decade-long space race against the Russians. That year, 1969, also saw the birth of the Internet, originally a Cold War government project called ARPANET that connected four western American universities. It would grow substantially in subsequent years and explosively over the following decades.

Growing up global, I watched "The Big Blue Marble," "Animals, Animals, Animals," and other '70s children's shows that fostered an appreciation for other cultures, other species, and for the Earth itself. "Sesame Street" was a funky neighborhood in which folks of different ethnicities and ages chatted cheerfully with gigantic feathered friends and green grouches on the sidewalk of life, and Mister Rogers seemed to genuinely love everyone, including the quirky inhabitants of the Land of Make-Believe.

In the decades since the *Apollo 8* mission, images of the Earth have become all too common. We see them every day, plastered across buses and billboards, emblazoned on shopping bags, cereal boxes, candy wrappers, and toilet paper packages. Merrily our colorful planet dances and spins across television and computer screens, foreshadowing the latest morsel of international news or hawking environmentally friendly footwear. In our current era of eco-this and terra-that, it is all too easy to forget that our planetary worldview is a startlingly recent development; that our global perspective is unique in all of human history.

Most of us alive today take for granted the fact that we can complete in a few hours a journey that only generations ago took weeks or months. We can chat with a friend in Timbuktu whenever the mood strikes (usually on weekends or evenings after 9 p.m.) and learn about events occurring on the other side of the globe in virtually the same instant that they transpire. While our worldview continues to expand, our world keeps getting smaller; continents shrink and countries begin to disappear. Space contracts and time becomes measured in nanoseconds. Ours is an age in which information circles the globe at the speed of light and knowledge arrives from another hemisphere via next-day delivery. Wisdom, alas, seems to be lagging far behind. Although we are all on the way to full global citizenship, humanity is still waiting for its green card.

THE WEB THAT BINDS

Perhaps as much as images of Earth, the "worldwide web" has come to symbolize our emergent global awareness. With Internet connectivity comes instant access to mountains of information on virtually any subject imaginable, whether practical, sublime, trivial, or lurid. In a very real sense, the Web represents the entire database of human knowledge and culture from prehistory to the present, a vast repository that makes the ancient library of Alexandria seem like a dusty elementary school bookshelf by comparison. As a storehouse of our collective knowledge, the Internet grows as our knowledge grows, reaching into every last nook and cranny of the planet, every last sunlit meadow and dark crevasse of the human psyche. Indeed the Internet has been not only compared to but equated with a vast global mind, a layer of collective consciousness that the early twentieth-century French philosopher Pierre Teilhard de Chardin called the *noosphere* (NO-us-fear, from the Greek *nous*, meaning "mind").

While representing our nascent global awareness, the Internet also symbolizes our collective dilemma, one unique to this period in history but familiar to those who, like Teilhard de Chardin, are concerned with the process of human progress, in which a gain in one area often brings about a loss in another. The optimists among us are inclined to see the Web as an exciting and empowering development, a giant leap forward in human evolution that keeps us all more informed and interconnected, perhaps even makes us more cultured and intelligent. After all, we have at our fingertips a host of remarkably powerful and mercurial search engines, flashing lightning-like along the axons of the global brain to retrieve the knowledge stored in our vast and growing Wikipedian memory. We have Google Earth to show us increasingly detailed and up-to-date maps of every square foot of our planet, a virtual world in which we can hover above the Nile delta or fly Peter Pan-like down the streets of our town, perchance to catch a glimpse of ourselves through our own bedroom window. Through MoveOn, Avaaz, TrueMajority, and similar online initiatives, we can gather our political forces and rally for change on the virtual public square, often quickly and effectively. And we each have our community of acquaintances on Facebook, Twitter, and MySpace; our romantic prospects on eHarmony and Match.com; and our use-group and chat room associates throughout the world, all of whom are surely waiting for us to post another blog entry or forward a link to that sensational new YouTube video.

One must concede that in some ways we are more interconnected than ever as a human community. But in what ways have we sacrificed quality for quantity? How many of our online acquaintances even know the sound of our voice or our laughter, or the warmth of our embrace? And what about our connection to the non-human world, to other forms of life, to Nature, the Cosmos, and the Divine? As we marvel Google-eyed at the virtual Earth, how many of us are connected enough to the tangible world to identify more than a few varieties of flowers, species of birds, or constellations in the night sky, if indeed we can even see the stars through the light pollution hovering overhead? As we become increasingly connected to the Web, it seems that we are becoming ever more disconnected from the web of life.

In discussions of the Internet, one inevitably comes across the symbolic image of the "net of Indra," warrior king of the gods in the ancient Hindu Vedas. Indra's net was extraordinary in that it contained at each node or intersection a precious multi-faceted jewel, with each facet reflecting all the other jewels in the net in a comprehensive, holographic unity. The metaphor is a profound and elegant one, and the comparison to the Internet is certainly fitting. But isn't a net also something that captures and ensnares, usually catching its victims unawares, so that they may be tamed or imprisoned? As we gaze at the beauty and intricacy of a spider's web, it behooves us to remember that the word "captivating" has an alternate meaning, one not likely to be forgotten by the unfortunate fly or moth.

The dilemma presented by the Internet specifically and by technological innovation in general is one that seems intrinsic to the human story, an adventure defined largely by material progress on one hand and the evolution of consciousness on the other. While flowing together, these two cultural currents are engaged in an ongoing dialogue—both amicable and antagonistic—that has been called the "dialectic of progress." As the mean global temperature continues to escalate, so does the tension between these two streams, both of which seem to be gaining momentum as they rush headlong towards an uncertain future. As we approach what appears to be a turning point in history, a crossroads in the human journey, the debate between material progress and spiritual evolution—between matter and psyche—becomes vitally important to understand and participate in, for it tells us whence we came and, more importantly, where we might be headed.

THE BUDDHA'S WORLD AND LIFE

Sitting meditatively in stark contrast to our world is that of the Buddha, who lived on the Asian subcontinent about twenty-five hundred years ago. What we now call India was at that time not a unified country but a smattering of independent kingdoms, republics, and principalities, with most of the population living in small agrarian villages and conversing in their regional dialects. Within the Hindu caste system, one's station in life was pretty well determined at birth, with little or no opportunity to navigate among different social strata. Certainly there existed within the Brahmin or priestly class a high degree of learning and culture, but those on the bottom of the hierarchy knew comparatively little of the world beyond their own village or small town. Such was the case in other cultures at the time, and to a degree remains the case today in less developed regions of the world, particularly for those living on the far side of the digital divide.

The Hindu culture of 550 BCE was in some ways the mirror image of that of the modern West. Knowledge of the material world, the "outer" world of the senses, was less important than the inner wisdom gained through disciplined meditation, introspection, and contemplation. It was not uncommon, especially among those with few practical commitments and ample spiritual commitment, to withdraw completely from their families and day-to-day lives to pursue enlightenment, whether at the feet of an esteemed guru in the company of other seekers or alone in the wilderness, perhaps hidden away in some proverbial cave. Indeed the Indian tradition of renunciation continues to this day, as evidenced by the many wandering *sadhus* or holy persons often seen in the vicinity of sacred pilgrimage sites, their barefoot, half-naked bodies smeared with gray ash and adorned with sacred jewelry, knotted hair coiled high above their painted foreheads. Initially the Buddha-to-be, Siddhartha Gautama, followed this ascetic path but eventually rejected its otherworldly focus. After his awakening, he also rejected the traditional Hindu caste system, offering guidance to all earnest seekers regardless of social status.

Siddhartha Gautama was born in Lumbini, located just inside the southern border of present-day Nepal. As a prince, he spent the first part of his life enjoying the trappings of royalty, strolling idly through exquisitely manicured gardens and dining on sumptuous foods prepared for him by faithful servants. Eventually he became curious about the world outside his palace walls and insisted that he be allowed to venture beyond them, something that his father had always been careful to prevent. When finally Siddhartha and his entourage visited a nearby town, he was shocked and disturbed to see an old person hobbling painfully along the roadside. It was the young prince's first encounter with suffering. On subsequent excursions to the outside world, he witnessed sickness and death, sights which moved him deeply.

As a result of Siddhartha's exposure to the darker side of the human condition, he made a private vow to get to the bottom of it all, to discover the cause of suffering. Kissing his sleeping wife and son goodbye in the middle of the night, he set off into the forest, where he soon encountered a small group of mendicant monks. Their spiritual path involved near-constant meditation, prayer, and fasting, practices which Siddhartha immediately adopted and pursued with diligence and fervor. Gradually his body became emaciated and weak, until one day he accepted a bowl of food offered by a woman from a nearby village, much to the dismay of his fellow monks. Their assumption was that Siddhartha had abandoned his spiritual quest, while in actuality he had reached the profound realization that wherever the path of wisdom might lead, it surely did not involve starving to death.

Siddhartha Gautama in the earth-touching pose or Bhumisparsha mudra.

After regaining his strength, Siddhartha again set off on his own, resuming his mission to discover the cause of suffering. So strong was his resolve that he planted himself beneath a *bodhi* tree and vowed not to budge from the spot until he reached full realization. For forty days he sat in meditation, each day eating a handful of food, until he began to pierce the veil of unknowing. At that point, he was visited by Mara, the wrathful deity of illusion, who questioned Siddhartha's right to become enlightened. "Who in the world do you think you are?" Mara demanded angrily. "By what power are you impelled?" Undaunted, Siddhartha reached down to touch the ground beneath him. "By the power of the Earth," he replied. Instantly Mara disappeared like a cloud of smoke and Siddhartha attained enlightenment, becoming the Buddha, the Awakened One.

Venturing forth from his spot beneath the bodhi tree, the Buddha wondered about the value of his realizations concerning the nature of suffering. Surely they were too subtle to be understood by the average person caught up in the sordid affairs of the world, and perhaps too profound for the monks trying desperately to escape from them. What the Buddha had discovered was the wisdom of the Middle Way between the extremes of indulgence in sensuality and worldliness on one hand, and disassociation and escape on the other. He had grasped the profound truth of the co-dependent arising of knower and known, of observer and observed, of psyche and matter. He had understood that while ultimate realization involves the complete integration of such opposites, the path to wisdom demands an intricate balance between them, born from a calm, spacious mind and a loving heart.

Eventually the Buddha was persuaded to share his deep insights into the nature of the human condition. As a compassionate offering to the world, he gave his first teaching in Sarnath, a day's journey from the site of his enlightenment in Bodh Gaya, to the group of monks with whom he began his spiritual quest. His former teachers were so deeply inspired that they became his first disciples. Over the course of his long life, the Buddha gave many more teachings and amassed thousands of followers as he wandered across the central plains of the Indian subcontinent.

The Buddha lived during what historian Karl Jaspers dubbed the Axial Age, a pivotal period from 800 to 200 BCE during which many of the world's major religious and philosophical traditions were established independently and more or less simultaneously. Buddhism and Jainism arose in India alongside Taoism and Confucianism in China, while Zoroastrianism represented the emerging monotheism of the Middle East. In Greece, philosophers such as Heraclitus, Parmenides, Socrates, Plato, and Aristotle laid the groundwork for the Western worldview in which the vagaries of the gods were supplanted by natural, universal laws accessible to reason and logic. In the span of just a few hundred years, a handful of history's greatest minds built the spiritual foundations upon which human culture still rests.

Jaspers considers the Axial Age to be the birth of humanity's search for meaning. It is also widely recognized as playing a crucial role in the development of the collective human ego, which had

THE FOUR NOBLE TRUTHS

The Buddha's first teaching included that of the Four Noble (or Spiritual) Truths, which comprise the cornerstone of Buddhist philosophy and practice from which the title and structure of this book are derived. Simple yet profound, these truths can be compared to a medical or psychological exam given by the Buddha. They are presented here in highly condensed form, and will be elaborated upon in later chapters.

1. **The truth of suffering**
   (Recognizing the reality of the sickness and its symptoms)
2. **The truth of the cause of suffering**
   (Diagnosis: identifying the root problem)
3. **The truth of the end of suffering**
   (Prognosis, in this case a favorable one)
4. **The truth of the path to the end of suffering**
   (Treatment, prescription)

Fortunately, the Buddha was more thorough and holistic than many modern allopathic doctors, who too often lack the time or training to address the root cause of illnesses, frequently aiming to simply alleviate or suppress symptoms by prescribing medication. Like putting a band-aid on a cancerous lesion, this masking of the problem can only lead to its intensification, perhaps even creating unanticipated and harmful side effects. True healing, according to Dr. Buddha, requires both the wisdom to see the problem clearly and the compassion to treat the patient effectively.

In the context of this book, the patient in question is our world. The hopeful prognosis is that despite the growing severity of the disease, it is not terminal. Its causes can be isolated and overcome, and our world and worldview can be healed.

taken form roughly three thousand years prior, at the dawn of modern civilization. That evolutionary milestone, coincident with the development of writing and the appearance of city-states, marks the beginning of the world as we know it, and in some ways foreshadows the beginning of the end of that world. It initiates a fifty-five-hundred-year cultural enterprise known as history, which has been dominated by masculine,* analytical, linear thinking and increasingly defined by the aforementioned tension between material progress and psychic evolution. Ever since Mesopotamia, it seems, humans have been living and dying in the fertile realm between the Tigris and Euphrates of mind and matter.

In the formation of new philosophies and worldviews during the Axial Age, we can see the establishment of collective self-concepts and a major step in the human maturation process, which would appear to be entering its next phase even as we contemplate it now. As reflected in the rapidly changing landscape of planet Earth, the landscape of the human psyche is currently undergoing an important transformation, one that would seem to require the drafting of a new map of reality and a new way of understanding that map. The growing consensus is that this new worldview will incorporate not just the rational, left-brain, linear, solar mode of consciousness that has defined the last few millennia, but will also honor a more relational, right-brain, cyclical, lunar mode of awareness. If indeed humanity is able to change its mind as quickly as would seem necessary, the worldview that will finally emerge will be a truly integral one defined by a shared sense of global community and universal responsibility.

---

*Here and throughout the book, "masculine" is used in a traditional, limited sense, as is "feminine." The author recognizes the deeper ambiguity of gender terms and issues.

I do find it potentially significant that the human maturation process to which I allude—and indeed most of history—has unfolded within larger astrological cycles, particularly the 5,125-year "Long Count" calendar of the Maya, which according to most scholars began in 3114 BCE (quite close to the supposed beginning of the Hindu "dark age" or Kali Yuga in 3102 BCE). The Mayan calendar, as many know, is scheduled to "end" on the winter solstice of 2012 (actually, it's the present Long Count that ends as a new one begins), which for some spells apocalyptic doom and for others portends the dawning of a new era of global enlightenment. The present book, perhaps not surprisingly, takes the middle path, presenting a vision in which both scenarios—breakdown and breakthrough—are already occurring simultaneously, and in which neither is likely to reach complete fruition on the exact date in question.

The teaching of the Four Noble Truths is considered the first "Turning of the Wheel" of Buddhist teaching or *dharma*. The second Turning is said to have occurred almost five hundred years later, at about the time of Christ, with the birth of Mahayana Buddhism. While the original Theravadan Buddhist teachings speak of liberation from suffering in largely individual terms, the Mahayana traditions emphasize the liberation of the collective. As with Christ, the focus becomes universal love, as exemplified by the Bodhisattva, one who vows to take birth again and again until all beings are liberated from suffering. At the heart of the Bodhisattva's ceaseless action and boundless compassion is the realization of interdependence, the deep understanding that we're all in this together.

Author, eco-philosopher, and engaged Buddhist Joanna Macy, herself an embodiment of the Bodhisattva ideal, speaks of the current global ecology movement as representing a transition from the "industrial growth" society to the "life-sustaining" model. Calling this the period of the Great Turning, Macy frames it as the third great revolution in history after the Agricultural and Industrial revolutions, and as one that will be occurring much more quickly than the previous two, with an active and conscious participation on the part of humanity as a whole. Therein lies our collective challenge, as well as the basis for hope. Perhaps the Great Turning will be the next turning of the wheel of *dharma,* ushering in a new collective awareness of global interconnectivity of not just the mind but the heart. Perhaps the spirit of the future Buddha, the Bodhisattva Maitreya, has already begun to take form within us.

ONE
THE REALITY OF GLOBAL SUFFERING

Constantly regard the universe as one living being, having one substance and one soul; and observe how all things have reference to one perception, the perception of this one living being; and how all things act with one movement; and how all things are the cooperating causes of all things which exist; observe too the continuous spinning of the thread and the structure of the web.

—Marcus Aurelius (121–180 CE),
Roman Emperor and Stoic[1]

THE RADIANT CORE OF BUDDHISM

Before looking at the state of the world, I would like to address the widely held misconception that Buddhism, with its talk of suffering, is pessimistic or fatalistic in nature. This notion seems to be based in part on an unfamiliarity with the Second Noble Truth regarding the cause of suffering, which foreshadows the clearly hopeful Third Noble Truth that suffering can be overcome. Much of the blame for

Buddhism's bad reputation, however, clearly lies with the word "suffering," a common and somewhat clumsy translation of the Pali word *dukkha* (Pali being a Sanskrit vernacular in which the earliest Buddhist scriptures were written). While *dukkha* can be applied to all forms of suffering, including physical agony, sickness, aging, and death, it is just as often used to describe subtle feelings of psychological discomfort. A more nuanced translation of *dukkha* would be anxiety or stress, while a look at the etymology is even more revealing: The root, *kha*, means "space," and the negative prefix describes a crowded, contracted, or inharmonious space, the more profound implications of which will be touched upon later. Throughout this book and in this chapter in particular, I rely on the translation of *dukkha* as "dis-ease," a common neologism that suggests both a physical ailment and a psychological condition, the logic of which will, I hope, become apparent.

One of the Buddha's most inspiring insights was that despite life's unavoidable tribulations—not getting what we want, getting what we don't want, losing what we have—each of us is always in possession of a sparkling jewel of innate goodness and infinite wisdom. Beneath our individual egos, restrictive self-concepts, fickle desires, harsh judgments, and emotional baggage lies a divine and radiant essence: our enlightened Buddha nature, which just happens to be temporarily obscured like the sun on a cloudy day. Although we may sometimes lapse from our intrinsic godliness, we are always susceptible to relapsing into wise and compassionate behavior.

Having ideally dispelled a few of the dark clouds surrounding Buddhism, I feel compelled to warn the reader that the truth of global suffering is indeed a highly inconvenient one. As a growing number of people are aware, our world is in a bad way, a state of crisis that the more benign reading of "dis-ease" falls far short of describing. Many of us are more than just a little uneasy, which the

Buddha posited as the usual (though surmountable) human condition, and some of us are understandably terrified. Meanwhile the gross physical disease of our biosphere is rapidly worsening, which only adds to the sense of a world spinning wildly out of control.

Although this chapter addresses global suffering in concrete terms, it is not meant to be a definitive account of the state of the world, something best left to authors and organizations more knowledgeable than myself. In a rapidly fluctuating worldscape, statistics and percentages quickly become obsolete (too often changing for the worse), while generalizations and forecasts are iffy by nature. Chapter titles aside, my aim here is not to provide indisputable facts, figures, and details, but to paint a general picture of large-scale problems, perhaps more in the spirit of impressionism than photo-realism. Rather than examine each dab of paint up close, the reader is encouraged to take a few steps back in order to survey in its entirety the scene before us, as grim as it may appear.

CONFRONTING THE SHADOW

Given the extent and magnitude of suffering in the world, it is hardly surprising that many of us are usually reluctant to "go there." The tendency, in fact, is to retreat from global suffering into a private virtual world of television, video games, iPods, Internet porn, shopping, alcohol, drugs, or any number of the many distractions offered by modern culture. But if true healing is what we seek, we must remove the blinders and band-aids to look squarely and unflinchingly at the wounds of the world. As is the case with many recovery programs, the first challenging step is to openly admit that the problem exists.

Most of us are not accustomed to looking at the unsavory aspects of existence. They make us feel upset, frightened, anxious, disgusted, guilty, or otherwise uncomfortable, and we have generally become quite used to feeling comfortable, or in many cases comfortably numb. Symbolically, our own waste gets flushed away immediately and our garbage is hauled off every week, allowing us to pretend that there is in fact such a place as "away." We bury our nuclear waste deep underground, seemingly repressing our consideration for the Earth and its present inhabitants, perhaps denying altogether our responsibility for the welfare of future beings. If indeed there will be generations after ours, we rationalize, surely they'll figure out a way to clean up the mess we're making.

Similar feelings of discomfort arise when we encounter the suffering of others. Since humans are naturally compassionate beings, we cannot help but be moved and affected. Our first compulsion, apart from simply turning away, is often to try and patch up the problem immediately, to offer advice or platitudes usually designed to restore our own relative peace of mind. Another common way of coping with the discomfort of seeing others suffer is to distance ourselves from the unfortunate person or "poor thing," which is not compassion (literally: feeling or suffering *with*) but its less empathetic imposter, pity.

And as difficult as it is for most of us to contend with external suffering, we are perhaps even more reluctant to look at our own, often engaging in avoidance or escape, downplaying, or denial. We tell ourselves, our friends, and our families that we are doing fine, even when the truth is otherwise. In some cases we are not even aware of our own suffering; we have become emotionally detached, disallowing our feelings of pain and grief while forfeiting our capacity for joy in the process.

Even among those who consider themselves reasonably conscious, there is a tendency to gloss over the dark and difficult aspects of life.

Open air garbage dumps like this one in Jakarta, Indonesia, represent our collective shadow and remind us that there is no "away" in which to throw our trash.

Such people would rather not devote energy to ugly details, fearing that doing so somehow makes matters worse. While my intention here is not to dwell on the negative or over-dramatize the state of global affairs, I do feel that an honest look at the situation is an integral part of the healing process. Surely the Buddha would agree, as would Joanna Macy, who highlights the transformative power of ecological grief and frustration, which arise from our love of the world. Swiss psychologist Carl Jung, who coined the term "shadow" to refer to the unintegrated bogey of the unconscious mind, wrote: "One does not become enlightened by imagining figures of light, but by making the shadow conscious."[2] Jung regarded the shadow as not just a reservoir of darkness but a wellspring of creativity and healing.

In many ways the journey we are all being asked to take is that of the archetypal hero. This journey, conveyed in the myths of many different cultures, usually involves a descent into the underworld, to some dark and frightening place where the hero is forced to confront dangerous and life-threatening challenges. In some cases he may endure dismemberment or death, in order to be reborn as a more balanced and integrated being. Often the treasure that the hero retrieves is a vital part of himself from which he had been estranged. These age-old lessons seem more relevant than ever.

DISEASE OF THE BIOSPHERE AND PLANET

The term "biosphere" was coined by the nineteenth-century English geologist Eduard Suess to refer to the "place on Earth's surface where life dwells"[3] (*bios* is Greek for "life"). It can be conceived of as the outer shell of the spherical Earth, including the oceans (hydrosphere), the topmost layer of land (lithosphere), and lowest layer of the atmosphere, as well as all plant and animal life. A narrower definition includes only the living organisms (biomass), while a broader definition would include the planet's crust, home to trillions of microorganisms living deep underground, as well as the entire atmosphere, clearly crucial to life on Earth. From the broadest perspective, the biosphere might be considered synonymous with the Earth in its life-bearing entirety.

Another Englishman, James Lovelock, began advancing in the 1960s the notion that the Earth not only bears life but is itself a living organism of sorts, with all its components working together to create and sustain life in much the same way that different systems in the human body (respiratory, digestive, etc.) interact seamlessly to maintain health and homeostasis. Lovelock, who named his hypothesis (and the Earth) after the Greek earth goddess Gaia, conceived of the planet as a complex, evolving, self-organizing, self-regulating, self-perpetuating system—the same terminology used to describe any living being. Although Gaia is incapable of reproducing (for better or worse), this seems like a helpful and holistic conception of our unique and creative planet, a conception that might reasonably be extended to the universe as a whole. (Although as far as I know, the living Cosmos has yet to be given a proper name. Major religions typically deify the abstract forces *behind* creation.)

The important concept emphasized by Lovelock, his collaborator Lynn Margulis, and many other biologists is the intimate interdependence of Earth's creatures and natural systems. Living beings are shaped and modified by the non-living elements of the biosphere, while these elements are in turn shaped and affected by living organisms. The salinity of the seas and the composition of the atmosphere, for example, always remain within the narrow margin that supports life, largely because of homeostatic feedback loops among these systems and biota. As miraculously reliable as it seems, this life-sustaining interdynamic has actually had its imbalances, such as when the primordial population of one-celled prokaryotes grew to such an extent that these organisms hyper-oxidized the Earth's atmosphere and almost caused their own extinction. If not for the evolution of oxygen-consuming eukaryotes, life on Earth would have ceased about two billion years ago.

Certain biologists disagree with Lovelock's notion that living organisms participate in planetary maintenance in an altruistic way, arguing that most species are not only non-conscious but naturally competitive in regard to available resources. This criticism, I believe, is based on limited views of both consciousness and organic life, as consciousness can be seen to function throughout Nature (though not necessarily in a human way), while life can be seen to strive for its own perpetuation on Earth, even if individual organisms are *sometimes* competitive and definitely mortal.

True, in the epic of life's evolution, there have been major setbacks and dead ends, just as there have been unexpected creative breakthroughs. It seems as though Gaia (and perhaps by extension, the universe) works like a poet or a writer, trying out different themes and threads and making it up the story she goes along.

What cannot be argued is that life on Earth is primarily about relationships—between the living and non-living components, and among the Earth's many species, which have co-evolved in relation to each other and in response to the ever-changing environment. In this complex web of life, each species has an effect on every other, and on larger ecosystems. While this awareness of interdependence has been of central importance to traditional cultures, it seems to have been forgotten by the industrial human. Inasmuch as life on Earth is about relationships, our collective relationship to life on Earth has become imbalanced and unhealthy, leading in turn to imbalance and ill health in the natural world.

This book advances the conception of the Earth as a living being, one whose body has become diseased by the collective dis-ease of humanity. Our physical and psychological suffering is also a *result* of the planet's illness, a natural aspect of an intimate biofeedback process. Many of us do not have to be told that Mother Nature is sick; we feel it in our bones. For just as our skeletons provide support for our bodies, so too does Gaia provide support for life, and her vital structures are steadily crumbling beneath us.

The Human Factor

Although each species in the web of life affects all others, no single species (except, perhaps, prokaryotes) has ever had the dramatic and far-reaching influence that humans have. With our immense creativity and adaptability, we have survived Ice Ages and other formidable challenges, and have thrived to become the Earth's biggest success story. One might argue, however, that we have been too successful for our own good, for the welfare of other species, and for the well-being of the planet as whole.

Due in large part to the growth of our population, the human race has become powerful enough to influence the very dynamics of biological evolution, a process that for billions of years had been governed, at least in part, by the laws of natural selection as put forth by Darwin. In his conception, it is the environment that plays the primary role in "selecting" the species and the traits most fit for survival; genetic mutations that result in features advantageous to survival in a given environment, such as sharp claws or a long beak, will enable those organisms to live and pass along their DNA. Within the last century or two, however, humans have become more influential than the environment in determining which species will survive. We have dethroned Nature herself to become the new "selector."

Of course, humans have been selecting certain species for domestication from the very beginning of our evolutionary journey: dogs for hunting and companionship, sheep and goats for food and clothing, oxen and horses for labor and transportation, and countless plants for myriad uses. But with an exponential increase in human numbers comes an exponential increase in our influence on the natural world, which unfortunately has not been accompanied by an exponential increase in responsibility and wisdom.

Climate Change and Rising Seas

Of all large-scale crises, global warming is doubtless the most well known, having become a hot topic of casual conversation, serious concern, and partisan game-playing in recent years. Although first brought to light by NASA scientist and climate advisor James Hansen in 1988, the issue began gaining widespread public attention after the

2006 documentary *An Inconvenient Truth,* which received two Oscar awards and led to Al Gore sharing the Nobel Peace Prize in 2007.

It should be immediately emphasized that the ensuing storm of controversy surrounding climate change has been taking place not in the scientific sphere but in the popular media—mainly among politicians, pundits, and scientists with dubious credentials and/or direct ties to the oil industry.* Among mainstream scientists, global warming is considered "unequivocal" and mainly attributable to increasing greenhouse gases.[4] Such is the authoritative assessment of the 2,500-member UN Intergovernmental Panel on Climate Change (IPCC), with which Gore shared his Nobel. The conclusions of the IPCC have been backed up by dozens of leading scientific and academic institutions, including the national academies of science of every major industrialized country in the world.

Here are the basic facts:

- The average surface temperature of the planet has risen a little over one degree Fahrenheit over the past century, with most of that increase taking place in the past thirty years.
- The decade from 2000 to 2009 ranks as the warmest since record keeping began in 1880.
- 2010 was the hottest recorded year, with the hottest summer, and the hottest month (June).
- Warming trends have been most dramatic in the Arctic, where temperatures have risen 4–5 degrees Fahrenheit in the last 50 years.[5]
- The main culprit among greenhouse gases is atmospheric CO_2, up nearly 40 percent since the start of the Industrial Revolution.[6]
- Carbon dioxide levels are now higher than they have been in

---

*See www.exxonsecrets.org.

hundreds of thousands of years, having recently surpassed 390 parts per million, about 40 ppm above what Jim Hansen and his research team consider safe for human civilization.

- About 25 percent of the world's CO_2 is produced by the U.S., which contains only 4 percent of the world's population.[7]
- Greenhouse gases come primarily from the livestock industry, transportation, and coal-burning power plants.

While scientists strive to calculate the long-terms effects of global climate change, dire consequences can already be seen in the record-breaking heat waves, raging wildfires, unprecedented flooding, prolonged droughts, and extreme weather events occurring with increasing frequency across the globe. In the non-human world, climate change has shifted the timing of tree leafing and plant blooming, altered migration and breeding patterns, and diminished or destroyed the populations of certain cold-blooded species.

As pointed out in *An Inconvenient Truth*, the world's glaciers are retreating at an alarming rate. During the twentieth century, total glacial surface area decreased by half, and since 1980 the changes have become more rapid and widespread. Although glacial retreat is observable throughout the world, certain regions are of particular concern because of the human populations that rely upon glacial melting as a dry-season water source. Himalayan glaciers, for example, feed Asia's largest rivers such as the Ganges, Indus, Yangtze, Mekong, Yellow, and Brahmaputra, upon which 2.4 billion people depend (the Ganges alone provides water for 500 million Indians). As glaciers thaw, this area and others throughout the world could experience flooding followed by severe and prolonged drought.

While vital to certain human communities, glaciers in temperate regions of the globe account for only a small percentage of the

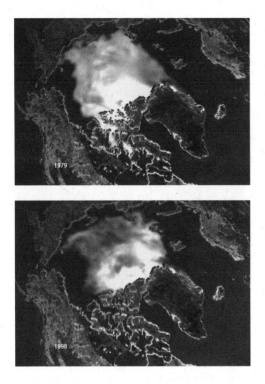

NASA images of the polar cap in 1979 (top) and in 1998 (bottom). More recent maps of the area indicate a shrinkage of 25 percent in the last three decades.

glacial ice on Earth. The vast majority exists in the polar ice sheets of Greenland and Antarctica, which are miles thick in some areas. Recent record-breaking changes in the Greenland ice sheet suggest that it is melting at the rate of almost 50 cubic miles per year, with some Greenland glaciers being among the fastest-moving in the world.[8] Rapid melting is also being observed in the ice sheets of Antarctica, which hold 70 percent of the Earth's fresh water. A 2006 UK report warned that the West Antarctic Ice Sheet, formerly considered a "slumbering giant" in terms of global warming, may in fact be starting to disintegrate. Arctic ice is also being affected, with predictions that by 2030 the Arctic could be ice-free for a portion of the year.[9] In 2007, Arctic ice retreated far enough for the Northwest Passage to be navigable for the first time in human history.

The melting of polar and subpolar ice sheets may affect sea levels in a dramatic way. If both the Greenland and West Antarctic ice sheets were to melt completely, seas would rise almost 40 feet, affecting at least one-tenth of the world's population.[10] While the IPCC has predicted a conservative rise of 8–24 inches over the next century, a more recent study doubles that estimate to more than 4 feet, which would affect 45 million coastal dwellers.[11] Perhaps most alarming is Hansen's observation that polar ice caps do not melt in a linear fashion but tend to flip suddenly between states, as occurred 14,000 years ago when sea levels rose about 20 meters in 400 years, or about 5 meters per century.[12]

Other scientists too speak of a "tipping point" in global climate change, leading to the suggestion that the process be called "climate shift." Certain effects of global warming introduce "positive feedback" into the process, causing further acceleration in warming trends. One example is the melting of permafrost peat bogs, such as the world's largest in Western Siberia, which would release into the atmosphere enormous quantities of methane, a greenhouse gas many times more potent than CO_2. The world's permafrost is thought to contain more carbon than is currently present in either the Earth's atmosphere or in all its vegetation. Methane is also present in methane hydrate, a form of ice that exists under the ocean floor, which may thaw as ocean temperatures rise. Some biologists theorize that a sudden release of undersea methane may have caused the most severe mass extinction in Earth's history, the Permian-Triassic event of 250 million years ago, also known as the Great Dying. Other forms of positive feedback include the melting of sea ice, which normally reflects a significant amount of sunlight back into space, and an increase in the number and intensity of forest fires, which release more carbon into the atmosphere.

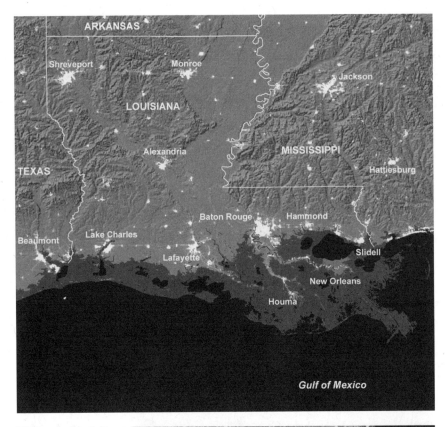

With a sea level rise of only one meter, large portions of southern Louisiana and Florida would be underwater.

If the term "climate shift" is more accurate than "climate change," global warming might instead be called "global weirding," as unseasonable, unreasonable weather is likely to become more common. The World Meteorological Organization and the U.S. Environmental Protection Agency have both linked global warming with the rising number of high-level hurricanes, and in 2004 Hurricane Catarina became the first recorded hurricane of the southern hemisphere. On land, higher temperatures mean increased convection and severe storms, while increased evaporation rates could lead to heavy rains and flooding in some areas, drought and desertification in others. Changes in weather patterns will of course have an enormous impact on the world's food supply and on agriculture in general, which itself affects the global climate through the release of greenhouse gases and modification of the Earth's topography.

Although the Cancún climate talks of late 2010 were widely considered more fruitful than earlier talks like those in Copenhagen, they also upped the publicity around an unexpected new threat: the increasing acidification and possible death of the world's oceans. According to an international panel of marine biologists, atmospheric CO_2 may destabilize ocean chemistry enough to cause the collapse of the world's fisheries, if not the entire aquatic food web.[13] An ever-growing body of evidence underscores the urgent necessity of not only curbing CO_2 emissions but also lowering the concentration of this gas in our atmosphere.

Mass Extinction of Species

The tremendous influence of humans on the biosphere is currently manifesting in a dramatic and disturbing way in what is being called a "mass extinction event" or simply a mass extinction. Although extinction is a naturally occurring phenomenon—perhaps 99 percent of all species that have ever existed on Earth are now extinct—there are certain periods during which a large number of species become extinct in a short period of time, in contrast to the usual "background" rate of extinction. We are currently in the midst of such a period: the Holocene mass extinction. Although the Holocene era began at the end of the last Ice Age about 12,000 years ago, the sharp rise in the rate of extinction appears to be directly proportional to the sharp rise in human population, making it essentially a modern crisis. Nobody knows for sure how many species exist on Earth, but the current mass extinction seems to be happening 100 to 1,000 times faster than the normal background rate.

Based on evidence from the fossil record, there have been at least five previous mass extinction events in geologic history, the most recent of which wiped out the dinosaurs during the Pleistocene era 65 million years ago. Significantly, however, the current event is the first one whose cause is well known, and the first one caused by just one species, namely *Homo sapiens.* Furthermore, the current die-off seems to be happening faster than any before. Estimates vary on the rate of extinction, but many biologists predict that 50 percent of extant species will disappear within the next 100 years, with some estimates being as low as 20 years for the same percentage.

One of the most authoritative evaluations of the Earth's biodiversity is the International Union for the Conservation of Nature's annual "Red List of Threatened Species." Of the world's known 1.9 million species, the 2008 Red List assessed more than 44,000 of them, concluding that more than one-fourth face extinction. One third of all amphibians, one third of mammal species, one eighth of bird species, and an alarming 70 percent of the world's assessed plants are in peril. Among mammals, primates are the most at risk, followed by marine mammals.[14] The 2009 Red List indicates that mass extinction "continues apace."

Given the magnitude of the crisis, one wonders why the current mass extinction is not a regular part of the nightly national news. A somewhat cynical supposition is that it has been deemed too distressing for the average viewer, and lower spirits might translate into lower ratings and advertising revenues. Although mainstream media are clearly wont to report a certain amount of bad news, apparently no major network wants to be the bearer of information so truly dire as to sound apocalyptic.

At the same time, mass extinction is hardly being kept a secret. Major print outlets have been sounding the alarm since the late 1990s:

- Fastest Mass Extinction in Earth's History (*Worldwatch Report*, September 16, 1998)
- The Sixth Extinction (*National Geographic*, February 1999)
- Human Impact Triggers Massive Extinctions (*Environment News Service*, August 2, 1999)
- UN Paints Grim Global Picture (United Nations Environment Program, September 22, 1999)
- Biodiversity: Vanishing Before Our Eyes (*Time Magazine*, 2000)
- One Quarter of All Mammal Species Face Extinction Soon (BBC, September 28, 2000)
- The Current Mass Extinction (*Scientific American*, October 30, 2000)
- Humans Moving Closer to Extinction, Study Says (*Seattle Post-Intelligencer*, January 5, 2001)
- Scientists Agree World Faces Mass Extinction (CNN, August 23, 2002)
- World's Ecosystems on Verge of Sudden Collapse (*Nature*, October 12, 2001)

- British Study Confirms Worldwide Mass Extinction (*Science*, March 19, 2004)
- One Quarter of Primates Will Be Extinct in 20 Years (*London Times*, April 7, 2005)
- United Nations: Humans Causing Greatest Mass Extinction in 65 Million Years (Reuters, March 21, 2006)
- Earth Faces Catastrophic Loss of Species (*UK Independent*, July 20, 2006)*

Although these headlines were culled from print and online sources (far less popular than television), the question remains as to why mass extinction has yet to take hold in the collective psyche in the way that global warming has. One can only speculate that the issue, even if experienced as depressing, is not understood as pressing. After all, most humans are understandably focused on human affairs, only occasionally extending concern to non-human beings apart from pets. Global warming seems a more urgent issue inasmuch as its effects can be experienced firsthand or seen in the faces of flood and tornado victims on TV, not usually because it is linked to the loss of unseen and unknown life forms.

What many people fail to consider is that the welfare of humanity is intimately linked to the welfare of other species; indeed our very survival depends on these relationships. The most obvious examples are the plants we eat, which in turn depend upon microbes in the soil and insects for pollination and protection, all of which depend upon other species for their survival. As the web of life steadily disintegrates, mutually supportive relationships will be destroyed, perhaps leading to a tipping point as with climate change, resulting in runaway species

---

*Headlines retrieved from www.massextinction.net, maintained by David Ulansey.

loss. At any rate, there is certainly no guarantee that in the current mass extinction, *Homo sapiens* will not be among the fallen.

In addition to fulfilling many of our physical needs, other species are deeply embedded in the human story. From time immemorial humans have sought to commune with and learn from animals, often adopting their appearances and mimicking their movements and calls in dance and ritual. Non-human beings wander about in the unconscious, often appearing in our dreams to impart forgotten wisdom. Animals are our only known living companions in the universe, and it is difficult and disturbing to imagine life without them. Of course, quite apart from their practical and psychological value to humans, other species possess their own intrinsic beauty, dignity, and preciousness.

Shrinking Forests and Expanding Deserts

One of the primary ways that humans contribute to the disappearance of other life forms is by destroying the ecosystems in which they live. Notable among these are the tropical rainforests, home to an estimated 50 percent of all the Earth's species of plants, animals, and insects. Each day, tens of thousands of acres of rainforest are cut down, with a corresponding loss of at least 100 species daily, and as many as 50,000 species annually.[15] The primary driving forces are commercial logging and clear-cutting for cattle grazing and agriculture.

Not only are rainforests rich in terms of biodiversity, they play a vital role in keeping greenhouse gases in check by converting carbon dioxide into oxygen. The Amazon rainforest alone produces 20 percent of the world's oxygen, for which it has been called "the lungs of the planet." Disturbingly, the Gaia's lungs are collapsing, driving

Arial views of Rondonia, Brazil, where deforestation has been particularly dramatic.

Above left in September 2000 and below left, September 2006.

the global temperature even higher in the process. The "slash and burn" method of agriculture common in these developing areas only worsens the problem by releasing more greenhouse gases into the atmosphere. Rainforests also help generate precipitation for neighboring arid regions. The near-total destruction of the rainforests of West Africa, for example, has been linked to a severe, two-decades-long drought in the interior of the continent.

Unfortunately, deforestation is not limited to rainforests. An estimated 80 percent of the world's forests, home to 70 percent of the world's flora and fauna, have been lost, with the rate of destruction showing few signs of slowing.[16] Along with loss of life, deforestation leads to a loss of soil nutrients and increased erosion, often resulting in desertification, an accelerating phenomenon in which areas once supportive of life are becoming barren wastelands. Unfortunately, when a desert begins to form or advance upon a neighboring eco-system, it is almost impossible to stop the process. A 2007 UN report warns that desertification could displace as many as 50 million people over the next decade.[17]

As habitats are degraded or destroyed by climate change, resource extraction, development, or tourism, animals too migrate to other bioregions in an attempt to survive. Such "invasive species" often upset the checks and balances of the new ecosystem by introducing unknown viruses or by overpopulating the area due to lack of natural predators. This can have a devastating effect on native species, some of which may already be threatened with extinction. Humans play a more direct role in this process by introducing species into non-native environments.

Topsoil Disappearance and Degeneration

Life in general, and human civilization in particular, rest on a thin layer of dirt—a rich mixture of inorganic minerals and tiny life forms that allows for the growth of plants, which in turn protect the soil from erosion. Throughout most of geologic history, soil erosion and formation have remained in balance, but modern agriculture, commercial development, and overgrazing have been causing topsoil to be blown and washed away many times faster than it is being replenished. At the rate of about 1 percent per year, our planet is being stripped of its living and life-bearing skin.[18]

Over the last four decades, almost one-third of the Earth's arable land has become barren. Needless to say, this poses a serious problem for the growing human population, which now relies heavily on industrial farming practices that can be fruitful in the short term but destructive over time. Pesticides meant to kill unwanted insects are often fatal to many other creatures that help keep the soil viable, while the tilling of large fields greatly expedites erosion. Fortunately, more and more farmers have been adopting no-till methods, practicing crop rotation, using natural fertilizers, and working to regenerate topsoil. Unfortunately, it takes several hundred years to produce one inch of topsoil.[19]

Air and Water Pollution

Another factor contributing to rapid species loss is pollution, which has increased greatly since the beginning of the Industrial Revolution. While carbon dioxide, methane, ozone, nitrous oxide, and other greenhouse gases are currently the most well-known forms of air pollution, the most visible form is smog, composed mainly of sulfur dioxide and particulates from automobiles and smokestacks. In addition to being irritating to the eyes (in more ways than one), smog can cause immune deficiency, respiratory problems, and death, particularly in young children and older adults, and particularly when air circulation is inhibited (i.e., during warm, sunny periods or in cities surrounded by mountains). An even more noxious and dangerous form of "photochemical smog," first witnessed in the 1950s, is caused by the reaction of sunlight with various airborne pollutants. Most major cities now use some method of determining and describing air quality on a given day, periodically warning citizens to remain indoors.

Unfortunately, the air quality is hardly much better inside, where modern humans spend most of their time. The World Health Organization (WHO) reports that 2.4 million deaths annually can be attributed to air pollution—more than the number who die in car crashes—and that at least half of these deaths can be linked to poor indoor air quality.[20] Buildings and houses often trap poisonous and carcinogenic gases such as radon from the Earth, formaldehyde from varnishes and sealants, lead dust from paints, asbestos from insulation, hydrogen sulfide from leaky sewer pipes, carbon monoxide from faulty vents, particulates from stoves and fireplaces, and volatile organic compounds (VOCs) from carpets, photocopiers, cleaning solvents, and paint thinners. The WHO estimates that 30 percent of all buildings suffer from "sick building syndrome."[21]

Unfortunately, air pollution does not simply linger indoors or hang in the air above cities; it eventually enters the atmosphere and the water cycle to become acid rain (and other forms of precipitation). Marked by high concentrations of sulfur and nitrogen compounds from cars and factories, acid precipitation can damage tree leaves and needles, slow the growth of forests and vegetation, destroy soil microbes and leach away essential nutrients, and kill fish and prevent their eggs from hatching. Sometimes air pollutants settle directly into the soil, combining with hydrocarbons and heavy metals from phosphate fertilizers, herbicides, and pesticides, all of which pollute rivers through agricultural run-off and seep into underground aquifers, thereby entering the food chain. A particular hazard is lead, which has a cumulative and permanent effect on the nervous and reproductive systems of humans and other creatures.

Ocean Pollution and Fish Decline

Air pollution accounts for almost a third of the ocean's pollution. The rest originates on land: sewage, garbage, and toxic waste from landfills, mines, factories, farms, houses, or coastal construction sites. Another major ocean pollutant is oil, about 700 million gallons of which enter the sea each year, less than 10 percent of it through natural geologic processes.[22] As horrifying and newsworthy as tanker spills are, they account for less than 10 percent of the annual total, most of the rest coming from automobile oil changes, road run-off, and industrial waste. More visible forms of ocean pollution collect along the average shoreline—tires, aluminum cans, styrofoam, synthetic fishing nets, plastic bottles, and other detritus. Some of these objects can be especially harmful to marine animals, which can be tangled in discarded netting, strangled by plastic loops, or suffocated by consuming indigestible material.

An apparently increasing percentage of trash gets dumped into rivers or directly into the ocean, often finding its way to the Central Pacific Gyre, a vast calm region known to sailors as "the doldrums." Here our plastic becomes part of what has been dubbed the Great Pacific Garbage Patch or Trash Vortex. Nearly as large as Europe and growing, the GPGP is undoubtedly the single largest body of pollution in the world. Unfortunately, plastic is not biodegradable but photodegradable, meaning that it resists bacteria and is broken down by sunlight, leaching toxic chemicals in the process. Over the course of about sixteen years, it degrades into smaller and smaller pieces that are often mistaken for food by fish, birds, seals, and whales.[23]

The illness of the Earth's oceans is reflected in the fish population, which has been declining rapidly, mostly due to over-harvesting. The UN Food and Agriculture Organization estimates that of the seventeen major fishing areas in the world, at least four are completely depleted and the others are either fished to capacity or overfished. The declining population of smaller commercial species like sardines and anchovies directly affects the deeper-dwelling predatory fish, whose numbers have dropped as much as 90 percent in some areas.[24] This is partly due to these fish being caught in nets that are being cast ever deeper as surface populations disappear. In many cases, such deep-sea trawling results in the destruction of entire marine ecosystems, as do the illegal but still relatively common practices of dynamite fishing and cyanide fishing. These seemingly desperate methods, and overfishing

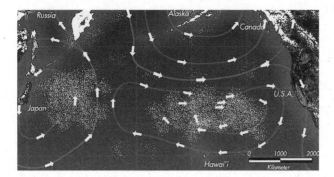

The Great Pacific Garbage Patch is an enormous, amorphous mass of plastic and other trash caught in the Eastern and Western Pacific gyres. Its depth is said to range from 30 to 300 feet.

in general, are the result of overwhelming consumer demands upon a non-renewable resource.

Irresponsible fishing techniques are also contributing to the loss of the planet's coral reefs, known as the "rainforests of the ocean" because of their impressive biodiversity. Although covering only 1 percent of the planet's surface, coral reefs support 25 percent of the world's marine life and are the largest, oldest living structures on Earth. Due to their presence in shallow tropical waters, coral reefs are also being dramatically affected by rising ocean temperatures, which cause coral to expel their algae in a die-off process called bleaching. Increased acidity also inhibits coral formation. Predictions are that if die-off and destruction continue at the present rate, most of the world's coral reefs will be gone in fifty years.[25]

Radioactive Waste and Electromagnetic Pollution

Perhaps the most disturbing form of pollution is radioactive waste. Although a certain amount of low-level waste is produced by the oil and medical industries, the most dangerous and prevalent forms are generated by nuclear power plants and weapons manufacturers. Among the most troublesome forms of radioactive waste is the main by-product of uranium enrichment, depleted uranium (DU), used by the military to make tank armor and armor-piercing munitions. When these high-density shells explode, they scatter particles of radioactive dust into the air, greatly endangering the civilian population. After the Gulf War, during which 320 tons of depleted uranium were used by the U.S., a United Nations subcommittee listed DU as a weapon with "indiscriminate effect, or of a nature to cause superfluous injury or unnecessary suffering," a.k.a. a weapon of mass destruction (WMD).[26] The European Parliament has passed numerous resolutions to ban DU, over the objections of Britain and France. Despite the unknown and indiscriminate effects, as many as twenty countries continue to use depleted-uranium weapons. Composed primarily of the isotope uranium-238, DU has a half-life of 4.5 billion years, the estimated age of planet Earth.

Other forms of radioactive waste include spent fission rods composed of uranium and plutonium, which account for most of the waste generated by nuclear power plants. The U.S. Department of Energy reports the existence of "millions of gallons of radioactive waste" and "thousands of tons of spent nuclear fuel," noting that "31 million pounds of uranium product and 2.5 billion pounds of waste" have been accumulated by one uranium processing plant alone (Fernald, Ohio).[27] Worldwide, the amount of high-level nuclear waste increases by about 12,000 metric tons every year, roughly equivalent to a two-story structure built on top of a basketball court.[28] Although some of this reactor waste can be repurposed, the vast majority of it is stored temporarily in spent fuel pools or dry casks to allow for the decay of short-lived isotopes, after which it is disposed of elsewhere. Debate continues worldwide over where that mythical "elsewhere" should be, whether underground, undersea, or out in space, all of which have serious drawbacks.

Much more pervasive in the modern world are the electric and magnetic fields (EMFs) emitted by televisions, appliances, computers, cell phones, radars, office machines, power lines, transformers, satellites, and automobile engines. Such devices produce a sea of alternating currents or pulses that interfere with the body's natural vibrations, thereby weakening the immune system, disrupting normal cellular activity, damaging DNA and RNA, and perhaps impairing brain function. Although a certain amount of low-level radiation is produced by the Earth and increasingly received from the Sun, the modern human is exposed to a growing number of artificial sources of non-ionizing radiation that contribute to a daily dose many millions of times more intense than anything experienced by previous generations.

While radiation and chemical pollution have been linked to birth defects, disease, depression, and other imbalances, their more insidious effects remain largely latent. The very language of life as present in the magical intricacy and artistry of Earth's genetic material—arguably the most precious resource in the universe—is being silently and irreversibly altered by the growing toxicity of our world. Although it may be impossible from our present vantage point to predict the exact effects of these mutations, future generations and perhaps life itself will undoubtedly be compromised as a result.

Overpopulation and Overconsumption

All of these biological diseases—climate change, deforestation, desertification, over-harvesting, and pollution—play a part in rapid species loss. They are all interrelated, and all of them are directly linked to the escalating population of humans and our increasing consumption patterns. Our needs are great, our desires are even greater, and our demands are slowly and surely overtaking Nature's ability to meet them. In fact, a 2002 study concluded that humanity surpassed the Earth's regenerative capacity around 1980, meaning that we have since been accruing ecological debt.[29]

At the time of this printing, the human population has topped seven billion, with estimates that it will reach nine billion within fifty years. To provide some perspective: humans have been around in their current form for at least forty thousand years. Only one thousand years ago the world's population was 250 million, less than the number of people currently living in the United States. That number had doubled to 500 million by the year 1600, doubled again to one billion by 1800, doubled again to two billion by 1927, and again to four billion by 1974. Thus during the thousand years leading up to 1974, each doubling of the population took approximately half as long as the previous doubling.

But certainly such exponential growth cannot continue unabated. At some point we will simply run out of non-renewable resources, by many estimates within this century. The question that looms large is whether the global population will naturally stabilize or level off in relation to available resources, or whether there will be a sudden population crash. Conceived graphically: will the population line continue as a smooth S-curve or a jagged J-curve? We can only hope for the former.

The exponential growth in population might be less alarming if not accompanied by an escalation in consumption rates, which are disproportionately high in affluent countries and rising in developing ones. Jared Diamond, Pulitzer Prize-winning author of *Guns, Germs and Steel* and *Collapse,* points out that consumption rates in the so-called first world—U.S., Europe, Japan, and Australia—are about thirty-two times higher than those in developing countries, which is like saying that each American, for example, equals about thirty-

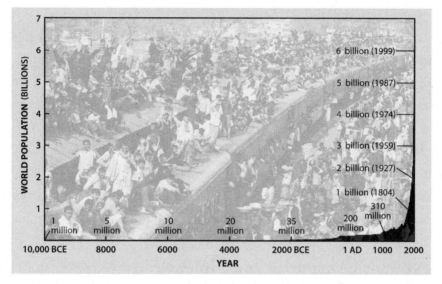

World population graph.

two Kenyans in terms of consumption.[30] According to Diamond's calculations, if the world were entirely populated by Americans, the global population would be more like 72 billion, a number that far surpasses our planet's carrying capacity. To accommodate that many people would require at least three Earths.

The unavoidable conclusion is that first-world consumption patterns are simply not sustainable for the planet as a whole. Even if the consumption rates of developing countries were to remain completely fixed, we would still effectively consume ourselves out of house and home. But of course nothing is fixed; developing countries like China and India are doing their best to achieve a first-world standard of living, and they are quickly catching up. The average Chinese citizen currently consumes about one-tenth as much as the average American, but China now has the fastest-growing economy in the world, as well as the largest population—about 1.3 billion, just ahead of India at 1.1 billion, together representing 40 percent of the world's people.

While population growth in affluent countries has slowed considerably in recent decades, growth in developing countries has increased, accompanied by increasing awareness of these tremendous disparities in living standards. Most Guatemalans, for example, have by now seen enough American television shows and music videos to develop a sense that they might be missing out on something. The chances that the average *campesino* would willingly curb his already low rate of consumption for the good of the planet are exceptionally slim—about as likely as the average first-worlder altruistically giving up her many creature comforts.

Economic Disparity and Violence

Given that the Earth cannot accommodate the current consumption rates of the world's one billion affluent people, let alone handle similar rates for the other six billion humans on the planet, it seems that serious changes must be made. Perhaps, as Diamond suggests, we could reach a global compromise in which all countries converge on consumption rates far below the current first-world levels. This would of course necessitate a lowered rate of consumption for people in developed nations, the question being whether they will elect to make this cutback willingly or be compelled to do so by extraneous forces.

Within recent decades there has been a movement in affluent circles towards voluntary simplicity, summed up in the bumper sticker slogan "Live simply so that others may simply live." Awareness of the extreme and growing disparity between the world's rich and poor has led many people to adopt more sustainable lifestyles in which walking, biking, thrift shopping, composting, gardening, and local farmers' markets all play a part. Ideally this trend, seemingly most popular among the educated middle class, will continue and catch on among the highly affluent, whose numbers are relatively small and whose influence is radically disproportionate.*

As noted, however, awareness of economic disparity is not limited to the developed, educated world. Residents of developing nations are becoming more aware of the obvious imbalance, and many of them feel understandably frustrated and powerless. In the extreme, a sense of frustration can lead to acts of desperation, namely violence and terrorism or support thereof. Of course many acts of terrorism are motivated by religious fanaticism, but in most cases an important psychological component is a sense of not being heard or recognized by much more powerful forces. Seen in terms of an extreme imbalance of power and wealth, such feelings of frustration are understandable, although violent actions are obviously pathological and deplorable.

From this perspective, it hardly seems accidental or insignificant that the most devastating attacks of 9-11 were directed at the World Trade Center, then headquarters of the global economy. In many poorer regions of the world, the engine of globalization is seen as a giant bulldozer, clearing ancestral lands to make way for export crops, often driving indigenous farmers into the nearest city slum to work long hours in unsafe factories or sweatshops. Whether or not one agrees with this caricature of globalization, the process is unarguably anti-democratic in nature. Members of the World Trade Organization, the International Monetary Fund, and the G8, three powerful groups which govern and regulate international trade and finance, are not elected but *selected* from among the world's most

---

*The World Institute for Development Economics Research reports that in the year 2000, the richest 1 percent of the global population owned 40 percent of all global assets, while the richest 10 percent owned 85 percent of the world's total assets. Looking at the situation from the bottom up, the poorest half of the global population owns less than 1 percent of global wealth.

powerful and elite figures. Furthermore, the decision-making processes within these organizations are heavily skewed in favor of affluent countries and influential corporations, with many important negotiations being conducted behind closed doors. These informal "Green Room" negotiations often exclude the delegates of developing countries altogether.

In many ways these global economic organizations have become more powerful than national governments. Certain international treaties like the North American Free Trade Agreement carry provisions that allow corporations to file suit against nations. If, for example, a CEO thinks that the profits of his company are being hindered by the labor or environmental laws of a given country, he may sue for profits lost—or not gained. In many such cases the corporate plaintiff has prevailed, and in some instances the laws in question have been undemocratically repealed. Given that such laws are meant to protect a nation's citizens, it is hardly surprising to see grassroots resistance to these global economic groups and treaties. One of the largest anti-globalization groups is the Zapatista Army of National Liberation or EZLN, which staged an indigenous uprising in Chiapas, Mexico, on January 1, 1994, the day that NAFTA came into effect. Despite the fact that the Zapatistas have since then been ideologically committed to nonviolence, they are considered by the American government to be a terrorist group.

Dwindling Water and Oil

Economic inequality means unequal access to resources, a situation that becomes more pronounced when resources are scarce. Even if increasing disparity does not lead directly to increased violence among humans, conflict over non-renewable resources can reasonably be expected to intensify in the coming decades as the global population continues to rise while resources decline.

In terms of fresh water, the Earth is already beyond its carrying capacity. The planet's finite supply of this vital resource, present in rivers, lakes, underground aquifers, and in the atmosphere as water vapor, is quickly being depleted. Experts from the UN Environment Program and other organizations have proclaimed a worldwide water crisis, predicting that more than half of humanity will be without potable water by the year 2025. Already more than one billion people are without access to safe drinking water, with another 2.6 billion— about 40 percent of the global population—lacking adequate sanitation, which compounds the problem as untreated sewage contaminates dwindling fresh water supplies.[31] Underground sources such as the once-great Ogallala Aquifer of the central U.S. are drying up, as are many above-ground lakes throughout the world. A particularly dramatic example is Africa's Lake Chad, which has shrunk 95 percent

Africa's Lake Chad has been drying up, causing conflict among neighboring countries.

in the last thirty years alone. As this formerly massive lake continues to disappear, conflicts are intensifying among the four countries surrounding it, namely Chad, Niger, Nigeria, and Cameroon. In the coming decades, water wars of this kind are expected to replace traditional conflicts driven by ideology or economic expansion.

As many people are painfully aware, the era of cheap oil is rapidly coming to a close, and global supply may have already peaked. As oil resources dwindle, prices will continue to escalate worldwide, with potential escalation in violence and warfare. Unfortunately, while the supply of oil appears to be in terminal decline,[32] global demand continues to grow, largely as a result of the population increase, with demand notably increasing in developing countries. As noted, the economies of the world's two most populous nations, China and India, are experiencing tremendous growth, accompanied by a proportional increase in demand for personal-use cars and trucks as well as for the transportation of goods. In China, which imports about half its oil, consumption has doubled in the past ten years, while India's oil demand is expected to triple in the next decade.[33]

Fossil fuels have played a major role in the world since the Industrial Revolution, particularly during the past century. Ease of transportation has been the most obvious benefit, but petroleum products in the form of plastics, fertilizers, adhesives, detergents, and solvents have become so ubiquitous that we tend to take them for granted. Oil has lubricated the engine of economic growth worldwide and in the U.S. in particular, to the point that dwindling resources will have an enormous impact on the global economy, perhaps leading to a worldwide recession, depression, or economic collapse. Meanwhile, given the dependence of modern agriculture on oil and gas, the end of peak oil may lead to skyrocketing food prices and perhaps a global famine. The severity of these changes will depend on the rate at which

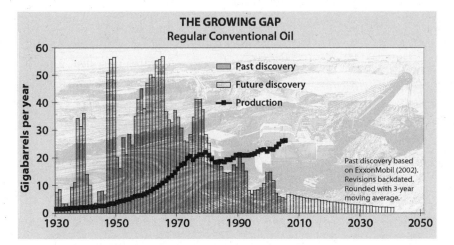

THE GROWING GAP
Regular Conventional Oil

Past discovery
Future discovery
Production

Past discovery based
on ExxonMobil (2002).
Revisions backdated.
Rounded with 3-year
moving average.

Although oil production (based on demand) continues to rise, new discoveries have been declining in both number and size since 1965. The latest "gold rush" is happening in Alberta, Canada, where oil is being extracted from tar sands (background). The process is extremely costly, both financially and environmentally, representing a seemingly desperate attempt to scrape the bottom of the barrel.

oil supply declines and on the development and availability of alternative sources of energy, as well as improvements in conservation.

Sprawl and Urbanization

One of the defining aspects of modern life is urban sprawl, which is marked by low population density in outlying suburban areas of a city. Because of a heavy reliance on automobiles, residents of these communities typically have large carbon footprints and higher rates of traffic fatalities relative to their urban counterparts. On the whole, they are also more prone to obesity and other health problems because of decreased walking, biking, and other forms of exercise. Suburban sprawl clears more farmland and forest per capita than urban neighborhoods, and it increases the chances of

invasive species migrating into remaining habitats. Sprawl also leads
to increased infrastructure costs and decreased water quality and
quantity as more concrete not only concentrates gasoline and oil
runoff but prevents water from being absorbed by local aquifers.
Perhaps equally tragic is the degradation of social systems and community interaction as private fenced yards and gated communities
replace public parks and open town squares.

Since the beginning of the Industrial Revolution, the steadily
growing human population has continued to migrate from rural
to urban areas, which have of course grown proportionally. One
century ago, only 10 percent of people on Earth lived in cities, a
figure which has risen to 50 percent as of 2008. For the first time in

Aerial view of suburban sprawl outside
of Albuquerque, New Mexico.

history, humans are primarily an urban species, with the percentage expected to reach 70 or more by 2050.[34] While this may not be an entirely bad thing in terms of energy consumption, the average city generates a great deal of pollution, which impacts both human and planetary health. Moreover, as the human race steadily migrates to cities and suburbs, our collective relationship with Nature continues to suffer.

Regional Conflicts

So far this chapter has remained focused on worldwide crises that are unique to this period in history. Unfortunately, wars, famines, diseases, droughts, floods, poverty, racial tension, violence, crime, and many other forms of suffering seem to be perpetual, omnipresent, and perhaps even unavoidable aspects of human existence. Certain problems that may not be global in scale nonetheless deserve mention because of their undeniable impact on the rest of the world.

The United Nations defines a "major war" as one inflicting more than one thousand battlefield deaths per year. So far this century, there have been at least eight major wars occurring at any given time, with as many as two dozen lesser conflicts brewing simultaneously. One tragic aspect of modern warfare is that in contrast to pre-1900 wars, during which non-combatants comprised a small percentage of the death toll, modern wars have claimed the majority of their victims from the civilian population, often affecting more children than soldiers.[35]

The ongoing war in Sudan, which has claimed at least 300,000 lives, has been called the "Darfur genocide" because of its basis in ethnic and tribal conflict. On one side are the Sudanese military and the Islamic, nomadic Janjawid, while the other side is comprised of rebel groups, such as the Sudan Liberation Movement, recruited from the non-Arab farming communities in the region. The conflict is partly caused and definitely exacerbated by drought, overpopulation, and desertification, as the camel-herding Janjawid are forced to seek water in the agricultural areas. An estimated 2.5 million people have been displaced since the start of the conflict in 2003.

At the time of this writing (2010), the war in Iraq has also been raging for almost seven years, during which at least 150,000 people have died violently, with some estimates as high as 1,000,000.[36] In addition to precious lives, the war has cost at least $600 billion total, with the U.S. Congressional Budget Office predicting the final cost to exceed $2 trillion, which amounts to over $6,000 per U.S. taxpayer.[37] According to the American Friends Service Committee, the money spent on the war in one day ($720 million) could buy health care for more than 420,000 children, new homes for 6,500 families, or outfit 1.3 million existing homes with renewable electricity.[38] When framed in this way, all war can be seen as a tragic opportunity cost affecting millions if not billions of people each day.

ONGOING WORLD CONFLICTS (2010)
Darkest areas = 1000+ deaths/year

Presently there are other wars ongoing in Somalia, the Philippines, Peru, Chechnya, Afghanistan, Pakistan, southern Thailand, Mexico, many parts of Africa, and at least twenty other areas of the globe. As exemplified by the Darfur genocide mentioned above, war is often accompanied by not only death but persecution and famine. The Four Horsemen of the Apocalypse usually ride together, and it seems that they are always on the move.

HUMAN DISEASE AND DIS-EASE

I hope it is clear that none of the large-scale diseases outlined above stands in isolation; they are all interrelated. Each part of the web of life affects all other parts, including humanity, and just as humanity affects all parts of the web (in a dramatic way), all parts in turn affect humans, both collectively and individually. Like the reflective jewels in Indra's net, we are each an integral part of an integrated whole. Writer Arthur Koestler coined the term "holon" (from the Greek word *holos,* meaning "whole") to describe this holistic or holographic quality of reality. While each of us is composed of smaller holons (cells, organs, and systems), we are also a part of the greater holon of humanity, a whole which is part of the biosphere, which itself is part of the planet, which is part of the solar system, the galaxy, etc.

Biologically speaking, our bodies are living extensions of the Earth. We were born from its basic elements and organic compounds, carrying the ocean's saltwater onto land within each of our cells, and have evolved into complex beings miraculously aware of our existence in the universe and on Earth. Given our origins, it is hardly coincidental that activities that benefit our bodies, such as walking, bike riding, and eating healthy, are usually good for the planet as well, just as unhealthy behavior can adversely affect Gaia's well-being.

When our individual bodies become stressed or compromised, they signal to us that something is wrong, and that things will get worse if we fail to rest and regain our balance. Often we ignore such feedback, continuing on our ego-driven way until we fall sick or perhaps even suffer a heart attack or similar systemic breakdown. In regard to the health of the biosphere, the signals are becoming increasingly obvious. It seems that our larger body, the Earth, has been urgently trying to tell us something, and we have only recently begun to listen.

Some might say that our species itself is the sickness, that humans are like so many abnormal cancerous cells that continue to multiply and threaten to overtake and kill their planetary host. While this analogy does have a certain ring of truth, it not only sells humanity short, it fails to take into account the remarkable resiliency and healing capabilities of the Earth, which has survived drastic climate shifts, atmospheric changes, and meteor impacts. Our planet will undoubtedly survive the onslaught of humans. Even if only bacteria and cockroaches were to remain after a devastating global nuclear war, Gaia will eventually regenerate herself and give rise to new forms of life. The more pressing questions are how many species will survive this intensifying onslaught on the biosphere, and whether the only known self-aware species in the universe will become aware enough on a collective level to prevent its own demise.

What Ails Us

Whether or not humans are a growing tumor on Gaia's body, we continue to be affected by cancer, the second leading cause of death worldwide. A 2008 study[39] reports that while the incidence rates of certain cancers are declining (fortunately), the prevalence of other forms has greatly increased within the last decade. Up dramatically since 1995 is the most dangerous form of skin cancer, malignant melanoma, associated with exposure to ultraviolet radiation in sunlight. Rates of this disease have doubled among women and tripled among men since the mid 1980s, likely because of the thinning and breakup of the ozone layer. The same study also found increases in the rates of mouth cancer (up 23 percent since 1995), liver cancer (up 33 percent), and kidney cancer (14 percent). These three diseases are linked with smoking and binge drinking, the latter of which appears to be an increasingly common behavior.

During the time period in question, uterine cancer rose 21 percent. This form of cancer is linked with obesity, which the World Health Organization (WHO) calls a global epidemic. More than one billion people worldwide are overweight, and 300 million are clinically obese. Rates have tripled or quadrupled in certain countries since 1980, mostly due to increased consumption of energy-dense and nutrient-poor "convenience" foods that are high in sugar and saturated fats. As the WHO reports, "economic growth, modernization, urbanization, and globalization of food markets are just some of the forces thought to underlie the epidemic."[40] Obesity is not restricted to affluent societies but increasingly affects developing countries. It cuts across national and socioeconomic boundaries and affects all age groups, with childhood obesity considered "one of the most serious public health challenges of the 21st century."[41]

These statistics suggest that now more than ever people seem to be overindulging in food and alcohol, paralleling the rising rates of consumption on the collective level. In individuals, overconsumption is often symptomatic of underlying psychological problems such as clinical depression, one of the most common forms of mental illness. While the prevalence of depression varies among different countries

from about 1.5 percent to 19 percent, worldwide rates have been rising over the last few decades, with the greatest increase among teen-
agers. Women are still almost twice as likely as men to experience
major depression, although the gender gap appears to be closing. The
WHO cited depression as the leading cause of disability in the U.S.
and other countries in 2000, with expectations that it will become
the second leading cause of disability worldwide (after heart disease)
by the year 2020.[42]

Symbolically it seems, heart disease is the leading cause of death
worldwide, claiming more than seven million lives per year (12 million if one includes stroke, 17 million including all forms of cardiovascular disease). In developed countries, heart disease causes about
one third of all deaths—about 2,600 per day in the U.S. alone.[43]
Major risk factors include high blood pressure and cholesterol,
obesity, smoking, and lack of exercise, all of which are on the rise
worldwide "as a result of industrialization, urbanization, economic
development, and food market globalization."[44]

No discussion of human disease would be complete without the
mention of AIDS. According to UNAIDS, this virus has claimed at
least 25 million lives since its discovery in 1981, making it one of the
most devastating epidemics in history. It ranks among the leading
causes of death worldwide, having claimed some 2.1 million lives in
2007, during which 2.5 million new cases were reported. Although
first noticed among the gay male population, the prevalence of HIV
among women has been rising since the mid-1990s, and most people
are infected through heterosexual sex.

The prevalence of HIV and AIDS is highest among teens and
young adults, especially in developing regions of the world. Most
dramatically affected has been Sub-Saharan Africa, where the disease
may have originated. Here at least 22.5 million people (7 percent of

TOP TEN CAUSES OF DEATH WORLDWIDE	Deaths (millions)	Percent
1. Coronary heart disease	7.20	12.2
2. Stroke and other cerebrovascular diseases	5.71	9.7
3. Lower respiratory infections	4.18	7.1
4. Chronic obstructive pulmonary disease	3.02	5.1
5. Diarrhoeal diseases	2.16	3.7
6. HIV/AIDS	2.04	3.5
7. Tuberculosis	1.46	2.5
8. Trachea, bronchus, lung cancers	1.32	2.3
9. Road traffic accidents	1.27	2.2
10. Prematurity and low birth weight	1.18	2.0

the population) are infected with HIV/AIDS, which in 2007 represented over two-thirds of the world's cases. Other hard-hit areas of the globe include the Caribbean and parts of Latin America, South Asia, and Southeast Asia.[45] Although incidence rates have leveled off in many countries, HIV/AIDS continues to be a major concern worldwide, with annual global spending on the disease estimated by UNAIDS to be around U.S.$10 billion—a figure that many health workers consider appallingly low.

Life, Liberty, and the Pandemic of "Happiness"

It seems tragically obvious that higher standards of living do not translate into physical and emotional well-being. If that were so, one would expect Americans to be the most healthy and blissful society in history, which unfortunately does not seem to be the case. Although certain polls indicate that most Americans do consider themselves happy,[46] the evidence would suggest otherwise. Increased use and abuse of prescription drugs and painkillers, world-record rates of violent crime, incarceration, and military spending, widespread heart disease and other stress-related illness, epidemic obesity, chronic over-consumption patterns, and other factors seem to indicate that in their relentless pursuit of happiness, many Americans have actually forgotten what the word means. To some, perhaps, it entails living comfortably in denial of personal and global suffering.

While denial may be one explanation for this emotional incongruity, my suspicion is that many people have become so estranged from their own deeper feelings that they are simply not aware of them. Recently a friend of mine, who had just entered therapy for the first time in her life, confessed to me tearfully that she hadn't even known that she had been unhappy. For many years she had somehow managed to conceal from herself what seemed all too obvious to others: a chronic malaise that manifested in the many physical ailments of which she often complained and in her frequent nightmares. With the help of her therapist, she became aware of her own dis-ease, which greatly accelerated her healing process.

Sadly, it seems that this kind of disconnect is not uncommon; in fact, it may be the dominant mode of being in affluent societies, if not a mode desired or even cultivated by those in power. An unaware and disconnected population is a complacent one that will support its leaders without question and "happily" uphold business as usual, even in the face of crisis and tragedy. Many readers will recall former President Bush's first address to the nation after 9-11—one of the worst tragedies in U.S. history—during which he essentially encouraged the public to continue shopping. Pundits have pointed out that he could have suggested mourning, grieving, praying, spending time with loved ones, or any number of healthy responses to overwhelming loss; instead he prescribed mindless consumption, thereby defining quite starkly the ideal of freedom to which America was apparently committed, one that suddenly seemed so vulnerable.

It is not my intention to pick on American leaders and citizens, nor portray the economic elite as dedicated to mass mind control. Even if politicians and advertisers do sometimes exploit the insecurities and unhealthy tendencies of the public, those weaknesses must exist in the first place in order to be exploited. The success of any marketing campaign, any piece of propaganda, any work of art, will be determined by how effectively it taps into the *zeitgeist* or current mood of the population, whether fearful, hopeful, depressed, or happy. My own sense is that the prevailing mood in the United States is one of hidden dis-ease masquerading as superficial contentment, while my fear is that the rest of the world is dying to live like Americans.

To want to be happy is hardly unusual. In fact, taught the Buddha, this abiding desire is shared by all sentient beings. Nor is it uncommon to shy away from the negative and gravitate towards the positive; this is the primary tendency of the body-mind. But to habitually acknowledge only pleasant feelings and ignore or repress unpleasant ones can easily result in a narrowing of the range and intensity of emotions, which of course is not true happiness but a mental condition called "flattened affect." This can also be a side effect (or the intended effect) of certain antidepressants, the use of which has nearly tripled in the last decade. Whether through denial, disconnection, drugs, or other means, habitual avoidance of feeling "bummed out" has resulted in millions of people being "numbed out" instead.

Apathy and Alienation

In addressing a woefully serious problem I will pass along a joke: What is the difference between ignorance and apathy? Answer: I don't know and I don't care. The "pandemic" described above could be seen as a kind of unknowing, a disconnection from one's own rich emotional core. It can also be understood as a form of apathy—not an *unwillingness* to extend concern as the word is sometimes used, but an *inability* to feel deeply. While the latter connotation may evoke a more sympathetic response, both describe states that are undesirable and unfortunate, in contrast to the original connotation of apathy. The Greek word *apatheia* was used by the Stoics to describe an emotional stability based on wisdom and clear judgment, similar to the equanimity cultivated by Buddhist practitioners. Apathy is essentially a negation of the word *pathos* (translated as "passion" or "suffering"), indicating that it was once considered a desirable state of serenity.

Just as the word "stoic" has developed a negative connotation, apathy has since come to mean something quite different than wise emotional distance. Psychologically speaking, apathy is a reaction to stress, associated with a condition of learned helplessness in which a person feels a lack of control over a given situation. Apathy can also be caused by more acute stress or trauma, such as that experienced by soldiers who become so accustomed to violence and killing that they become emotionally dead. Even if the cause in each case is different, the effects (and affects) are similar and equally unfortunate. The same is true for other forms of emotional disconnection, repression, denial, alienation, or numbness: all are forms of suffering warranting compassion, and all are disturbingly common in today's world, which is being greatly affected by this collective flat affect.

Many people who report being abducted by UFOs describe their alien captors as detached and unemotional. Even while performing bizarre and cruel experiments upon their hapless subjects, these otherworldly beings remain strangely aloof, often appearing to hover just above the ground. Without commenting on the reality of extraterrestrials, I will say that I see an interesting parallel between their alleged behavior and that of humans in regard to the biosphere. As we perform our ongoing experiments, we seem to be hovering above the Earth, ignoring the objections of other life forms while watching from a curious emotional distance. On the whole and in general, we have become alienated from our deepest emotions, from Nature, and from our Buddha nature.

The truly bizarre thing is that people really do care deeply about the Earth. Nearly everyone enjoys spending time in natural settings, whether roughing it in the remote wilderness or strolling through a city park, and surely very few people are eager to see the disappearance of terrestrial life. Deep down, everyone is an environmentalist, even if he or she has never planted or embraced a tree. We all love Mother Nature, which makes our collective estrangement from her all the more strange and tragic.

The Uniqueness of Our Situation

Whether or not we care or are even aware of it, the truth is that we are living at a most unique time in history. Although there have been many groups in the past that have proclaimed the end of the world, usually from a religious standpoint, never before has the prospect been spelled out in sober scientific data, devoid of spiritual meaning. As Joanna Macy writes:

> With isolated exceptions, every generation prior to ours has lived with the assumption that other generations would follow . . . that the work of our hands and heads and hearts could live on through those who came after us, walking the same Earth, beneath the same sky . . . Now we have lost the certainty that there will be a future for humans. I believe that this loss, felt at some level of consciousness by everyone, regardless of political orientation, is the pivotal psychological reality of our time.[47]

Fortunately for the planet, more and more people are in fact becoming consciously aware of the magnitude of the ecological crisis.

Unfortunately, awareness of the global crisis is often accompanied by a personal crisis marked by a sense of helplessness, hopelessness, or despair. These feelings can be so overwhelming to those who have heard the alarm that they are compelled to hit the snooze button and go back to sleep. Some may fall under the spell of apathy as defined by a lack of control or a sense of futility in the face of a seemingly impossible task: that of stopping or turning around the juggernaut of human progress, need, and greed.

For those committed to staying awake and present to the stark reality of our times, other psychological challenges are likely to arise: a desperate sense of urgency that something be done quickly, often combined with a confusion about where to start or how to proceed. With so many options to consider, so many issues to address, and so many causes to support, one might easily feel overwhelmed or become emotionally burnt out.

The sense of urgency that many people share stems from an awareness that the actionable window of opportunity seems to be closing, compounded by a feeling that time itself seems to be speeding up. As human needs and numbers grow exponentially, so do the problems we face, leading to a sense of contracting space and time, the very definition of *dukkha*. In our individual dis-ease and anxiety, we might well wonder if we are simply contributing to the woes of the world.

While striving to be part of the solution, some may feel like Chicken Little crossbred with the Greek prophet Cassandra, blessed with the ability to see the future and cursed with the inability to alter the outcome or to convince others that the sky is falling. But convince others we must, if life on Earth is to survive. Somehow we must find a way to translate our collective desperation, anger, alienation, and grief—as well as our individual gifts, our passion, and compassion—

into wise and skillful action, and we must do so relatively quickly. For the optimist, the hourglass is half full, while the realist perceives that it is at least half empty.

This book rests on the assertion that we as modern humans must not only change the way we act, but also the way we think. We must transform our collective worldview, our conception of the universe and our own place in it. For at its essence the global crisis represents a spiritual crisis and a species-level identity crisis. Who are we? Where have we come from? Where are we in our evolutionary journey and where might we be headed?

Important questions like these have been addressed by countless philosophers and sages throughout the ages, and by a growing number of new-paradigm thinkers in recent years. By delving into some

of them in the following chapters and endeavoring to help redefine the way we humans conceive of ourselves, my deeper aim is to help change how we *feel* about ourselves. This will naturally affect our relationships: with other human beings, with other forms of life, with the Earth, and with the Cosmos as a whole. My hope is that these relationships will become richer and more intimate, enabling humanity to find and retain a deep sense of community, connection, and belonging, a sense of being at home on a precious and sacred planet in an enchanted and revelatory Cosmos.

TWO
THE ROOTS OF GLOBAL SUFFERING

What were we doing when we unchained this earth from its sun? Whither is it moving now? Whither are we moving? Away from all suns? Are we not plunging continually? Backward, sideward, forward, in all directions? Is there still any up or down? Are we not straying as through an infinite nothing? Do we not feel the breath of empty space? Has it not become colder? Is not night continually closing in on us?

— Friedrich Nietzsche[1]

So how is it that we find ourselves in such a frightening situation?

From a Buddhist perspective, the question itself contains the source of dis-ease, on a personal level at least. The cause of individual suffering, according to the Buddha, lies with the notion of selfhood, particularly in the idea that there exists a fixed, independent self or soul that endures forever in the same state, a metaphysical position usually called eternalism.

It should be noted right off that the Buddha did not explicitly deny the existence of the self, which would have meant opposing eternalism with nihilism, a stance he considered equally problematic. Regardless of the name later given to his teachings, the Buddha was not concerned with "isms" or metaphysical positions that need defending, but with freedom from these and other mental constraints. When asked about the ultimate reality of the self, he preferred to keep silent.

What the Buddha *did* espouse was that the conventional view of self is not quite right, that sentient beings live in a state of *avidya* or "unknowing" (the less polite translation being "ignorance" or "delusion"). His point was that the "I" that each of us tends to think of as a static, monolithic structure is really just a conglomeration of ever-changing thoughts, emotions, concepts, memories, sensations, urges, bodily functions, and other parts that don't really add up to a lasting and substantial whole. Looking deeply into his own mind, the Buddha could find no firm foundation on which to build a home, no particular component of experience that remained unchanging against the ceaseless flow of phenomena he called the "mindstream."

Of course, in our daily lives, it is perfectly natural and useful to refer to "ourselves" as the agents of activity. The real problem is not that we use the word "self" but that we too often think of it as something real and lasting and therefore become attached to it. And the degree to which we identify with or cling to any particular aspect of our fluctuating experience, even a pleasurable one, is the degree to which we are bound to suffer. As William Blake wrote, "He who binds to himself a joy, doth the winged life destroy; but he who kisses the joy as it flies, lives in eternity's sunrise."

Along with a definite, objectified self or "I" comes a definite, objectified not-self. Every other entity suddenly appears as either desirable (helpful to the self, to be acquired or used for its reinforcement) or undesirable (harmful to the self, to be avoided or actively fought). When trapped in this mindset, a person experiences the world as a place of stark dualism in which self and other, good and bad, mind and matter, or any number of pairs of opposites exist in varying degrees of imbalance, tension, or conflict.

Once the "I" has taken form, it begins to gain weight, so to speak, to grow in strength and solidity through the accumulation of self-concepts, which form the basis of stories that get acted out. A person who believes herself to be a "good daughter," for example, will tend to behave accordingly, as will a "bad son" or "the life of the party." Depending on the strength of attachment to one's self-concepts, any inability to adequately enact them will result in some degree of distress. Even if performed wonderfully, many roles of the solidified self or ego clearly have less-than-wonderful effects.

So far I have been speaking of the ego in individual terms. What I hope to convey in this chapter is that the process just mentioned can also be seen to apply to the formation and solidification of a collective sense of self or cultural identity, introducing imbalance and dis-ease on a much greater scale. To find the roots of this collective imbalance, we will be traveling back to the origins of the human race, indeed to the birth of the universe itself. The journey will be a long and ideally fruitful one, during which we will discover not one single, solitary source of global suffering but a confluence of many tributaries entering and impelling the larger collective mindstream.

IN THE BEGINNING...

Buddhism is unique among world religions in that its scriptures make no mention of a creator god. The Buddha himself, who is not usually worshiped as a divine being but venerated as a teacher and a symbol of innate wisdom, was reluctant to engage in metaphysical speculation about the origin of the universe. Nevertheless, there does exist in the *Agganna Sutta* a Buddhist creation story, which is meant to be understood metaphorically:

> In the beginning of a world cycle, neither beings nor their world had solid form or distinctive features. Weightless, luminous, and identical, the beings wafted about over a dark and watery expanse. When a frothy substance appeared on the waters, they tasted it. It was delicious, and for its sweet honey flavor a craving arose.
>
> As the beings consumed more and more, both they and their world changed, both becoming more distinct. The beings began to lose their identical luminosity, and as they did, sun, moon, and stars appeared, bringing with them the alternation of day and night. The beings began to solidify and vary in appearance.
>
> Pride and vanity arose as they compared their beauty, and the savory froth vanished. The beings bewailed its loss . . . In its place, on an earth that was now firmer, mushroom-like growths appeared of similar tastiness—only to disappear as the creatures fattened on them and changed. The mushrooms were replaced by vines, and these, in turn, by rice. . . .
>
> When rice first grew, it was without husk, and after being harvested would grow again in a day. A lazy person, to save effort, decided to harvest two meals at once. Soon all beings were harvesting for two days at a time, then four days, then eight. With this new practice of hoarding, the rice changed: a husk appeared around the grain and the cut stem did not grow again. It stood only as dry stubble. So the people divided and fenced the land, setting boundaries to ensure their private source of food.
>
> Soon a greedy one took rice from a neighboring plot. Admonished by the others, he promised to refrain but he took again, repeatedly. Since admonishment was of no avail, he was beaten. In such fashion, with the institution of private property, arose theft and lying and abuse and violence. . . . [2]

In this allegory, manifestation begins with desire, which brings about the separation of sun and moon, which can be regarded as symbolic of psyche and matter, respectively. The story illustrates how the formation and solidification of the ego are processes that occur over time, resulting in jealousy, competition, and greed, eventually manifesting in social unrest, theft, and violence. The story also describes how psyche and matter, although split, are interdependent; that the world takes on various forms in relation to the thoughts, desires, and actions of the beings inhabiting that world. This is not an echo of the postmodern belief that each of us creates our own reality; rather it suggests that all beings participate in the *co-creation* of what might be called reality through their interactions with the environment and with each other. Such dynamic interdependence can be observed directly in the process of biological evolution and in the web of life, in which each species—indeed each organism— both influences and is influenced by other species and individuals, while also altering and being altered by the environment. These concepts are of central importance to this book, and to this chapter in particular.

Evolution, Involution, and The Fall

A variation on the Buddhist creation myth can be found in the biblical story of Genesis in which Adam and Eve eat from the Tree of Knowledge of Good and Evil (duality), leading to their banishment from Eden, that place of unity and peace. They cover their genitals because they have become "self-conscious"; they have lost their connection with their own true nature (divine innocence), with their biological nature, and with Nature as a whole. Adam is forced to work the land for food while Eve is condemned to a different kind of labor, that of bearing children. She begets Cain and Abel, who introduce competition, jealousy, and warfare into the human equation. After that, things get much more complicated, as we shall see.

While both the Buddhist myth and the Eden story tell of human creation, each also presents a condensed, symbolic account of human evolution, from original unity to increasing disunity, alienation, and antagonism. More accurately, these myths describe de-volution or involution, a symbolic Fall from a state of grace, innocence, or non-dual awareness. As pure consciousness or spirit splits from its divine source and becomes further removed and alienated from its original essence, it becomes progressively more isolated, dense, and solid, a process reflected in the increasing solidification of the world at large. With increasing density of both self and world comes a sense of *dukkha*—of contraction, crowdedness, and disharmony—which can intensify and eventually manifest in conflict and violence.

Another conception of cosmic evolution is known as the "Great Chain of Being." In this framework, developed by classical thinkers and favored by many religious traditions, reality is seen as being arranged into a unified hierarchy of matter, body, mind, soul, and spirit. These levels are imagined as being either stacked on top of one another or nestled within each other like a set of Russian dolls, giving rise to an alternate term: the Great Nest of Being. These conceptions of evolution lend themselves to spatial depiction and to a metaphoric language of luminosity, such as the term "enlightenment," which may refer to either a gradual process or a sudden revelatory experience of "seeing the light."

Science also favors a model of evolution or progress, although soul and spirit are set aside (or dismissed altogether), while mind or psyche remains the subject of much confusion and controversy. The general consensus among the scientific community is that in the course of

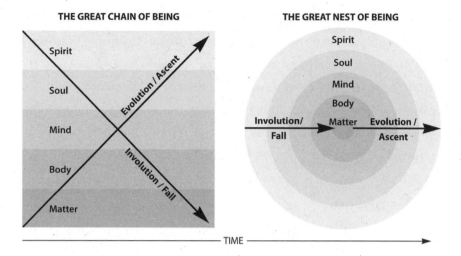

Whether one favors the idea of evolution or progress over that of involution or entropy, the truth is that both processes are happening simultaneously.

evolution, consciousness arose rather suddenly in the human brain as a kind of mutation or accident, an aberration in an otherwise unconscious universe composed of lifeless matter and quantifiable energy. In this view, humans alone possess consciousness; everything else functions essentially like a machine (the strict materialist insists that even the human mind can be reduced to its chemical interactions). In addition to raising more questions than it answers, this perspective privileges the human being (with negative consequences for other species, namely extinction) as psychologically alone in the universe (with negative consequences for humans, namely alienation). A more holistic view, known by many traditional cultures, ancient philosophers, mystics, shamans, and poets, and advanced by a growing number of modern thinkers, is that consciousness is and always has been present throughout the universe; indeed the Cosmos itself is something of a conscious entity, an evolving, self-organizing system that is alive with creativity and meaning.

Both evolution and involution are understood as unfolding over time, usually in a more or less linear (or spiral) fashion. As noted, both processes can also be conceived of spatially, in terms of ascent and descent, or visually in terms of increasing or decreasing light. In any case, once the initial split from unity has occurred, the tension of opposites arises and, unless kept carefully in balance, begins to mount. The stage has been set for our cosmic drama to unfold.

Cycles of Four

The Hindu tradition speaks of time in terms of cosmic cycles or *mahayugas,* each comprised of four *yugas* or ages, with each of these being different from one another in duration and character. Often compared to the Gold, Silver, Bronze, and Iron ages of classical antiquity, each *yuga* can be seen to represent a decrease in value, a contraction and corruption—a step down, as it were, from the previous period. Along with this condensation of space comes a contraction of time, as each age is also said to be shorter than the one preceding it. This system demonstrates a deep understanding of the evolutionary/involutionary dynamic with which we are concerned.

According to Hindu cosmology, we are currently living in the last and darkest age, the Kali Yuga, characterized by conflict and discord. The diabolical ruler of this age is Kali, not to be confused with the goddess Kali, who is usually depicted wearing a garland of severed heads and sticking out her bright-red tongue. The male demon Kali, who at the end of the age will face off against the tenth and final incarnation of Vishnu (named Kalki, to further confuse matters), is described as a huge, soot-colored, foul-smelling ogre who resides in unwholesome places such as taverns, casinos, and slaughterhouses, while the *yuga* itself is thought to be characterized

In this card from the classic Rider-Waite tarot, the four fixed signs of the zodiac (Aquarius, Taurus, Leo, and Scorpio) are depicted by a human, bull, lion, and eagle respectively. The same symbolism can be found on the Wheel of Fortune card, while a variation on this theme appears on the front cover of this book.

THE WORLD.

by greed, warfare, environmental degradation, murder, deceit, lust, intoxication, and meat eating.

As exemplified by the four seasons, the division of time into quadrants or cycles of four is a common practice throughout the world. As noted, the ancient Greeks and Romans used a system of four ages—Gold, Silver, Bronze, and Iron—that parallels the Hindu system, although in the classical version the ages are shorter and of equal duration, perhaps reflective of the Western predilection for order, regularity, and literalness. The classical system may have been derived from earlier astrological systems of the ancient Near East, in which the zodiac was divided into four elements—air, earth, fire, and water—and four fixed signs: Aquarius, Taurus, Leo, and Scorpio. A symbolic depiction of this can be found in "The World" card of the Tarot, in which an hermaphroditic figure is shown surrounded by four heads: that of a human (Aquarius), a bull (Taurus), a lion (Leo), and an eagle (Scorpio). These four figures, sometimes correlated with the four evangelists Matthew, Mark, Luke, and John, also show up in the Book of Revelation, suggesting their connection with a cycle much longer than a single year. This will be elaborated upon in a later discussion of astrology.

From a scientific perspective, the universe is regarded as having evolved from lighter elements into progressively heavier ones, as in the Buddhist creation myth and the Hindu *yuga* cycle. In an abstract sense, the evolution of the universe can also be divided into four epochs of increasing density, symbolized by the classical elements of Fire, Air, Water, and Earth. In this hypothetical model, the epoch of Fire would correspond with the initial, sudden expansion of the primordial fireball and the formation of the lightest elements of hydrogen (which, being comprised of one electron and one proton, introduces a primary duality) and helium; the epoch of Air would correspond to further cosmic expansion and the formation of heavier elements as well as galaxies, stars, and planets; the epoch of Water correlates with the formation of Earth's oceans and the appearance of life; and the Earth epoch would begin with the population of the continents and the evolution of increasingly diverse and complex forms of life, including humans. The history of our own species can in turn be broken down into the aforementioned "Ages of Man," those of Gold, Silver, Bronze, and Iron, or any number of other divisions used to describe human evolution. All such evolutionary models are, of course, highly abstracted. The transitions between periods are rarely distinct, and the progression hardly linear, with diversions and dead ends along the way. Nonetheless, the evolutionary process does seem to happen in phases, often punctuated by relatively sudden phase shifts or quantum leaps, a concept important to bear in mind when considering our current planetary crisis.

The Story of the Universe, Condensed

According to the modern cosmological conception, it all began about 14 billion years ago with a Big Bang—a strange name, given that no sound travels in space, which was in fact created in that instant, as was time. But such are the limitations of language outside the context of conventional reality. In the terms of modern cosmologist Brian Swimme, the universe "flared forth" from a point of zero size and infinite creative potential, "unfurling" in all directions through (and *as*) space. The first atomic particles stabilized within the first second, forming immense clouds of hydrogen and helium destined to become galaxies.

After about a billion years, stars began to form as portions of each cosmic cloud coalesced and collapsed into burning balls of gas. Heavier elements were forged within these nuclear furnaces, some of them large and intense enough to burn up their own fuel after only several billion years. These huge stars collapsed upon themselves and exploded into gigantic supernovae, scattering stardust out into space. These supernova clouds birthed second and third generations of stars, comprised of heavier elements like carbon, oxygen, and nitrogen.

One of these stars became our own sun, forming about 4.5 billion years ago near the edge of the Milky Way, a spiral galaxy some 100,000 light years in diameter. During the half-million years of the sun's formation, the spinning disc from which it was born divided into distinct planets: Mercury, Venus, Earth, Mars, Jupiter, Saturn, Uranus, Neptune, and Pluto. Originally they all churned

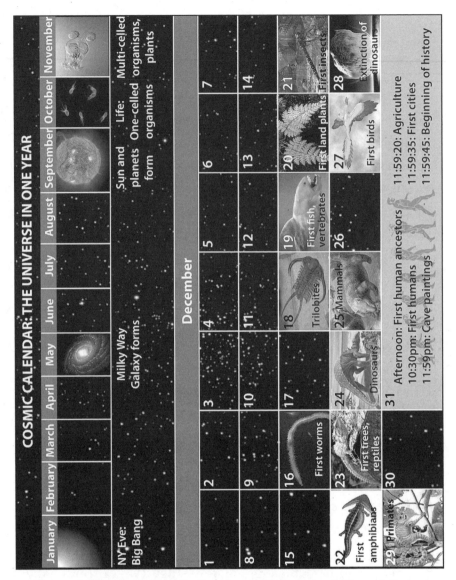

COSMIC CALENDAR: THE UNIVERSE IN ONE YEAR

First put forth by Carl Sagan, the "cosmic calendar" represents the evolution of the universe as compressed into a single year. In this scheme, the birth of the solar system occurs in September, life emerges in October, vertebrates appear on December 19th, mammals on Christmas Day, and modern humans at about 11:54 p.m. on New Year's Eve. All of recorded history transpires during the 15 seconds before midnight.

with chemical activity, but within a few hundred thousand years, all but one of them had stabilized into either gaseous balls or rocky wastelands.

Owing to its position relative to the Sun, as well as its own internal dynamics, the Earth remained a fecund combination of solids, liquids, and gases that continued to interact, creating the ideal conditions for the formation of life. About four billion years ago, the first one-celled prokaryotes arose and thrived in the nutrient-rich oceans of Earth, followed two million years later by eukaryotes capable of combining their DNA to create new forms of life. This led to the appearance of the first multi-cellular organisms some 700 million years ago, and eventually to fish, insects, and plants, the last of which began filling the slowly shifting continents of Earth. The first amphibians crawled onto shore about 370 million years ago, evolving into reptiles and then into dinosaurs about 235 million years ago. Mammals appeared soon thereafter, about 215 million years ago, in the form of small marsupials, which took to the trees to become early primates (about 70 million years ago) and then monkeys (about 36 million years ago).

Proto-humans emerged about four million years ago as *Homo habilis*, the tool maker, followed two million years later by the upright-walking *Homo erectus*. Early humans, *Homo sapiens*, arrived on the scene about 200,000 years ago, evolving distinctly modern features by about 40,000 years ago, while the first cave paintings date back 18,000 years. After millions of years of hunting and gathering, humans began domesticating plants and animals about 10,000 BCE, leading to the first human settlements. The birth of civilization as marked by written language and the appearance of city-states occurred about 3,500 BCE in Sumeria in the Fertile Crescent, followed by the cultures of ancient Egypt and the Indus Valley in modern-day Pakistan, as well as that of the Olmecs in Mesoamerica. Ancient Greek culture flourished during the aforementioned Axial Age until being supplanted by the Roman Empire.

The rest, as they say, is history. It is a rich, complex, and colorful one marked by wars, revolutions, inventions, achievements, discoveries, and ideas that changed the world, for better and for worse, all of which are well known to the historian and the scholar. As neither, my primary concern here lies not so much with the specifics of human history, fascinating though they may be, but with the general and gradual transformation of human consciousness, a process that influences—and is influenced by—historical and cultural developments.

THE UNFOLDING OF CONSCIOUSNESS

This book adopts the metaphysical position mentioned above, that the material universe is conscious in its own mysterious way. The appearance of human beings on planet Earth does, however, mark a significant development or perhaps a quantum leap: the genesis of self-reflective awareness. As a species, *Homo sapiens* ("knowing man"), we are not only aware of ourselves, but as modern humans, sometimes called *Homo sapiens sapiens,* we are aware that we are aware. In this regard we may be special among Earth's creatures, or at least we think that we are, which has been of no small consequence in our collective cultural adventure. Caveats aside, humans do seem unique in many ways, most notably in our ability to compose music and poetry, plan for the future or reflect on the past, marvel at the sublime beauty of a sunset, or ponder the origin of the universe or of suffering.

Looking at the situation from a more cosmic perspective (and setting aside considerations of extraterrestrial intelligence), human consciousness represents the universe becoming aware of itself for the first time in its 14-billion-year existence. From another point of view: human beings, having evolved from uniquely terrestrial elements, represent Gaia becoming aware of herself for the first time in her 4.5-billion-year life. In either case, humans do appear to represent the evolutionary avant-garde, the frontier of consciousness, a position that seems to be both a blessing and a curse. While our specialized form of consciousness allows us to ascend to great heights and commune with the Divine, it also can separate us from our earthly biological roots and from the natural world.

Again we are brought back to the analogy of Eden, that mythic place in which the Tree of Life grows beside the Tree of Knowledge of Good and Evil. But we have eaten the forbidden fruit of the latter and been banished from the Garden, condemned to live in conflict between our divine or Buddha nature and Nature herself, between psyche and matter. As has been suggested, the human story can be regarded as unfolding within this figurative nether region, a purgatory that is beginning to look and feel increasingly hellish.

Structures of Consciousness

Human evolution has been studied by countless sages and scholars in many different contexts (biological, sociological, philosophical, spiritual), each employing a different model in which the process is usually divided into successive stages. The integral philosopher Ken Wilber has done an impressive job of comparing and correlating many of these models, the results of which appear in his book *Integral Psychology*. Wilber's own comprehensive, "all-quadrant-all-level" (AQAL) model lays out the evolutionary process along four main lines of development: interior-individual (the quadrant of psychology and

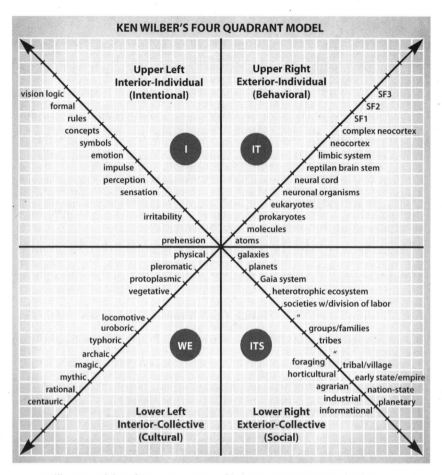

KEN WILBER'S FOUR QUADRANT MODEL

Upper Left
Interior-Individual
(Intentional)

Upper Right
Exterior-Individual
(Behavioral)

vision logic
formal
rules
concepts
symbols
emotion
impulse
perception
sensation

I

IT

SF3
SF2
SF1
complex neocortex
neocortex
limbic system
reptilan brain stem
neural cord
neuronal organisms
eukaryotes
prokaryotes
molecules
atoms

irritability

prehension

physical
pleromatic
protoplasmic
vegetative

galaxies
planets
Gaia system
heterotrophic ecosystem
societies w/division of labor
"

locomotive
uroboric
typhoric
archaic
magic
mythic
rational
centauric

WE

ITS

groups/families
tribes
"
foraging
horticultural
agrarian
industrial
informational

tribal/village
early state/empire
nation-state
planetary

Lower Left
Interior-Collective
(Cultural)

Lower Right
Exterior-Collective
(Social)

In Wilber's model, Gebser's structures of human consciousness—archaic, magic, mythic, mental, and integral (here called centauric)—are located in the lower left quadrant.

spirituality), exterior-individual (science), interior-collective (world-views), and exterior-collective (social structures). These four quadrants are divided into different levels, each of which finds correspondence in the other quadrants. Wilber's conception of reality is far more detailed and profound than what is presented here, and readers are encouraged to explore his work further.

In his studies of collective consciousness (lower left quadrant), Wilber has been influenced by the work of Jean Gebser, a twentieth-century philosopher born in Imperial Germany (now Poland) who conceived of consciousness as unfolding into five different "structures," namely the archaic, magical, mythical, mental, and integral. As we touch briefly upon each of these modes of awareness, it is important to bear in mind that within a given structure, the more fundamental ones continue to function. In other words, although we as individuals may operate primarily within a mental structure of consciousness, we can also consciously access—or unconsciously lapse into—archaic, magical, or mythical awareness. Although the more fundamental structures may not have access to successive ones, they are not to be thought of as more primitive in the derogatory sense, but as entirely different modes of perception. To discourage hierarchical thinking, Gebser described the transitions from one structure to the next as "mutations" rather than progressions, and stressed that each structure represents a kind of enrichment as well as an impoverishment due to an increased remoteness from spiritual origin. The figures on page 83 should provide some clarification of these key concepts.

Archaic: In his masterwork entitled *The Ever-Present Origin,* Gebser explains that in the archaic structure, consciousness remains undifferentiated from the world. The individual is motivated primarily by immediate needs for food, shelter, and warmth, much like an infant during the first months of life. Inasmuch as an archaic person forms an identity, it is based on being part of a collective or tribe, which is in turn embedded in the immediate environment or ecosystem. Archaic consciousness might be compared to a form of non-dual awareness in which a self-concept has not yet been formed. To quote the Buddhist creation myth: "Weightless, luminous, and identical, the beings wafted about over a dark and watery expanse."

Gebser likened archaic consciousness to a state of deep sleep and described it as follows:

> It is origin. Only in a terminological sense is it a "first" structure emanating from that perfect identity existing "before" (or behind) all oneness or unity which it initially might have represented. It is akin, if not identical, to the original state of biblical paradise: a time where the soul is yet dormant, a time of complete non-differentiation of man and the universe.[3]

Although it cannot be securely situated in time, the archaic structure presumably extends far back into the mists of ancient prehistory, out of which our earliest ancestors emerged. Their eventual invention of stone tools ushered in the Paleolithic era, during which hunting and gathering became the dominant means of subsistence. Such a lifestyle could hardly be considered idyllic, yet, contrary to Thomas Hobbes' description of "primitive" peoples living "solitary, poor, nasty, brutish, and short" lives, they undoubtedly enjoyed much more leisure time than the average industrial human. Also, despite the common but not universal division of labor along gender lines, hunting and foraging societies (a few of which survive, though archaic consciousness does not) tend to be largely egalitarian and non-hierarchical, due primarily to the absence of material possessions or ownership of land.

Magic: With this structure of consciousness, the individual begins to feel a basic sense of self, but the separation between psyche and cosmos has not fully occurred. The individual may feel somewhat distinct from the world but remains in continual communication and

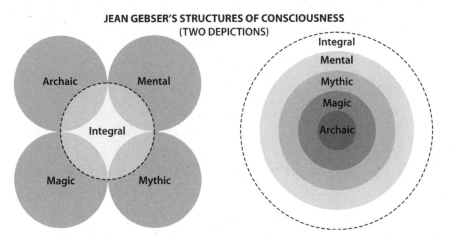

JEAN GEBSER'S STRUCTURES OF CONSCIOUSNESS
(TWO DEPICTIONS)

Although Gebser normally depicted his structures of consciousness as on the left, the other version harkens the Great Nest of Being and emphasizes the idea that within a given structure, the more fundamental structures continue to function.

communion with it. Similarly, she feels an identification with her tribe or ethnic region and a deep connection with Nature, which is thought to be governed by spirits—of wind, rain, plants, and other natural elements. These spirits can be invoked through ritual and prayer, called upon to confer blessings and curses, or to heal sickness, which is usually believed to be the result of demonic possession.

Gebser describes the magic as "a world of pure but meaningful accident; a world in which all things and persons are interrelated, but the not-yet-centered Ego is dispersed over the world of phenomena."[4] Everything exists in space-less and time-less unity in which any object or action can be interchanged with any other, independent of rational, causal connection. The intertwining of human and Nature is reflected in the earliest art and cave paintings, in which human forms share the same plane as animals and plants; there is no background, for none was perceived. Humans were sometimes depicted

with glowing auras, suggesting a greater sensitivity to psychic phenomena, and usually without mouths, which assume much greater
importance within the mythic structure.

Due in part to its timeless character, the magic structure, like the
archaic, resists strict chronological placement. Still, one can safely
say that the Agricultural Revolution of roughly 10,000 BCE initiated
the decline of hunter-gatherer societies and of magical consciousness in its pure form. (It does survive in certain traditional cultures,
although primarily in what Gebser would call its "deficient" form,
having been devitalized by contact with industrial culture.) In contrast
to the cosmic orientation of the archaic mind, the magical imagination is aligned primarily with the energies of Nature. Archaeological
evidence suggests that before the Neolithic revolution and the incep-
tion of farming, warfare was relatively rare.

Mythic: From the standpoint of this author, it is within this structure
that the real drama begins, for mythic consciousness marks the birth
of the human ego on a collective level. The process of human individuation here surges forth, as reflected in the earliest written myths,
which feature masculine, kingly, hero figures as in the Sumerian epic
poem of Gilgamesh or in Homer's tales of Odysseus. In contrast to
the creation stories of pre-literate cultures and periods, these myths
tell of specific individuals (even if semi-divine) who struggle against
various forms of adversity—a narrative structure that has been
employed in nearly every subsequent story, play, and movie.

In the earliest myths, a common theme is that of the sea voyage,
which represents a gradual mastery over the psyche or soul, often
associated with water. Whereas the magic structure brought about
an awareness of the external world, the mythic structure leads to an
awareness of the internal world, and "what is viewed inwardly, as in

	ARCHAIC	MAGIC	MYTHIC	MENTAL	INTEGRAL
Symbol	None	Point •	Circle ○	Triangle △	Sphere ●
Essence	Identity	Unity	Polarity	Duality	Transparency
Orientation	Cosmic	Terrestrial	Psychic, we-oriented	Egocentric, I-oriented	Ego-free
State	Deep sleep	Sleep	Dream	Wakefulness	Lucid dream?
Mode	Latency	Emotion	Imagination	Abstraction	Concretion
Emphasis	Unconscious spirit	Nature	Soul/psyche	Space/world	Conscious spirit
Time consciousness	Pre-temporal	Timeless	Past-oriented	Future-oriented	Time-free

Gebser's Structures of Consciousness.

a dream, has its conscious emergence and polar complement in poetically shaped utterance,"[5] i.e., myth. Indeed Gebser described myths as collective dreams, and likened mythic consciousness to a dream state, which to the mythic mind was as vivid as what we call "reality." Waking consciousness and dream were polar complements, just as myth was the complement of life. Such polarity is characteristic of the mythic structure, which can be symbolized by a circle, the nearly universal, age-old symbol of the mythic focus: the soul. As will be discussed, the mental structure divides this polarity or complementarity into an oppositional duality.

Another striking theme of the earliest myths is that of aggression or anger. The Indian epic known as the *Mahabharata* (the well-known Bhagavad Gita is a small part of

Mythically, anger is associated with the god Mars. His symbol has come to represent masculinity, which during the mythic structure came to predominate over the feminine. This symbol also prefigures the birth of the mental structure: breaking out of the mythical circle with outward-directed energy and discursive thought, as conveyed in the myth of Athena, goddess of reason, who springs from the head of Zeus.

this larger epic) tells of a major battle, while the original Western myth, the *Iliad*, begins: "Sing, goddess, the *wrath* of Peleus' son Achilles." As exemplified by the rebellious teenager, anger seems to be an important emotion in the process of individuation, as Gebser suggests:

> Anger is the force that bursts the confines of community and clan, to the extent that it manifests the "hero" in the individual and spurs him on towards further individuation, self-assertion, and consequently Ego emergence.[6]

Mythic man's newfound awareness of his individuality is reflected in myth as well as in the art of the ancient world. Ordinary mortal humans begin to appear as distinct from the first natural backgrounds, common objects become valid subjects, and ancient Greek sculpture captures the human form with unprecedented realism.

With the arrival of a central figure in the form of human ego, we now have our protagonist and antagonist rolled into one. As the story continues to unfold and the plot thickens, so do the psychological structures in tandem with the structures of the material world. Recalling the Buddhist creation myth, we have reached the point at which solidified beings begin to put up fences, both psychological and literal. Historically, humans have by this point begun to form permanent settlements and city-states, requiring the division of labor, hierarchical power structures, and armies for both protection and conquest. The ego requires a great deal of maintenance, and the more solidified it becomes, the more maintenance it requires.

The Mythic Mind and Monotheism

In regard to the story of consciousness, we now return to our discussion of the mythic structure. As noted, it was within this definitive form of consciousness that the first civilizations arose (associated

CALL HIM ISHMAEL . . .

In his popular book *Ishmael,* Daniel Quinn writes about the division of the world into the "Leavers" and the "Takers," the former group corresponding with traditional hunter-gatherers and the latter with settled or "civilized" agricultural societies. According to the title character, Ishmael (a telepathic gorilla), the Leavers live "in the hands of the gods" or in harmony with Nature, taking only what they need and leaving the rest for other creatures. The Takers, on the other hand, hoard surplus food and practice "Totalitarian Agriculture" in which they assert complete control over the Earth's food supply.

Ishmael explains that the Takers behave in accordance with their interpretation of a story they have been told about themselves. Their story appears in Genesis, in which God grants humans "dominion . . . over every living thing that creeps upon the earth." In this biblical myth, Cain is described as a sedentary farmer, while his brother Abel is a nomadic shepherd. Cain the Taker kills Abel the Leaver, presumably in order to steal his land or his livestock, making Abel the first martyr and Cain the prototypical evildoer.

In emphasizing the fact that a culture is defined by its story or self-concept (i.e., its worldview), Ishmael says:

> There's nothing fundamentally wrong with people. Given a story to enact that puts them in accord with the world, they will live in accord with the world. . . . And, given a story to enact in which the world is a foe to be conquered, they will conquer it like a foe, and one day, inevitably, their foe will lie bleeding to death at their feet, as the world is now.[7]

Ishmael later gets to the heart of the matter by saying: "The premise of the Takers' story is 'The world belongs to man' . . . The premise of the Leavers' story is 'Man belongs to the world.'"[7] The difference between these two ideologies is profound, with painfully obvious implications for the world at large.

herein with the birth of human ego), along with writing and the earliest sacred texts. The oldest of the world's religions, Hinduism, began in the Indus Valley sometime between 1700 and 1100 BCE, during which time the Vedas are thought to have been composed. Debate exists about whether these scriptures were created by the original Indus Valley civilization, by their predecessors, or perhaps by the "arya" people to whom the texts repeatedly refer. In Sanskrit, *arya* simply means "noble" or "spiritual" (as in the Four Noble Truths), but evidence suggests that the Aryans were actually an ancient Indo-Iranian race that migrated or invaded from somewhere near the Caspian Sea. The language of the earliest of the four Vedas, the *Rigveda*, is closely related to that of the ancient Andronovo people (a Caspian-area culture that may have invented the chariot, first mentioned in the Vedas), and to Avestan, the language in which the sacred writings of Zoroastrianism were composed.

Although the ancient Iranian prophet Zoroaster is often cited as one of the world's first monotheists, an earlier proponent was the Egyptian ruler Amenhotep IV, who lived during the fourteenth century BCE. Also centered on a single god (and the fatherly figure of Abraham, progenitor of Judaism, Islam, and Christianity) was the Hebrew Bible, written between 1300 and 400 BCE. Apart from these early exceptions, polytheism prevailed in the Ancient Near East, or more accurately a system called henotheism or monolatrism in which each city-state worshiped its own local deity while also acknowledging the existence of other divinities. Rivalries among city-states seem to have existed in much the same way that inter-city sports rivalries exist today, with everyone idolizing their home team but enjoying the competition nonetheless. Such was the mythic mindset, which was unacquainted with the notion of absolute truth that would all but define the emerging mental structure of consciousness.

During his reign, Amenhotep IV, the likely father of Tutankhamen, made the historically crucial declaration that the sun god Aten was not only the highest god but the *sole* god. Changing his name to Akhenaten, he ordered the defacing of temples dedicated to other deities and the removal of all inscriptions mentioning "gods" in the plural. Akhenaten's firm insistence on monotheism is echoed in the biblical story of Moses and the golden calf, which represents idolatry or the "false gods" of a bygone age. It seems significant that this central patriarch's angry denunciation of polytheism occurred after his descent from Mount Sinai with the Ten Commandments, for here we see the institutionalization of an all-powerful "sky god" and His immutable laws—another example of human consciousness becoming aligned with the transcendent, ever-radiant Sun, the light of which drowns out that of all other heavenly bodies.

As the Western spirit was being formed by Judaism, the Western mind was being defined by the ancient Greeks, who may have inherited some of their sky gods—most notably Zeus—from the nomadic warrior cultures that swept into Greece from the north. During this period the Greek pantheon, always in a state of creative evolution and flux, took on a distinctly patriarchal character. Eventually the goddesses became subordinate, and the worship of older female deities like Isis and Ishtar went underground. This movement towards masculine dominance, which occurred in many cultures during the mythic phase, was accompanied by a disenchantment of the earthly realm.

Thus the gods began to migrate from the Earth to the heavens, from immanence to transcendence, while humans were undergoing their own transition into a new structure of consciousness. This liminality was reflected in the stories of the Greek gods and goddesses, who lived and moved between the divine and earthly realms, meddling in human affairs and often behaving in capricious and even immoral ways. Likewise, the God of the Old Testament was at times vengeful and cruel, indicating that a full separation between good and evil had not yet occurred. During the transition from mythic to mental, the human mind continued to exist in a state of polarity or equilibrium of opposites rather than being defined by the dualism and absolutism that would eventually prevail. In the ancient Near East at least, the forbidden fruit was slowly being passed around.

The Birth of the Mental

The mutation from mythic to mental is anticipated in the biblical story of the Tree of Knowledge (of duality) and symbolized more graphically in the Greek myth of Athena, goddess of reason, who emerges or leaps from the skull of Zeus. Athena is described as owl-eyed, possessing the ability to see clearly that which had formerly been shadowy, amorphous, and obscure. In light of this, it could hardly be coincidental that Athens became the center of the awakening of the Western mind to philosophy and rational thought.

The root of the word "mental" is *ma/me,* from which come the words matter, material, meaning, measure, and meter, all of which are relevant to this mode of perception. The root appears in Athena's Roman name, Minerva (originally Menerva), her mother Metis, her mid-husbands Prometheus and Hermes, and in the names of the earliest historical kings, namely Menes of Egypt, Minos of Crete, and Manu of India, whose name means "man, thinker, and measurer." As Gebser writes:

> Even if we recall only the most important of these words . . . we can circumscribe the essence of this mental structure: it is a world of man, that is, a predominantly human world in which "man is the measure [and measurer] of all things."[9]

Like Moses, the ancient patriarchs mentioned above were also the upholders of laws, which assume greater importance within the mental structure. Of course, the ascendance of codified law parallels that of writing, which during this period of transition underwent its own mutation. On the temple of Apollo at Delphi, the definitive phrase "Know Thyself" was inscribed from left to right, defying the tradition of writing either vertically (as in the Far East) or from right to left (as in the Middle East). This signifies a psychic reorientation to the side of the body related to consciousness and wakefulness, in contrast to the left side, that of the unconscious and unknown. Masculinity too is usually correlated with the "right," which in English also means direct and correct.

Athena, copy of fifth-century BCE original (Greek).

The transition from the mythic to the mental structure is the only one that has occurred within the historical period, specifically during the Axial Age. Although the shift occurred over centuries, Gebser points to the statement of the early Greek philosopher Parmenides that "thinking and being [are] one and the same." A later variation on this idea is Descartes' famous phrase, "I think, therefore I am," in which thinking is identified not with Being in general (i.e., existence) but with the being of an isolated individual. The *logos* (divine reason) was to be further diminished and dissected by the English thinker Thomas Hobbes, who asserted that "thinking is calculation in words." As will be discussed, this change in focus from essence or quality to mere quantity indicates a shift into what Gebser called the rational phase of the mental structure. In Latin, *ratio* (RAH-tee-oh)

The Taoist symbol of Tai Chi captures the harmonic polarity of yin and yang. In the East, the side of light and consciousness usually appears on the left.

means "to calculate, to understand," while in English, to ration is to divide. Similarly, in mathematics a ratio represents a relationship that can also be divided or reduced to a specific number or quantity.

To get some sense of the difference between the mythic and mental structures, consider the symbol of the former: the circle. The ratio of circumference to diameter is represented by *pi,* an *irrational* number that never reaches resolution. It lies beyond rational comprehension and can only be represented in symbolic form, like the amorphous beings of mythology and dreams. By contrast, the symbol of the mythic structure is the triangle, comprised of three straight lines and three angles that always add up to 180 degrees. The triangle was regarded by Plato as the fundamental form from which matter is constructed, and it can be considered the base upon which rest the mental structure and the Western worldview, to which we now turn our attention.

THE WESTERN WORLDVIEW

Many authors have attempted to isolate the cause of the current global crisis, often identifying a particular point or period at which things began to degenerate. Some say The Fall occurred with the invention of tools or fire, which set humans apart from animals; others point to written language, which introduced symbolic thinking; others blame agriculture, which led to classism and sexism; still others focus on patriarchal religion, colonialism, capitalism, or industry. The seemingly unavoidable fact is that every historical development has its pros and cons, that each movement towards something (individual autonomy, for example) is also a movement away from something (e.g., collective cohesion).

Inasmuch as a single source of global suffering can be named, it involves a psycho-spiritual imbalance of humanity in regard to Nature and the Cosmos. Although this imbalance has prehistoric roots, it began to manifest most strongly in the historical period, during which the mental structure of consciousness has been predominant. This form of perception has not only dominated but perhaps even defined the Western psyche, which has in turn played a dominant role on the world stage, particularly during the modern period and the continuing era of globalization. It is primarily in the West where the structure of consciousness that Gebser called the "efficient mental" would become the rational or "deficient mental," representing an extreme imbalance with roots that we will be tracing in the following pages. (In Gebser's view, the mental structure is divided into the efficient and deficient phases. The latter he also calls the rational phase.)

The evolution of Western thought is a rich and fascinating story that has been told in various ways by sundry scholars. Of particular depth, clarity, and inspiration to this author is Richard Tarnas' *The Passion of the Western Mind*, which presents the evolution of the Western worldview as a colorful narrative thread running from ancient Greece to the postmodern present. Rather than recount this entire epic, I will be focusing on particular aspects of the Western worldview which seem to me to have become especially deficient or imbalanced in regard to the world at large, upon which these imbalances have had dramatic effects.

It should go without saying that many aspects of Western thought continue to benefit the world in innumerable ways, as all worldviews have their strengths and weaknesses, their insights and oversights. Our present concern, however, lies with the roots of global suffering, which in turn lie within a worldview that has become so vastly influential that its particular shortcomings are now painfully apparent on a global scale. As we continue our evolutionary/involutionary journey, the following aspects of the Western worldview should also become apparent: an increasing emphasis on individuality leading to isolation, a loss of feminine wisdom and balance, a gradual disenchantment of the natural world, an intensifying contraction of the collective psyche, and a growing antagonism between the sacred and the secular.

Ancient Greece and the Rise of Reason

Standing on the cusp of the mental structure were the earliest Greek philosophers, who endeavored to access universal truths through observation and reason rather than religion or ritual. Still, their thinking was infused with a mythological flavor, as exemplified by the assertion of Thales that "All is water, and the world is full of gods."[10] Thales was followed by other thinkers who likewise attempted to explain the ceaseless change of the phenomenal world in terms of underlying substances. For Anaximenes, the fundamental principle was air; for Heraclitus it was fire; for Empedocles it was earth, air, fire, and water; for Anaximander it was a substance without qualities called the *apeiron;* for Pythagoras it was number. Anaxagoras, postulating the existence of tiny seeds moved about by a universal mind, prefigured the atomists Leucippus and Democritus, who in turn inspired the later scientific venture.

These and other early thinkers struggled to answer one of the most basic and enduring problems confronting humankind: that of The One and The Many. The basic question is whether there exists something eternal and unvarying behind the change that we observe in the material world. If so, how and why does this ultimate unity (which a theist would call God) express itself in multiplicity and change? The secular world tends to focus on The Many while ignoring The One or rejecting it as unreal, while religion worships The One while downplaying The Many or rejecting it as mere illusion. The tension between these two positions is illustrated in the differing philosophies of Parmenides and Heraclitus, the former of whom argued that change is logically impossible, the latter of whom emphasized perpetual flux by stating that "it is impossible to step in the same river twice."

The ideas of these two philosopher-mystics are more nuanced than caricatured here; Heraclitus in particular retained much of the mythic polarity in his paradoxical statements such as "we both are and are not" and "the way up and the way down are one and the same."[11] His thinking has a distinctly Eastern flavor, and his description of reality as "Plenum-void" is resonant with the core insights of Buddhism. But this indeterminacy was criticized as "that on which mortals wander knowing nothing"[12] by Parmenides, whose either-or logic indicates a turn towards the mental structure of consciousness.

Tellingly, however, the Greeks mentioned thus far are categorized as "pre-Socratics," for it is Socrates who is widely considered the founder of Western philosophy, despite the fact that he wrote no philosophical texts. His single-minded pursuit of truth involved rigorous dialogue and debate, constant questioning, and self-critical reflection, all combined with a moral fortitude that remained unwavering, even in the face of execution for corrupting the youth of Athens. By choosing hemlock over exile, Socrates became a reluctant martyr whose death marks the symbolic demise of the mythic imagination.

Most of what we know about the enigmatic Socrates comes through his student Plato, who formulated the notion of Ideas or Ideals—transcendent principles or forms that are reflected in the material world. In the infamous allegory of the cave, sensory phenomena are likened to shadows on the wall as viewed by prisoners who cannot see the true source of their visions. In this conception, known as Platonic idealism, humans experience beauty, for example, due to the existence of the *archetype* of Beauty in the transcendent realm. Whereas most people perceive particular manifestations of beauty, the true nature or essence of Beauty, symbolized by the goddess Aphrodite, can only be accessed via philosophical insight.

Plato's student, Aristotle, disagreed with this metaphysical model, insisting that what is truly real is not the world of transcendent Ideas but the world of immanent substances, which possess particular qualities that are recognizable by the senses. In Aristotle's view, substances are expressed in forms, which are not to be thought of as external templates of perfection but as indwelling developmental potentials, as in the form of an oak tree being present in an acorn, or a Buddha being present in each sentient being.

In the differing philosophies of Plato and Aristotle, we see the familiar tension between One and Many, ideal and real, spirit and matter, that would come to plague the Western psyche. Centuries later, this tension would become an estrangement, as religion and science branched off from philosophy and parted ways. The rivalry between these two estranged siblings continues today in the debate between creationism and evolution, the former being more aligned with Plato and his unchanging Ideals, the latter allied with Aristotle and his evolving potentials. But it is from the ancient Greeks in general

In this detail of Raphael's painting *The School of Athens,* Plato points to the heavens while Aristotle gestures toward the Earth, each indicating his philosophical focus.

that the West acquired the essential character of its worldview, the basis of its collective self-concept, the premise of its story: henceforth, the human would no longer experience magic or co-create myth; he would systematically and individually seek truth.

The Stoic Sensibility

Before leaving the ancient Greeks, I would like to elaborate upon Stoicism, a philosophical tradition that has been mentioned in passing. This school of thought was founded in Athens in the third century BCE by Zeno of Citium, who advocated self-knowledge and self-control or *apatheia* (absence of the passions, then understood as lust, greed, anger, etc.) and stressed the importance of ethics and universal love. Much like the Buddha, Zeno and his followers believed that true freedom was born from wisdom and clear perception of the sensory world, without which a person is held captive by mental conditioning and is subject to suffering. The Stoics advocated a simple, virtuous life in harmony with natural and universal laws and in recognition

97

of the essential goodness and equality of others, as well as diligent spiritual practice that included self-reflection and concentration on the present moment.

Although Stoicism and Buddhism are similar in spirit, they differ considerably in several important ways. Whereas Buddhist cosmology describes a multiverse of different levels or states of existence into which consciousness is reincarnated, the Stoics were essentially pantheists who conceived of the universe itself as a kind of sentient Being, a.k.a. God or Nature, which was composed of both matter and universal reason or *logos*. This active principle of the universe, which the strictly deterministic Stoics also called Fate, was thought of as a primordial fire, of which the souls of living beings were emanations. While Buddhism speaks not of a soul but of a mindstream that carries *karma* from lifetime to lifetime, the Stoics believed that after death the soul was completely subsumed by the greater fire.

I mention Stoicism not only because of certain parallels with Buddhist thought and with a more integral cosmology, but also because of its influence on the later Greco-Roman empire, during which it was the most popular philosophy among the educated classes. Alas, the schools of Stoicism were closed in 529 CE by the Roman Emperor Justinian, a Christian who felt threatened by what he perceived to be Stoicism's pagan orientation. The Stoics are now little more than a historical footnote, mischaracterized as unfeeling or arrogant.

Had the Stoic tradition been allowed to continue, we might now be living in a different world, perhaps one more balanced and holistic. As mentioned, the Western mind instead took a different path, or rather two divergent paths: Plato's idealism, which had a profound influence on Christian thought, and Aristotle's practicality, which paved the way for science and secularism. While the Stoics integrated these two streams in their thought, the Western worldview has since been defined by a dualism between psyche and matter that has resulted in an ambivalence towards Nature. In general, the religious side lacks connection to the immanent, corporeal world and to certain forms of knowledge, the secular side lacks connection to the ineffable, transcendent realm and to a certain form of wisdom, and both sides sorely lack connection to each other.

Christian Vision and Revision

Although Christianity arose in the context of Judaism, it was the Greco-Roman world that ultimately embraced this new religion. Specifically, it was the Roman Emperor Constantine who converted to Christianity in 312 CE after a revelation he received by looking up at the Sun. Through the Edict of Milan, Constantine effectively established Christianity as the central worldview of the West, although it was the Emperor Theodosius who later made Christianity the official state religion, banning paganism in the process.

Pagan mythology nevertheless had considerable influence on the early Church. An obvious example appears in the symbolism of Christ and his twelve disciples, which call to mind the twelve months of the year or signs of the zodiac, with the "Son" at the center and a lunar figure in the person of Mary Magdalene. Other pagan parallels exist in the themes of the virgin birth and the resurrected deity, present in many pre-Christian myths including those of the Egyptian god Horus, the Greek god Dionysius, and the Persian god Mithra.

Philosophically speaking, it was the ancient Greeks who would most profoundly affect Christian thought in the centuries after Christ. Especially influential was the philosophy of Plato, which inspired the Neoplatonists, particularly the third-century thinker Plotinus, who advanced the notion of a transcendent and supreme "One"

In this detail of a painting by Raphael entitled *The Vision of the Cross*, the Roman Emperor Constantine is shown in the midst of a revelation that inspired his conversion, and that of the West, to Christianity.

from which the universe emanates. Still, the philosophy of Plotinus, which included an emphasis on the soul's flight from the body and a concern about the evil inherent in matter, represented a break from Greek rationality into a more thoroughly religious spirit, or what could be considered a trans-rational mysticism.

Although rationality and reason were valued by early Christian theologians, they slowly became subordinate to personal revelation and intimate communion with God. The conversion of Augustine, one of the greatest of Christian theologians, involved overcoming his intellectual pretensions and humbly accepting Christ, after which he proclaimed "I have faith in order to understand"—a statement that even Plato would likely have flipped around. Augustine deemed it unnecessary for Christians to learn astronomy or biology or to "probe into the nature of things," writing: "It is enough . . . to believe that the only cause of all created things . . . is the goodness of the Creator, the one true God."[13] The laws and processes of Nature were seen as dependent upon God's will, while the Bible was regarded as the unchanging repository of Truth—the last Word.

Another important way in which Christian philosophy diverged from classical thought was in its conception of time. While the ancient Greeks and Romans generally conceived of history as cyclical, the Judeo-Christian sense of time was linear and progressive, an unfolding of God's ultimate plan for humanity. History itself was seen as a context for God's incarnation in human form, His creation of an increasingly universal or catholic Church, and His eventual return for the faithful. This radical remodeling of time was made official in the fixing of the calendar relative to the birth of Christ, an idea proposed by the Scythian monk Dionysius Exiguus in 525 CE and adopted throughout Europe over the subsequent centuries.

Before the *Anno Domini* ("Lord's Year") system, a common convention had been to orient the calendar in relation to the reign of a given king or emperor. In a way, the AD calendar operates on the same principle, elevating Christ as the "king of kings" whose birth marks the beginning of history itself, whose power is absolute, and whose reign is ongoing. Thus Christianity dramatically altered not only the content and character of the Western psyche, but the very context within which it was to function.

Space and Time Redefined

One of Gebser's major insights, one in fact central to this book, was that each structure of consciousness (archaic, magic, mythic, mental, integral) has its own unique way of experiencing time and space. Magical consciousness, for example, which Gebser described as timeless and one-dimensional, relates to all objects and events as different only in quality; no quantitative difference is perceived between now and then or here and there. To the mythic mind, time is experienced as rhythmic or cyclical, as reflected in the recurring movements of the Sun, Moon, and stars, while space is perceived as finite and enclosed.

Within the mental structure, time becomes linear and directional, as noted; the arrow of time flies in only one direction, from past to future. Time is also understood as ordered and structured, reflected in the increasingly sophisticated calendars and devices that measure time in individual mathematical units. Likewise, space is regarded as consistent and mathematical, as symbolized by the Greek geometric forms and later by the three-dimensional graph of Cartesian geometry. Within this space, the mental human has believed, events occur over time, in accordance with definable and immutable laws governing linear cause and effect. These conceptions of space and time, so crucial to the advancement of science, have been subject to radical revision by the discoveries of modern physics, as will be discussed.

The calendar in use at the time of Dionysius Exiguus was the Julian calendar, introduced in 46 BCE during the reign of Julius Caesar. This system, which uses a 365-day year divided into twelve months with an intermittent leap year, was later revised by Pope Gregory to become the calendar used today throughout most of the world. Both the Julian and Gregorian versions are solar calendars that use the Sun and its cycle as the central ordering principle of time, activity, and thought. Although solar calendars had been in use in Egypt, India, and other parts of the ancient world before Caesar, these cultures also used lunar calendars and so-called lunisolar calendars, in apparent recognition of the need to incorporate both masculine and feminine viewpoints in attempting to describe reality. Lunar systems were also in wide use in the Greco-Roman world until the time of Caesar.

With the adoption of the Julian calendar and the *Anno Domini* system, Christendom established it solar prominence in the ancient Western psyche. The world of human affairs became oriented around the Son, even if the actual Sun was still believed to revolve around the Earth. In contrast to the Moon, whose changing face reveals only vague, nebulous forms, the Sun illuminates all in its unwavering and eternal progress through the heavens. Symbolic of reason and comprehension, the Sun sheds light on specific and well-defined subjects, leading to a more enlightened way of thinking.

Given all this, it seems ironic that the Christian Era is nearly synonymous with what was once routinely called the Dark Ages. Although this pejorative term fails to capture the brilliance of a period during which religious art, architecture, and scholasticism flourished, it does describe the relative homogeneity of the medieval era. During this period, the largely illiterate masses fell under the oppression of feudal lords and the authority of the Church, the latter of which came to define not only the dominant worldview but the structure of Western society as a whole. While Christ the Son was regarded as the center and savior of the world, the Pope was recognized as having supreme theocratic power over earthly affairs. Apart from Mary the Virgin and Mary the prostitute, feminine symbols all but disappeared, and with them feminine wisdom, lunar creativity, and psychological balance. By narrowing its focus to one single, steadily cycling, male, solar symbol, the medieval mind became effectively spellbound, even as Christianity and its many cathedrals dedicated to *Notre Dame* provided a rich and beautiful context for life and worship. Not until the Renaissance and the Protestant Reformation did the Western psyche begin to awaken from its collective trance and regain its creative and intellectual diversity and dynamism, a development that of course had its own consequences for the Western worldview and the world at large.

THE PERSPECTIVAL WORLD

Gebser assigned great importance to perspective (from the Latin *perspectiva,* meaning "seeing through") as conveyed through the art of various cultures and time periods. He made a basic distinction between "pre-perspectival" and "perspectival" perception, outlining an incremental transformation in the human understanding and depiction of space. Although the breakthrough into the third dimension had occurred much earlier, it was Leonardo da Vinci—artist, scientist, and engineer in one—who was the first to successfully systematize perspective and to fully comprehend space rationally. This was circa 1500, the beginning of the modern era, which brought tremendous advancements in the understanding and conquest of both terrestrial and cosmic space, as reflected in navigation and astronomy. The negative result has been a restriction and narrowing of perception to a limited segment of reality; that is, a single perspective. While human horizons expanded, mental man's focus—and worldview—became increasingly narrow.

Perspectival perception and thinking have remained dominant since Leonardo. Breakthroughs into "aperspectival" consciousness have, however, occurred through the art of Picasso and other twentieth-century artists capable of depicting subjects from multiple points in space and time, and through the ideas of quantum physics, which also undermine perspectival notions of time and space.

In his iconic painting of the Last Supper, Leonardo da Vinci used a grid of converging lines to convey depth and to draw the eye to the face of the central figure, Christ.

Rebirth, Reform, and Individualism

If matter and flesh had been demystified during the Greco-Roman era, they were further depreciated and even demonized during the medieval era. Although considered part of God's creation, the world was viewed as a kind of hell, a type of purgatory, or simply irrelevant in terms of spiritual salvation. The focus of the human was primarily on the heavens above and secondarily on other humans, not on the Earth beneath one's feet. There did exist exceptions to this attitude, most notably St. Francis of Assisi, now considered by Catholics the patron saint of the environment. Also, a twelfth-century discovery of some of Aristotle's writings sparked a resurgence of the study of Nature in Paris. Aristotle also served as a great inspiration to the Dominican monk Thomas Aquinas, who is said to have "converted Aristotle to Christianity and baptized him,"[14] just as Aristotle's empiricism had a secularizing influence on medieval Christian thought.

The great rebirth of classical philosophy and human creativity did not truly begin, however, until the latter part of the fifteenth century, during which Leonardo da Vinci, Michelangelo, Raphael, Magellan, Columbus, Machiavelli, Luther, Shakespeare, and Copernicus all lived and thrived. Indeed the Renaissance is perhaps best remembered through the accomplishments of such geniuses, who revived an enthusiasm for independent thought, individual creativity, and courageous action. Particularly in the works of the great artists of this period we can see the skillful integration and synthesis of opposing elements: Christian and pagan, scientific and religious, secular and sacred, classical and modern. Characteristic of this era, such intermingling also reflected the ambiguity and paradox of the Renaissance, situated as it was on the cusp of modernity. The masterpieces of Michelangelo and da Vinci, often depicting otherworldly mythic or Christian themes like the Last Judgment, also demonstrate a new-found understanding of the laws of perspective, human anatomy, geometry, and *chiaroscuro* born from careful empirical observation. Thus even as Renaissance art celebrated the glory of the Church, it paved the way for the further advancement of science and for the mathematization of Nature.

Alongside the artistic innovations of the Renaissance came a number of technical inventions or acquisitions that would also have a secularizing influence on the Western world. Among them were the printing press, which exposed an increasingly large portion of the populace to literature and learning; the magnetic compass, which opened the door to global navigation, exploration, and conquest; and gunpowder, which contributed to the fall of feudalism and the rise of nationalism. Most relevant to the present discussion was the invention of the mechanical clock, which officially freed—and disconnected—humans from the rhythms of nature and dramatically transformed the human relationship to time, which likewise came to be regarded as mechanical, mathematical, and divided into small, discrete units. The clock became the model for all subsequent machines, as well as the modern metaphor for the functioning of the universe as a whole, with God recast in the role of "cosmic watchmaker."

In the midst of this dynamic transition from medieval to modern, Martin Luther nailed his 95 Theses to the door of the Castle Church in Wittenberg, Germany, in 1517, thereby initiating the Protestant Reformation. Although Luther was motivated by a conservative religious impulse to restore a Biblical-based Christianity, the ultimate effect of the Reformation was to move the West as a whole towards liberalization, secularization, and modernization. The movement had another profound effect, seemingly antithetical to Luther's intentions but in keeping with the heightened individualism of the Renaissance:

truth became an increasingly subjective affair, and the individual became empowered to define his own inner truth and determine his own personal direction.

The increased emphasis on individual autonomy and achievement that arose during the Renaissance and Reformation and intensified during the modern era can be seen to correspond with the gradual individuation of humanity as a whole. Although the power and importance of the individual were relatively limited during the Middle Ages, history in the abstract represents an ongoing psychological process in which our species has become more and more independent from its family of origin. While creating the conditions for a host of remarkable cultural advancements, this natural if not inevitable process of *differentiation* has lapsed into an unnatural and unfortunate *dissociation* of humanity from its biological and communal origins. Although personal alienation would come to find its most poignant expression in existential philosophy (as we shall see), our collective alienation from Nature has since continued to intensify into a crisis with wide-ranging effects.

Planetary Revolutions

An important subject not yet addressed is astrology, a field of inquiry that permeated and in some ways defined the pre-Christian West. Indeed astrology played a major role in the development of the Western psyche, even after the rise of Christianity. Throughout the Middle Ages it remained an integral part of medicine and science, and its connection to mathematics is apparent in the title *mathematici* assigned to medieval practitioners.

The earliest known astrological text, dating from about 1600 BCE, came from the Babylonian culture, which deified the heavenly bodies we know as the sun and the moon, Mercury, Venus, Mars, Jupiter, and Saturn (the outer planets, not visible to the naked eye, were discovered much later). From this cosmological system came the seven days of the week, and from the Babylonians also came the convention of dividing the ecliptic (the apparent, annual, circular path of the sun through the constellations) into twelve zodiacal signs of 30 degrees each.

Babylonian and Assyrian high priests used astrology primarily to ascertain the will of the gods, schedule important public events, and divine the future. The idea of the personal horoscope would not come about until many centuries later, perhaps indicating an emergent individualism with which this chapter is partly concerned. In any case, the ancients understood terrestrial events as being intimately connected with those of the divine realm. It was the luminous gods and goddesses whose recurring journeys through the heavens created night and day, initiated the change of seasons, caused floods, wars, and famines, and determined political fortunes.

Astrology was greatly revised by the ancient Greeks, who retained many of the mythological components but also sought an intellectual understanding of the *planété* or "wanderers," so called because of the movement of these bodies against the background of seemingly stationary stars. The errant planets presented a disturbing problem for the ancient Greeks, who had conceived of the universe as being composed of two concentric spheres: an outer sphere of fixed stars that revolved westward around the immobile Earth, and an inner sphere of the Sun, Moon, and planets that moved gradually in the opposite direction. Particularly confounding to the Greek mind were the erratic cycles of the planets, which appear to slow down, stop, or reverse directions while also increasing and decreasing in brightness, thereby defying the perfect symmetry and regularity of the *kosmos.*

Many great classical thinkers devoted themselves to finding a

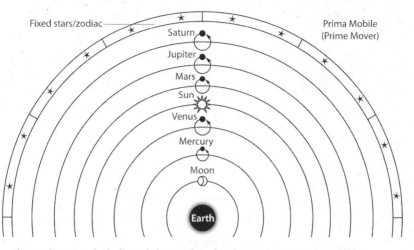

The ancient Greeks believed the Earth to be the stationary center of the kosmos. Above is a simplified version of Ptolemy's astrological scheme, in which the irregular movements of the planets were explained by epicycles—smaller cycles within revolutions around the Earth.

rational explanation for the odd behavior of the planets. Among them was Plato, whose firm belief in the perfect mathematical symmetry of the universe led him to theorize that the planets do in fact move in perfectly circular and regular orbits, according to as-yet-undetermined mathematical principles. In keeping with Plato's Idealism, the role of the philosopher became that of seeing through the veil of seeming disorder to comprehend the underlying divine order.

Although Ptolemy did succeed in developing an elaborate and durable model of circles within spheres to explain planetary motion, the problem in question was not actually solved until two millennia later during the Renaissance, when Nicholas Copernicus presented his heliocentric model of what we now call the "solar system." This conception was supported by Galileo Galilei, who in 1610 published *Siderius Nuncius* (Starry Messenger), an account of observations that

Copernicus, Galileo, Kepler, and Newton, initiators of the Scientific Revolution.

he had made with his newly invented telescope. Among these were the moons of Jupiter (which contradicted the notion that everything revolved around the Earth), the phases of Venus (impossible in a geocentric solar system), the uneven landscape of the moon (previously thought to be a perfect sphere), and the individual stars of the Milky Way, which suggested a much larger universe than previously thought. Finally, Johannes Kepler introduced his laws of planetary motion and advanced the notion of elliptical orbits of the planets, paving the way for Isaac Newton's sophisticated laws of motion and universal gravitation, which were applied not only to celestial bodies but to objects on Earth. While Copernicus is thought to have initiated the scientific revolution, Newton, the so-called father of science, successfully defined the dynamics of that revolution.

It is worthwhile to note that the concept of a moving Earth was first put forth by the Pythagoreans and elaborated upon by one of Plato's students, Heraclides, and that the heliocentric model was first proposed by the ancient Greek astronomer Aristarchus. Initially these ideas were rejected, not simply because they contradicted observation and common sense, but because they undermined the philosophical convictions of the Greek scholars and later the religious convictions of the Christian fathers.

Copernicus himself was a devout Catholic whose fears of persecution led him to delay the publication of *De revolutionibus orbium coelestium* (On the Revolutions of the Celestial Spheres) until just before his death in 1543. Galileo too was a Christian who obeyed the suggestion of church authorities not to "hold or defend" the heliocentric theory, although the circulation of his *Dialogue Concerning the Two Chief World Systems* led to his being accused of heresy by the Inquisition in 1633, condemned by the church, and placed under house arrest until his death nine years later.

Although Galileo was forced to recant his position, the proverbial cat was out of the bag. Word of the heliocentric theory quickly spread throughout the European intellectual community, in which scientific methodology and inductive reasoning were already beginning to take hold. By the end of the seventeenth century and increasingly thereafter, the relationship between science and religion became more antagonistic, with each side claiming the more intimate relationship to Truth.

Rationalism and Empiricism

In discussing science and religion here and elsewhere, I hope to make it clear that I do not take sides, except perhaps in my support of an evolutionary cosmology (which is certainly not exclusive to science). My belief is that both science and religion are valuable and that both are incomplete. Each offers an important partial truth, while neither holds the complete Truth, which can hardly be expected of any single system of thought. One of my intentions in this chapter is to show how the Western worldview has been partly shaped by this increasing tension and eventual conflict between science and religion, conceived of more broadly as reason vs. faith and even more abstractly as matter vs. psyche (understood as an intangible, intelligent, animating force). The animosity between these two streams is not only unfortunate but unnecessary; ultimately the dichotomy is a false one, as psyche and matter are interwoven and interdependent on the relative level and unitive on the absolute level.

As noted, the Western worldview has taken form primarily within the mental structure of consciousness, which Jean Gebser further divided into the efficient mental and deficient mental (or rational). An important characteristic of the rational mode is the tendency to make unequivocal and extreme statements about Truth and Reality, as opposed to speaking in terms of multivalent truths or multiple realities. Advocates of a particular rational viewpoint generally see any argument as binary: one side is right (usually theirs) and the other is wrong; there are no partial or coexistent truths. While binary logic was initially codified by Aristotle in his Laws of Thought,* it was further formalized by seventeenth-century rationalists like René Descartes, Baruch Spinoza, and Gottfried Leibniz, the last of whom developed the binary number system upon which modern computers rely.

It was Descartes who made the famous statement "I think, therefore I am." Like many subsequent philosophers of the Western world, Descartes based his identity—indeed his very existence—on cognition alone. Note that Descartes did not say, "I relate, therefore I am," or "I dream, therefore I am," as a magic or mythic mind might have said (if forced to make a definitive personal statement).

---

*The Law of Identity (A is A), The Law of Non-contradiction (A is not not-A), and the Law of the Excluded Middle (there is no other possibility). Although useful in many contexts, these laws do not accommodate the paradoxes of modern physics (e.g., light as both particle and wave) or the subtleties of a more inclusive or integral system of thought, as will be discussed in Chapter 3.

Even Plato or Aristotle would likely have affirmed, "I philosophize, therefore I am," which would have carried an entirely different meaning. To the ancient Greeks, philosophy was a holistic, interdisciplinary pursuit involving reason (the True) as well as ethics (the Good) and art (the Beautiful). The very word "philosophy"—a combination of the Greek words *philos,* meaning "love," and *sophia,* meaning "wisdom"—indicates that the ancient love of wisdom was partly an emotional if not erotic affair, with wisdom itself encompassing not just rationality and logic but intuition and creative inspiration. Modern rationalism, by contrast, views the emotional, relational, and imaginative aspects of human nature as distortional and therefore dispensable.

Descartes believed that the soul was situated in the pineal gland. His mistaken belief that animals lack this organ led him to conclude that they lack subjectivity and cannot feel pain.

Although Descartes made other contributions to Western thought, including a theory of inertia that heavily influenced Newton, he is best remembered for his "Cartesian dualism." By identifying exclusively with the mind, the so-called father of modern philosophy thus drove the final wedge between consciousness and matter, between subject and object, between "in here" and "out there." Descartes made a clear distinction between *res cogitans* (thinking substance) and *res extensa* (extended substance), the former being restricted to human awareness. In contrast to ancient ideas, the material world was viewed by Descartes as entirely devoid of subjectivity, spirit, or ultimate purpose, functioning essentially like a machine created by God and then left alone. So committed was Descartes to a strictly human subjectivity that he explained the cries of animals being beaten as simply the squeaks of malfunctioning machines.

Descartes' philosophy was born from skepticism, a wiping clean of the slate in order to determine what, if anything, is truly knowable by the human mind. Although Descartes was a Christian whose philosophy included a logical argument for God's existence, his ideas ultimately helped to liberate the modern rational mind from former philosophical and theological preconceptions. Another philosopher who helped make a clean break from the past was the seventeenth-century Englishman Francis Bacon, best known for his advancement of empiricism and the scientific method. In likewise striving to develop a reliable method of obtaining certain knowledge, Bacon was critical of previous thinkers for their reliance on deductive reasoning, which proceeds from a given premise rather than attempting to develop a new one based on careful and unbiased observation of the real world. Bacon's viewpoint was that "the true philosopher does not attempt to narrow down the world to fit his understanding, but strives to expand his understanding to fit the world."[15]

Given this position, it seems ironic that Bacon's empiricism had the ultimate effect of greatly narrowing the focus of the Western mind, with science becoming the only source of "objective" truth (an objectivity that would later be challenged). Contemporary thinkers like Ken Wilber have pointed out that at this stage of Western intellectual development, the Great Nest of Being—which includes body, mind, soul, and spirit—became collapsed into matter alone, as a radical reductionism came to dominate the Western psyche. No longer were great minds concerned with metaphysical issues or questions of cosmic purpose; the focus shifted from the *whys* of the universe to the *hows* of the material world and to mechanical processes that could be directly observed and measured.

Another effect of these two philosophies, especially rationalism, was to continue the trend of increasing individualism being described in this chapter. Descartes' famous statement can be understood as:

> ... the prototypical declaration of the modern self, established as a fully separate, self-defining entity, for whom its own rational self-awareness was absolutely primary—doubting everything except itself, setting itself in opposition not only to traditional authorities but to the world, as subject against object, as a thinking, observing, measuring, manipulating being, fully distinct from an objective God and an external nature.[16]

Yet another effect of empiricism and rationalism was to reinforce a linear conception of time. Bacon in particular believed that the ongoing pursuit of science, which he regarded as a religious obligation, would lead to man's increasing dominion over nature and ultimately to the end of human suffering. This idea, conceived as a counterpart to God's plan of spiritual salvation, in turn served as further justification for European expansionism and imperialism, which was initiated in the fifteenth century, first by Portugal and then by Spain's conquest of the New World. Bacon equated knowledge not with virtue as had Socrates, but with power, and the technologically advanced Europeans generally met with modest opposition in their collective colonial exploits. To the Western psyche, unlimited progress and growth—not only intellectual but economic—now seemed inevitable if not pre-ordained by God, an idea that has had a profound effect on our world.

Science vs. Religion and the Death of God

Like Descartes and Bacon, the post-classical intellectual and artistic figures that have been mentioned so far were Christians. Even if many of these thinkers also had ties with esoteric societies, their primary allegiance lay with Christianity, as did that of the pre-modern West as a whole. During the modern era in general and the eighteenth and nineteenth centuries in particular, however, that allegiance shifted from Plato's otherworldly idealism to Aristotle's this-world empiricism; the material gained importance over the spiritual. While medieval Christianity taught the Western mind that the material world was irrelevant, in later centuries science deemed God or spirit unnecessary, and neither religion nor science has demonstrated an abiding respect for Nature.

Even if certain individuals did not explicitly take sides between science and religion, a definite division took place during the transition into modernity (and the deficient mental structure). Religion was increasingly "seen as relevant less to the outer world than to the inner self... less to this life than the afterlife, less to everyday than to Sunday."[17] This schism in the individual psyche was reflected collectively in the splitting of not only religion from science but of metaphysics from physics, astrology from astronomy, and theology from philosophy. The last of these, which to the ancient lover of wisdom had included all the aforementioned fields of thought and then some, was reduced to the study of ideas, with an even more specific focus on rationality, logic, linguistics, and epistemology (the study of knowledge and belief). Philosophy lost its vitality and soul to become a theoretical science.

Perhaps more than anything, it was a newfound awareness of the structure and size of the universe that altered the early modern mind. In contrast to the geocentric *kosmos* of the ancient and medieval eras, which was finite in scope and hierarchical in nature, with a definite division between the stationary Earth and the dynamic heavens, the modern cosmology posited a spherical Earth moving through an infinite, empty space in accordance with the same natural laws and mechanical forces that moved all objects. On a physical level at least, the distinction between heaven and Earth had disappeared.

The psychological effect of this radical revision of the universe can hardly be overstated. Like a slow-motion one-two punch, Copernicus' heliocentric model and Newton's universal laws dislodged the Earth from the center of creation, in the process unmooring the Western mind from both religious tradition and psychological security. For not only had the Earth suddenly lost its uniqueness and significance, becoming just another planet among many in an expansive solar system within an incomprehensibly vast universe, humankind too lost its centrality, its home in the *kosmos*. Especially after Darwin, *Homo sapiens* became just another species, not one more noble or spiritual but simply more fit for survival in its terrestrial environment. This dramatic shift not only had profound consequences for the Earth, which had already been subordinated during the medieval era, it altered humanity's conception of itself and of the Divine. The seventeenth-century mathematician and religious philosopher Blaise Pascal captured the spirit of his era with his admission, "I am terrified by the eternal silence of these infinite spaces."[18]

During the seventeenth and eighteenth centuries, many intellectuals struck a compromise between the scientific and religious viewpoints by conceiving of God as existing outside history or time, a first cause or divine inventor who created the world as a perfect machine, the functioning of which should be studied. In what seems like a clear projection of the modern mind, God was regarded as primarily a rational or supra-rational being, an objective and distant observer, rather than as an intimately involved, loving, guiding principle of everyday life. The Holy Spirit as an animating force was replaced by natural and mechanical laws, while Christ as the Son of God became increasingly implausible to the rational mind, particularly in light of scholarship that revealed the Bible's human sources and imperfections.

Eventually, God as "first cause" would likewise be dispensed with as unnecessary. The eighteenth-century Scottish thinker and historian David Hume refuted Descartes' logical argument for the existence of God, as did the German philosopher Immanuel Kant, despite his being a Deist who favored an impersonal God but eschewed religious authority or dogma. In the nineteenth century, Karl Marx described religion as an "opiate of the masses" that ultimately benefited only the ruling class, and finally Friedrich Nietzsche proclaimed the "death of God" to overthrow what he considered not only a religious illusion but a "worldview that for too long had held man back from a daring, liberating embrace of life's totality."[19]

Thus in the course of the unfolding of the Western psyche, divinity was relocated: from this-worldly immanence during the magical stirrings of civilization, to mountainous elevation within the mythic structure, to heavenly transcendence during the classical and medieval eras, to extra-universal detachment during the modern period, and to total departure and death by the twentieth century. While Nietzsche and other modern philosophers may have regarded God's gradual disappearance as personally liberating, many modern humans have experienced this lack of universal order as contributing to a sense of alienation and uncertainty. Perhaps it is hardly surprising that the twentieth century, with its world wars, holocausts, and atomic explosions, has the distinction of being the most violent in human history.

The Enlightenment's Shadow of Subjectivity

With all aspects of existence suddenly subject to rational analysis, the increasingly self-absorbed modern mind inevitably turned its attention towards its own machinations and to the critique of knowledge and science. While rationalists and empiricists initially enjoyed a certain kinship, these schools of thought eventually came into conflict as each asserted the central role of either the mind (rationalism) or the senses (empiricism) in acquiring knowledge. Although the English philosopher John Locke agreed with Bacon that nothing can exist in the mind that has not been obtained through the senses, he saw no guarantee that internal ideas of things had any genuine correspondence with external objects themselves. To overcome this subjectivity, he made a distinction between an object's primary qualities—those that could be accurately measured or weighed—and its secondary qualities such as color and taste. With this distinction, he believed, knowledge could be established and science could proceed.

Locke's position was critiqued by Bishop Berkeley, who insisted that *all* qualities perceived by the mind, both primary and secondary, could never be said to represent actual objects, and therefore one can never be certain of the existence of an objective, "real" world apart from one's subjective experience. In order to establish the validity of science, the religious Berkeley placed the human mind in the context of a universal mind (i.e., God) that allowed the individual to perceive regular, recurring qualities and thereby discover the laws of Nature. Hume in turn critiqued Berkeley's metaphysics, insisting that the mind perceives not universals but particulars, from which it can only draw inferences. In Hume's view, cause and effect were also inferences based on mental associations, as were the ideas of time and space, previously assumed to be external realities in Newtonian cosmology. Hume wrote that

119

"the intelligibility of the world reflects habits of the mind and not the nature of reality."[20] His philosophy amounted to a critique of inductive reasoning, the very basis of empirical science.

Thus science, like religion, was proven fallible during the European Enlightenment. Previously thought to be aligned exclusively with reason, science was revealed to rest on a faith of its own, namely the assumption that objective truth could be determined through subjective experience. Another attempt to restore the validity of individual perception was made by Emmanuel Kant, who suggested that the mind does not passively receive sensory data but actively structures them, and that reality can be understood only to the extent that it matches the structures of the mind itself. In other words, "the mind does not conform to things; rather things conform to the mind."[21] Kant also insisted that space and time were not inferences as Hume had suggested, but pre-existing categories of human experience, as were the principles of cause and effect. Observations of the world, argued Kant, could never be neutral; they always include the observer's own assumptions and judgments, a concept that would later find support in postmodern theory and quantum physics. Although Kant succeeded in reuniting the mind and the senses, he ultimately failed to establish any basis for subjective certainty, as pointed out by later critics of science like Karl Popper and Thomas Kuhn.

Enlightenment thinkers Locke, Berkeley, Hume, and Kant.

The modern trend of increasing subjectivity combined with growing uncertainty was furthered by psychology, which emerged as a systematic study in the late nineteenth century, largely through the work of Sigmund Freud. It was Freud who first recognized the structure and function of Id, Ego, and Super-Ego, disclosed the role of dreams, fantasies, and mythological symbolism, demonstrated the importance of both sexuality and early childhood experience in conditioning the adult personality, and brought forth a host of other insights that are now widely taken for granted. While illuminating the depth of the individual psyche, however, Freud denied its transpersonal height, dismissing all spiritual beliefs and experiences as infantile fantasy.

Although Freud's investigations were in keeping with the rational spirit of his time, his discoveries ultimately undermined rationality by revealing the unconscious: a powerful repository of non-rational forces, hidden motivations, and bestial urges, which together all but overshadowed the significance of the fragile and newly formed human ego. Just as Copernicus had dislodged Earth from the center of the *kosmos*, and Darwin deposed humanity from the center of creation, Freud unseated the ego from its position of central importance in the mind. If humans were largely under the control of unknown, animalistic, psychological forces, they risked losing not only their divinity but their humanity. Moreover, in the shadow of the unconscious, the sense of personal freedom for which the modern mind had fought so valiantly suddenly appeared as perhaps just another illusion.

Modern Revolutions

While the radical subjectivity and individualism of the modern era came at the price of alienation, they also led to an increased emphasis on individual, unalienable rights. In the West, the idea of "natural rights" was first articulated by John Locke, who identified these as "life, liberty, and estate," an idea that set the context for the American and French revolutions. While both of these defined themselves in opposition to the aristocracy, they differed in their overall tone, with the latter being more Romantic in inspiration and character. The rallying cry of the French Revolution, *"Liberté, Égalité, Fraternité"* (Liberty, Equality, Fraternity), was penned by Jean-Jacques Rousseau, a Swiss philosopher who challenged the so-called divine right of kings, asserting that government can only be legitimate if sanctioned by the people. In his seminal work *The Social Contract,* which begins with the famous phrase "Man is born free, yet everywhere he is in chains," Rousseau spoke of humankind's innate goodness being corrupted by society, with its laws, hierarchies, and divisions of labor inevitably promoting inequality and strife.

Rousseau's ideas served as an inspiration for the European Romantics, who shared a similar longing for a simple life in harmony with Nature and who sought to restore the primacy of emotion, inspiration, and imagination over impersonal rationality and materialism. It was this reframing of subjectivity that shaped the spirit of the American and French revolutions, more so than the political theory of Rousseau, who placed very little emphasis on individual rights and whose ideas were more in keeping with socialist ideals than the Republicanism upon which the United States was founded. The U.S. founding fathers held it self-evident that "all men are created equal, endowed by their Creator with certain unalienable rights," a sentiment that also made its way into France's 1789 "Declaration of the Rights of Man and of the Citizen."

Unfortunately, these bold declarations on the equality of "all men" did not extend to slaves or women, a fact recognized by Olympe de

Gouges, a French journalist who in 1791 wrote the "Declaration of the Rights of Woman and the Female Citizen." In this treatise, addressed to Queen Marie Antoinette, de Gouges simply revised the language of the 1789 declaration to encompass the rights of women, including that of being equal in marriage. One year after de Gouges' treatise, the British philosopher Mary Wollstonecraft published "On the Vindication of the Rights of Woman," considered by many to be a pioneering work of feminism (a term that had not yet been coined). Tragically, the following year, 1793, de Gouges was guillotined, and her demands were not to be officially recognized in France until 1946. In America, women's suffrage was not extended until 1920, and the full equality of women in the U.S., as in most parts of the world, is still a dream yet to be realized, as is the equality of African Americans, homosexuals, and many other minority groups.

Mary Wollstonecraft's daughter was Mary Shelley, best known for her book *Frankenstein; or, The Modern Prometheus,* first published anonymously in 1818 and revised in 1831. Written by

Olympe de Gouges, Mary Wollstonecraft, and Mary Shelley.

Shelley at age eighteen, *Frankenstein* is largely a reaction to the Industrial Revolution of the late eighteenth century, with Victor Frankenstein cast as the heedless scientist whose horrific creation (never actually given a name) ends up causing unintentional harm, including murder. In the spirit of Rousseau, however, by whom Shelley was influenced, Dr. Frankenstein's monster is actually quite gentle and virtuous by nature and only becomes violent and irrational in the presence of humans.

While spawning both the horror and science fiction genres, Shelley's masterpiece also offers a critique of science, which had gained supremacy by the time of the Industrial Revolution. Considered by historians to be as momentous as the Agricultural Revolution that sowed the seeds of civilization, the Industrial Revolution initiated a complete reorientation of the human towards the machine, reflected in increasing automation, standardization, and uniformity. Society itself came to be regarded as a kind of machine, with its smooth operation depending on the conformity and cooperation of the individual cogs and the absence of the "squeaky wheel." As with previous shifts in human consciousness, the Industrial Revolution brought with it an increasing regularity and constriction of time, with an emphasis on smaller and smaller units: seconds, tenths of a second, hundredths of a second, etc. Eventually the cyclical nature of time, symbolized by the circular clock, would be all but forgotten as the digital wristwatch came into fashion, representing a personal obsession with time and its increasing commodification, culminating in the phrase "time is money." To the industrial human, productivity is paramount, and time is a *thing* to be kept, killed, bought, spent, or squandered.

During the early twentieth century, time would undergo a radical remodeling through the discoveries of physics, as would science itself. In the theories of Albert Einstein, Max Planck, Neils Bohr, Werner Heisenberg, and others, the modern Cartesian-Newtonian cosmology broke down. No longer were space and time independent entities, as had long been assumed; they became relative aspects of a four-dimensional space-time continuum, with time flowing at different rates for different observers moving at different speeds, slowing

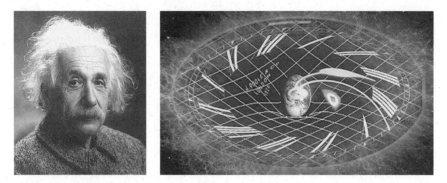

Albert Einstein, whose theory of relativity overthrew the Newtonian-Cartesian paradigm.

down near dense objects and even stopping inside black holes. Supposedly solid atoms were discovered to be almost entirely empty, and subatomic particles, which could also be observed as waves, could only be measured in terms either of location or velocity, not both simultaneously. Mechanistic causality was undermined by the observation of non-local connections between particles, and the speed of light as the ultimate threshold of communication was contradicted by the observation of instantaneous connections between particles. In these and other ways, quantum physics affirmed the central role of the observer in determining reality, which was recognized as radically indeterminate and relative. This new conception of the universe was disturbing to even the father of Relativity, who wrote: "It was as if the ground had been pulled out from under one, with no firm foundation to be seen anywhere upon which one could have built."[22]

Existentialism and Postmodernism

As Tarnas points out in *The Passion of the Western Mind,* each of the epochal shifts in the Western worldview has been accompanied by a kind of archetypal sacrifice, the martyrdom of a central prophet of the age. Socrates was tried and executed at the beginning of the classical period, Jesus' trial and crucifixion marked the birth of the Christian era, and Galileo was tried and condemned at the birth of the modern period. The central prophet of the postmodern period would have to be the existentialist philosopher Friedrich Nietzsche, who eventually succumbed to insanity, signed his last letters "The Crucified," and died at the dawn of the twentieth century.

Nowhere was the prevailing mood of the twentieth century better captured than in the writings of Nietzsche and other existentialists such as Kierkegaard, Sartre, Heidegger, Camus, and Kafka, whose outlook is in turn deftly captured and articulated by Tarnas:

> . . . the existentialist addressed the most fundamental, naked con-
> cerns of human existence—suffering and death, loneliness and
> dread, guilt, conflict, spiritual emptiness . . . the void of absolute
> values or universal contexts . . . Man was condemned to be free. He
> faced the necessity of choice and thus knew the continual burden
> of error. He lived in constant ignorance of his future, thrown into
> a finite existence bounded on each end by nothingness . . . only his
> existence was given, an existence engulfed by mortality, risk, fear,
> ennui, contradiction, uncertainty . . . There was no eternal design
> or providential purpose. Things existed simply because they existed,
> and not for some "higher" or "deeper" reason. God was dead, and
> the universe was blind to human concern, devoid of meaning or
> purpose . . . To be authentic one had to admit, and choose freely to
> encounter, the stark reality of life's meaninglessness. Struggle alone
> gave meaning.[23]

In contrast to the rationalism of Descartes, which posits consciousness as the primary reality, existentialism asserts that what is
primary is existence. Heidegger, who spoke of "being in the world,"
also used the term "thrownness" to describe the idea that humans are

cast into existence without having chosen it. In his novel *Repetition*, Søren Kierkegaard asks: "How did I get into the world? Why was I not asked about it and why was I not informed of the rules ...? Why should I be involved? To whom shall I make my complaint?"[24]

Given this "thrownness," the task of existence is to create or invent meaning for one's self, a prospect that became further complicated by the ideas of postmodernism. One hesitates to call this movement a philosophy, since it is defined more than anything else by a radical relativism and perspectivism, a sense that all meaning and understanding is socially constructed and constrained by idiosyncratic filters of race, culture, language, context, worldview, symbols, personal bias, etc. Reality is subjective, interpretive, and radically ambiguous. As suggested by modern physics, the world does not exist as a "thing-in-itself" but only comes into being through interpretation, and the mind can never stand apart from the world, judging from an external vantage point. Postmodernism thus stands in opposition to the early modern, scientific

Existentialists Friedrich Nietzsche, Martin Heidegger, and Søren Kierkegaard.

worldview, and it goes even further by denying the presumptions of Western culture altogether. To the postmodernist, there is no such thing as "Truth," and "Progress" too is nothing more than fiction, and a destructive one at that. Any attempt to articulate a cohesive worldview or "meta-narrative" is not only self-deceptive but dangerous, particularly to those not aligned with that way of understanding the world.

Under the cloak of Western values, too many sins have been committed. Disenchanted eyes are now cast onto the West's long history of ruthless expansionism and exploitation—the rapacity of its elites from ancient times to modern, its systematic thriving at the expense of others, its colonialism and imperialism, its slavery and genocide, its anti-Semitism, its oppression of women, people of color, minorities, homosexuals, the working classes, the poor, its arrogant insensitivity to other cultural traditions and values, its cruel abuse of other forms of life, its blind ravaging of virtually the entire planet.[25]

THE AMERICAN MINDSET AND GLOBALIZATION

While I hope it is interesting in itself, this relatively brief, highly over-simplified, and necessarily incomplete history of the Western worldview is intended to draw out a number of themes that I believe have contributed to the kind of global suffering referred to in the quotation above. To rephrase, these themes are: increasing individualism leading to alienation and the loss of inter-subjective communion, the disenchantment and mechanization of Nature and the Cosmos, the degradation of the feminine, growing antagonism between matter and psyche (or science and religion), and a shared sense of the increasing constriction of time and space.

These interwoven threads run throughout the Western narrative, which represents a protracted process of psychological development in which the Western mind has separated from Nature and tradition to become autonomous, self-directed, and isolated. Of course, the West can hardly be said to represent the whole of humanity, and even less do the relatively few philosophers, prophets, artists, writers, and scientists—most of them male—mentioned in this chapter. Nor is the West itself a stable or monolithic entity. Nevertheless, the human individuation process, as characterized by the themes listed above, has found its most forceful expression in Western culture, which continues to have a substantial effect on the rest of the world.

If human individuation can be understood most clearly in the story of the West, it has undoubtedly reached its most dramatic culmination in American culture, which to much of the world has become symbolic of—if not synonymous with—Western culture as a whole. Certainly as the reigning global superpower of the twentieth century, the United States of America has exercised an influence that all but eclipses that of its European and Mediterranean forebears, of which it can be seen as an extension. On the other hand, American culture is clearly distinct, with its own unique structures and sensibilities, its own guiding principles and core values, its own definitive ways of thinking. Given the profound and ongoing influence of the U.S. on the world at large, it seems important to explore the essence of the American mindset.*

America Means Business

As noted, the United States of America was founded upon principles that emerged during the Enlightenment and the Romantic movement, namely a concern with personal liberty and individual rights. More specifically, the founding fathers were inspired by the tenets of Republicanism, which include sovereignty of the people, rule of law, disdain for corruption, and civic virtue and participation. The last

---

*While I recognize that the word "America" encompasses an entire hemisphere, I use it here to refer to the United States, with apologies that the term "American" must be restricted to citizens of the United States, for whom there is not a more accurate name. Similarly, when used as an adjective, "American" refers to features of the United States.

of these requires that the individual place collective concerns ahead of personal ones.

Given this emphasis on "the general welfare," it seems somewhat incongruous that the United States would adopt as its economic model capitalism, which stresses competition above *égalité* and *fraternité*. Certainly tremendous advances have been made under capitalism, promoting as it does individual creativity and entrepreneurship, but in many other ways capitalism has been disastrous for the planet as a whole. It has led first of all to enormous economic disparity, within the U.S. as well as between the developed and developing nations of the world, with tens of thousands of children starving each day while others eat their way to obesity and poor health.

Meanwhile the biosphere has been decimated under capitalism, which thus far has been operating under a number of dangerous assumptions. The first of these is that the natural world is nothing more than a repository of resources simply waiting to be harvested and converted into products for human consumption, with every mountain representing a potential mine, every forest a grazing spot, every tree a ream of paper or furniture set, every animal a piece of food or clothing, every river a toxic dumping ground. While this mindset has some basis in a Cartesian dualism in which everything apart from human consciousness is regarded as lacking in soul and subjectivity, it is also fueled by another dangerous assumption of capitalism: the idea of unlimited progress, itself linked to a strictly linear conception of time. The idea of industrial growth lies at the heart of capitalism, as reflected in the modern corporation, which has as its only objective the generation of wealth for its shareholders, regardless of "externalized" costs and consequences. Here we can make an important distinction between wealth as simply money, which has only extrinsic, agreed-upon value, and wealth as something with intrinsic

value, such as the richness of the soil or the wealth of the environment. Unfortunately, capitalism makes no such distinction and in fact
values most that which actually has no intrinsic worth.

Essentially, the central focus of American society is commerce.
Americans worship money, and in this sense they are as religious as
any culture in history. As Joseph Campbell and other cultural historians have pointed out, the values of a given society are usually reflected
in its architecture, with the tallest and most conspicuous buildings
representing that society's most elevated principles. While the ancient
Greeks celebrated the goddess of reason in the elegant symmetry
of the Parthenon, and the Christian world built majestic cathedrals
with heavenward spires, the modern city is dominated by its financial
center, in which tall buildings scrape the sky and often prohibit visual
access. If all Greek citizens were welcome in the Parthenon and all
Christians were welcome in the Gothic cathedral, the modern corporate building welcomes only those who have business being there.

While corporations have been around since the Middle Ages, they
have certainly gained prominence in the world since the Industrial
Revolution. One important development came in 1886 when the
U.S. Supreme Court designated corporations as "legal persons,"
thereby extending to them many of the natural rights and freedoms
already enjoyed by individuals. Before that time, the corporations
had already been widely referred to as "artificial persons," which
brings to mind the image of Dr. Frankenstein's monster, assembled
out of disparate parts, given life, and then set loose upon the world. A
more contemporary metaphor is that of a robot, similarly assembled
out of smaller parts and issued only one directive: venture forth and
profit. In either case, although our artificial person intends no harm,
its crimes eventually come back to haunt its creators, even if they are
not directly liable for the creature's actions.

Corporations have since grown into transnational behemoths, arguably more powerful than governments and certainly wealthier, with the top corporations generating more revenue annually than many countries. Notably, of the top ten wealthiest corporations of 2009, all but two of them (Walmart and ING) are either oil or auto companies. Second on this list is Exxon Mobil, which in 2008 (when it ranked first) generated more than $40 billion in profits, the largest annual reported net income in U.S. history.[26] Because of this spectacular earning power, corporations exercise immense political influence, with (for example) lobbyists effectively obstructing the signing of the Kyoto Accord to curb greenhouse gas emissions, opening up protected lands to oil drilling and other exploitation, reversing environmental and labor laws, disallowing struggling countries from declaring bankruptcy, or, in the case of pharmaceutical companies, preventing developing countries from loosening their patent laws to allow wider access to antiretroviral drugs for HIV/AIDS patients. In a textbook example of value-free or amoral capitalism, so-called "Big Pharma" tends to devote most of its efforts to top-selling drugs like Viagra rather than to the curing of tropical diseases that affect most of the world's population. Similarly, a disturbing percentage of the world's scientists—some

TOP 10 WEALTHIEST COMPANIES	Country	2009 Rev. (billions U.S.)
1. Royal Dutch Shell	Netherlands	458
2. ExxonMobil	U.S.	443
3. Wal-Mart Stores, Inc.	U.S.	405
4. British Petroleum (BP)	Britain	367
5. Chevron	U.S.	263
6. Total S.A.	France	235
7. ConocoPhillips	U.S.	231
8. ING Group	Netherlands	226
9. SInopec	China	208
10. Toyota	Japan	204

of the most brilliant minds on Earth—work for the military in some capacity.

Whereas technology has traditionally been linked with knowledge and the common good, it has become more closely linked in the American mind with individual profit. In this scheme, the value of any innovation lies not so much in its advancement of understanding or enhancement of well-being but in its ability to generate money, even if its ultimate effects might be detrimental. Although it is easy to appreciate the argument that technology itself is value-neutral, that humans alone determine how a given invention will be used or abused, it is more difficult to accept this argument when considering automatic rifles, chemical weapons, and atomic bombs. As many readers are undoubtedly aware, the U.S. spends more money on its military than much of the rest of the world combined—more than $700 billion per year. Of the top ten weapons manufacturers worldwide, the majority are American, and the U.S. is also the top exporter of weapons in the world.[27] To recall the Hindu scheme of increasing density of matter: the U.S. arsenal represents the highest-ever concentration of iron, lead, plutonium, uranium, and other heavy metals.

One of the United States' own top-ten defense contractors is General Electric, which also operates a multi-billion-dollar media

TOP TEN DEFENSE CONTRACTORS		Country	Revenue (billions U.S.)
1.	Boeing	U.S.	30.5
2.	BAE Systems	UK	29.9
3.	Lockheed Martin	U.S.	29.4
4.	Northrup Grumman	U.S.	24.6
5.	General Dynamics	U.S.	21.5
6.	Raytheon	U.S.	19.5
7.	EADS	EU	13.1
8.	L-3 Communications	U.S.	11.2
9.	Finmeccanica	Italy	9.9
10.	Thales Group	France	9.4

empire that includes NBC, CNBC, Telemundo, Bravo, msnbc.com, and Universal Studios. Here we see just one example of the intermingling of military and commerce (the military-industrial complex) with the media, which in any case continue to be consolidated in the hands of fewer and fewer corporations. This development has had a dampening effect on freedom of speech in general and investigative journalism in particular, the latter once considered crucial in a democratic society to keep the populace well informed and the government accountable (one of the central concerns of the founding fathers). Still, the United States has witnessed its share of scandals in the last few decades: Watergate, Iran-Contra, the Clinton Whitewater affair, the savings and loan debacle, the corporate accounting scandals of Enron and Harken Energy, the Yellowcake forgery, the Valerie Plame leak, and the Abu Ghraib torture and abuse scandal, not to mention the deception, secrecy, cover-ups, cronyism, and voting irregularities that characterized the Bush administration.

The Three Poisons

The core values of the United States are reflected in its three most powerful complexes—industry, military, and media—all of which have become increasingly consolidated, interrelated, and globalized. While each of these on its own is unrivaled in human history in terms of power and influence, together they have allowed the U.S. to become the most dominant, defining force in human, if not geologic, history. One would be hard pressed to find a place on Earth not affected by at least one branch of this mighty American triumvirate.

Germane to this discussion is the idea that these three main driving forces of the American enterprise can be equated with what in Buddhism are called the "three poisons" of greed, hatred, and

In this detail from a traditional Buddhist painting or thangka (left), the three poisons of greed, hatred, and delusion are symbolized by a rooster, snake, and pig respectively, all located at the center of the wheel of cyclic suffering. A variation on this traditional image is shown on the right, in which the three poisons are represented by a dollar bill (greed), a tank (hatred), and television set (delusion). A larger version of the traditional wheel of life appears on page 268.

delusion. Alternatively translated as desire, aversion, and ignorance, these poisons are said to be the root causes of suffering. Although interrelated, primary emphasis is placed on delusion, which gives rise to selfish desire and aversion (as has been discussed). In the American model, desire manifests as consumerism and unbridled capitalism, hatred finds expression in militarism and violence, and delusion is symbolized by the media, which reinforce the other poisons through advertising and various forms of propaganda.

While the power of the media in shaping public opinion and perception has been compellingly put forth by Noam Chomsky, Amy Goodman, Arundhati Roy, and many others, I wish to point out here its more subtle yet profound role in constructing and reinforcing a particular way of thinking. In some ways a newspaper or a television broadcast can be said to represent a worldview, not only in the information it divulges but in the way it divulges that information and perhaps most importantly in what information it leaves out, whether consciously or unconsciously. Again, in order to avoid sounding con-spiratorial, I will divulge my own belief that the influence of the media is not one-directional; the general public also plays a role in shaping the content and character of media, if only in its ability to choose what information it consumes. Unfortunately, the U.S. public relies almost exclusively on television for news, more specifically on the "big four" media outlets: ABC, NBC, CBS, and FOX.

In terms of America's three poisons, it seems relevant that the terrorist attacks of September 2001 were directed at the World Trade Center (symbol of desire) and the Pentagon (symbol of aversion), and that shortly thereafter, deadly anthrax spores were sent to vari-ous media outlets on the East Coast. Needless to say, this wave of attacks was devastating for many families and deeply disturbing to the American public, whose worldview was quickly and dramatically altered. These were the first attacks on U.S. continental soil, and they introduced an unfamiliar sense of vulnerability and uncertainty to the typically insulated and isolated American. Suddenly the world seemed larger and more mysterious, populated perhaps by shadowy and sinister enemies but also filled with the prayers, support, and shared anguish of millions of allies across the globe. Beneath the grief, or perhaps because of its uniting influence, there arose a brief, hopeful sense of national and international kinship.

Due in part to the overbearing response of the U.S. government, whose representatives immediately began speaking in stark absolutes of good vs. evil, the national mood quickly changed into one of fear and indignation. America's pride had been damaged, and the country needed to reassert its global superiority in a dramatic display of aggression. It would not rely on international courts of law, nor would it politely petition the world community for assistance. Instead its president would demand allegiance to the "war on terror" by threatening, "You're either with us or against us." Least of all would U.S. leaders and citizens seek to understand the root causes of terrorism or address the complaints of the perpetrators, which were clearly outlined in a number of videotapes that surfaced after 9-11. All these responses would have required a kind of humility and introspection with which the United States of America, the world's strongest ego structure, is largely unfamiliar. Before long it was back to business as usual: hyper-individuality and alienation reinforced by consumerism; xenophobia and suspicion; commodification and constriction of time; denial of death and repression of the shadow; mental myopia and psychic contraction; dis-ease and *dukkha*. That these psychological defenses and states have become commonplace in a country with such a dark and violent past is hardly surprising.

A Sort of Homecoming

Perhaps no phrase has shaped the American psyche more than the one appearing at the beginning of the Declaration of Independence: "the pursuit of happiness." Likely taken from Thomas Paine's 1776 treatise *Common Sense*, it was used to replace the last of Locke's unalienable rights, "life, liberty, and estate," a revision suggested by Thomas Jefferson but opposed by other founding fathers. In the true spirit of America, the phrase in question was left completely open to interpretation, and therein lies its potency. One could argue, however, that "the pursuit of happiness" has been interpreted by many Americans to mean the gratification of one's desires, whatever the consequences. Eating sumptuous meals, wearing designer clothing, driving big cars, and buying expensive toys—this is how we Americans pursue happiness, while much of the rest of the world continues to struggle with life and liberty. We have been told that purchasing power translates into freedom, the irony being that millions of Americans are so figuratively burdened with debt that literal imprisonment looms as a possibility.

I am speaking in broad generalities and do not wish to blame the victim. Americans are not universally or especially greedy, nor are they the only culture prone to seek out pleasure, which is deeply rooted in human nature (as has been discussed). My main point is that the structure of American society as a whole promotes the pursuit of happiness through consumption, and it does so with historically unprecedented effectiveness and relentlessness. Additionally, American culture fails to provide its citizens with an effective means of initiation into adulthood, resulting in a valuation of youth, fame, sensory stimulation, and instant gratification above wisdom, humility, peace, and patience. These factors, combined with a general cultural isolation and a nascent worldview lacking broad context and connection to other perspectives and periods, have helped foster a habitual consumerism that is causing so much suffering throughout the world.

Fortunately, the tide seems to be turning, however slowly. Partly because of the events of 9-11 and increasing concerns about climate change and other large-scale crises, Americans on the whole have become more worldly within recent years, more conscious of their place in the global community and in the tide of history, more conscientious and compassionate. A growing number of people are realizing that a lavish lifestyle does not translate into happiness, and may even contribute to a sense of meaninglessness and scarcity. Perhaps most hopeful is a growing hunger in all quarters for genuine spiritual wisdom and integral philosophy to replace the religious dogma and political debate that we see tediously represented by ongoing holy wars and predictable clashes between fundamentalists and secularists, Republicans and Democrats. Whether consciously or intuitively, more and more people are beginning to feel that a new and broader worldview is required: a way of thinking, feeling, and acting that is at once more holistic, more balanced, more enlightened, and more aligned with the natural and universal orders.

Indeed just such a worldview has been taking shape over the last decades, although it draws much of its inspiration from earlier eras. Its spirit has been forged by Romantics and revolutionaries, its ideas articulated by deep-thinking psychologists and far-seeing physicists, its character shaped by Old World philosophers and New Age visionaries, its aesthetic influenced by indigenous shamans and ingenious artists and engineers. This new way of seeing and being is taking hold among young activists, middle-aged intellectuals, elder ecologists, and everyday people from all cultures and walks of life. Slowly and surely, the world is waking up. To quote again from Nietzsche: "It is returning, at last it is coming home to me—my own self and those parts of it that have long been abroad and scattered among all things and accidents."[28]

SOMETHING OF A SUMMARY

In an abstract way, the 14-billion-year evolution of the universe can be seen as a maturation process in which the Cosmos has become progressively more conscious of its own existence. This process took a dramatic leap forward with the appearance of *Homo sapiens*, blessed and cursed with the capacity for introspection and a newfound understanding of context. Initially our context was deeply relational and communal, but as our numbers grew and our minds evolved, we started to notice distinctions with which we began to identify and through which we began to disassociate. We became members of a specific tribe or a specific race, with a specific way of seeing the world. About 5,500 years ago we began to form permanent settlements and cities, which required armies of conquest and protection, these born from our fundamental impulses of desire and aversion. As beings of ego, we wore our self-concepts as clothing, uniforms, and both literal and figurative armor that became denser as we began acting out our stories on the world stage.

Where once we had danced and celebrated together beneath the Moon, we eventually came to identify with the solemn solar hero in his lone struggle against adversity. Some heroes journeyed bravely into the depths of the psyche, there finding profound truths that were preserved in sacred texts meant to be shared, recited, and remembered. We feared forgetting, because already the voices of the animals, plants, trees, mountains, and rivers had become difficult to understand, and the gods and goddesses had begun to leave our world for the heavens. As the stories in the stars grew more and more faint, we began searching for the brightest of lights to guide us.

Aligning our minds with the Sun, we came to believe in a single expression of the Divine, although we called it by different names. To some the world seemed like a mere shadow of this light, to others the Divine remained bound up in matter, whose secrets awaited discovery. In Nazareth, the Divine announced its presence in human form, and was put to death by those who did not believe. But a growing number of people did believe, and soon everything, including history and time, became organized around this prophet, Jesus. False gods were banished, and the one transcendent God was accessible only through Christ. The Earth, like the body, became a decisively unholy thing.

Under powerful popes and kings, the Western mind was placid for many centuries, knowing essentially only one story about itself and about the universe, which lost most of its magic and mystery.

Eventually a rebirth came about through men of genius, who saw with fresh eyes a rich, colorful, and spacious world that awaited discovery and conquest. But by this point the powerful Western ego, already disconnected from Nature and her cycles, had also become blind to the beauty and subjectivity of other peoples, whose lives seemed less important than personal glory and wealth.

Copernicus, Galileo, Kepler, and Newton initiated the Scientific Revolution by proving that the Earth revolves around the Sun and that the whole universe is governed by the same fundamental laws. While liberated from ancient ideas, the Western mind was also disoriented, since humanity had lost its cosmic importance, as had the Earth. Eventually the human became just another animal on just another planet, and the universe was seen as nothing more than a machine. Descartes argued that animals too were machines, and that the only thing of value in all the universe was the human mind, which became increasingly isolated and self-absorbed.

During and after the Industrial Revolution, even people became more like machines, clocking in and out of routine assembly-line jobs and defining their worth by the hour, the quarter hour, and the minute. Vitality was traded for money, which soon became the measure of all things. During the twentieth century, alienation found expression in horrific world wars and shocking atrocities, proving that on the whole the human could no longer recognize himself in others. Nor could the twentieth-century human see value in Nature, which it began pillaging with relentless efficiency. Nothing was sacred, and a sense of meaninglessness prevailed. The world's youngest country, the United States of America, emerged as a global superpower, partly by converting the immense creativity of its citizens (as well as the blood, sweat, and tears of those never recognized as such) into the largest military arsenal of all time.

In their intense individualism and single-minded pursuit of happiness, Americans became isolated from the rest of the world and removed from large-scale violence and death. Thus they were deeply affected by the events of 9-11, and for many the world has since seemed like a very different place. Yet that psychic shift has also been accompanied by a sense of open-ended possibility and a growing desire for a more integrated, balanced, and peaceful world. Perhaps the story of human becoming, in which the deeply connected nomad has transformed into the darkly disconnected monad, is now entering a new and more hopeful chapter.

THREE
THE RELIEF OF GLOBAL SUFFERING

We are living in what the Greeks called the kairos—*the right moment—for a "metamorphosis of the gods." Coming generations will have to take account of this momentous transformation if humanity is not to destroy itself through the might of its own technology and science . . . So much is at stake and so much depends on the psychological constitution of modern man . . . Does the individual know that he is the makeweight that tips the scales?*

—Carl Jung[1]

THE POTENTIAL FOR PROGRESS

Had the Buddha been a pessimist at heart, he might have been daunted when taunted by Mara to abandon his pursuit of enlightenment. Certainly he would never have agreed to turn the wheel of *dharma* and teach the Four Noble Truths, or perhaps he would have dwelt solely on suffering and its causes without acknowledging the possibility of emancipation. Fortunately, however, the Buddha's successful awakening included the essential insight that while life is indeed fragile and fraught with difficulty, it is far from hopeless. In fact, the Third Noble Truth can be viewed as the Buddha's favorable prognosis, an optimistic declaration of the potential to be free of dis-ease in all its 10,000 forms (a number used frequently in Eastern traditions to connote "a great many").

The freedom promised by the Third Noble Truth is linked to the cessation or extinction of grasping or craving, put forth in the Second Noble Truth as the root cause of suffering. So powerful is this self-centered desire that the Buddha was inspired to use the word *trisna*, translated as "thirst"—clearly one of the most basic biological urges. But as strong as this addiction of the body-mind might be, it can be overcome by an even stronger desire to relinquish it, to kick the habit of clinging or attachment. Here the Buddha placed emphasis on the powers of will, intention, and choice, which together generate the potential for liberation.

Central to the Third Noble Truth and the possibility of spiritual awakening is *karma*, a concept developed by the Hindu traditions and later appropriated by Buddhism. It has since become a term commonly used in English, and just as commonly misunderstood, by Eastern and Western minds alike. If forced to define the term, most people are likely to reply that *karma* means either "fate" or "the law of cause and effect," neither of which quite hits the mark. In the first instance, fate usually implies predestination, the notion that events have been ordained by some higher power to unfold in a particular way, that in some sense the future already exists and is simply "waiting" to happen. In ancient Hindu culture, *karma* was often used in this limited and limiting way to justify the inequalities of the caste system: social standing was simply a matter of *karma*, something outside one's control, and given the rigidity of the system the best thing to do was to accept one's lot, however undignified or miserable. To the Buddha, who rejected predestination and believed the highest authority to lie within, *karma* was a much more empowering concept that allowed for the possibility of liberation from not only social but psychological restrictions, and hence he defied tradition and offered teachings to people from all walks of life.

Another, less metaphysical way to define *karma* is "the law of cause and effect," a definition that is still misleading as it suggests a strictly linear relationship between events. Especially in Western culture one is tempted to think of cause and effect in scientific terms, perhaps imagining billiard balls ricocheting off one another in mathematically predictable ways. In Buddhist thought, however, the relationship between two events (A and B, for example) is neither strictly linear (as in A directly affects B), nor strictly deterministic (as in A directly affects B in a specific, predictable way). Rather, A and B are linked or correlated through *karma*, as in "when A is present, B may arise," similar to the way in which a seed (A) is likely to become a plant (B), given the right causes and conditions (namely sunlight, water, and nutrients). The difference between the mechanistic and organic metaphors is profound, for the latter emphasizes the intricate web of relationships within which we are embedded and the larger context within which our thoughts and actions manifest. Such a conception of *karma* is more in keeping with the deeper dynamics of the universe as revealed by modern physics, implying a greater sense of possibility, fluidity, creative dynamism, and freedom, both within our lives and in the Cosmos as a whole.

In what may be the most open-ended definition of *karma*, the Buddha is alleged to have told his disciples that "*karma* is choice," his apparent point being that choice is key, for where there is choice there exists the possibility of liberation. Even on a moment-to-moment basis, each choice that we are faced with, however minor, represents an opportunity to move towards greater freedom and wakefulness, an idea captured in what the Buddha called "skillful" choices or actions (those leading to liberation) versus "unskillful" choices or actions (those leading to suffering). Although simple in theory, this distinction is quite difficult to make in practice, given that we rarely if ever know the ultimate effects of each of our choices or actions. But according to the Buddha, we do in fact know the difference between what is skillful and unskillful, or more accurately we *feel* the difference on a deep, intuitive level. Particularly when the options before us are clear, our wise inner voice tells us the right path to take. Note that in the Buddhist context, "right" is understood not as the opposite of "wrong" in the strict moral sense, but more like the opposite of "left." The important idea is that we always have the power to choose and the wisdom to act skillfully, especially when our mind is calm, spacious, receptive, and anchored in the present moment.

Unfortunately, this is rarely the case. Like a singles bar on a Saturday night, our mind is usually too active, too crowded, and too loud to permit us to hear that relatively quiet inner voice, and even when we do hear it, our ego is often too strong to really listen to its subtle directives. More often than not, the shouting of the mind prevails over the whispering of the heart, and we end up making unskillful choices that cause suffering for ourselves and others, sometimes with a sense of regret that we chose to ignore our intuition. Of course, to a large extent poor judgment and mistakes are inevitable; we are after all "only" human, always learning and deserving of compassion. At the same time, we are not *merely* human; we also possess an innate divinity and a host of amazing, superhuman capacities, including the ability to make wise choices and even overcome suffering altogether.

In fact, in Buddhist thought, humans are seen as more capable of attaining enlightenment than all other types of sentient beings, including gods and demi-gods who are inclined to languish for eons in the pleasurable heavenly realms, where they nevertheless suffer from pride and jealousy. Although we endure certain uniquely human tribulations, each of us has been blessed with a "precious human rebirth," said to be as rare as the likelihood that a sea turtle, surfacing every hundred years from the depths of a vast ocean, will put its head through a single small ring floating on the surface. On top of that, many of us are fortunate enough to possess the time and ability for spiritual practice, so it would be skillful to take advantage of our unique situation and orient our heart-minds towards the cessation of suffering for ourselves and others. The choice is ours in every moment.

HOPE, OPTIMISM, AND FAITH

On an individual level we have reason to be grateful for our present situation and hopeful if not optimistic about the future. Cessation of clinging *(nirodha)* and liberation from suffering are possible given our Buddha nature, our precious human rebirth, our freedom of choice, and our ability to make wise decisions and take skillful action. But is it reasonable to be hopeful about the future when considering suffering on a global scale? Does it make sense to be optimistic about the *karma* of humanity as a whole, which is presently manifesting in such a dramatic and disturbing way? Can we in good faith offer a favorable prognosis for the survival and recovery of planet Earth? This chapter will address these questions by considering the monumental changes taking place in our world and attempting to place them in a broader—and I hope more optimistic—context.

Before proceeding, it may be useful to define the words hope, optimism, and faith, all clearly related but different, at least in terms of degree. The first of these, hope, may be the most limited in that it involves a personal desire for future events to unfold in a certain way. Usually one is hopeful about a particular situation, and the hope involves a specifically desired outcome, as in "I hope I pass the test." Here the implication is that not passing the test will result in an expectation remaining unmet, a desire not being fulfilled, and hence disappointment and dis-ease. We might conclude that hope, at least as commonly used, is connected to the ego and its trademark insistence that things should or should not be a certain way.

Optimism, by contrast, seems to describe a general outlook or attitude, a certain openness of the heart as opposed to a narrowness of vision. One may be an optimist by nature, meaning that she is always inclined to look on the bright side, to expect the most favorable outcome, or to believe that whatever the present situation, it is the best possible one. An optimist is generally not attached to a particular outcome and is given to interpreting any development in a favorable light, including unfortunate ones that could nevertheless be seen as necessary and valuable life lessons. To the true optimist, "it's all good" (whereas the realist might add: "except for the bad parts").

To have faith is to possess a kind of optimism on the most profound level. Indeed the word is frequently used to indicate specific religious traditions, most often the Christian and Jewish faiths. In this sense, faith is a deeply held conviction that a higher order is at work in one's life and in the world at large, even in times of difficulty and crisis and even when the purpose of such tribulation is not clearly understood. A person of faith does not usually question this higher order and in fact tries to align her own will with God's will, which may be extended to include all phenomena. Of course, faith is frequently used as an antonym for reason, sometimes in a derisive way to point out someone's lack of the latter. The person of faith may in turn feel contempt or pity for the secularist, who insists that belief requires external, verifiable proof. Thus goes the all-too-familiar debate between subjective and objective forms of truth, which could be traced at least as far back as the historical split between science and religion.

It should be noted that Buddhism is rarely referred to as a faith, and not always categorized as a religion. Often it is described as a philosophical tradition, or more accurately a number of them: Tibetan, Sri Lankan, Burmese, and Thai Buddhism; Theravada, Vajrayana, Zen, Pure Land, and Abhidharma, among others. In all of these related but distinct forms of Buddhism, the role of faith is a nebulous one, given that divinity is usually understood as being an innate potential, i.e., Buddha nature. With the possible exception of Pure Land and its emphasis on devotion, the Buddhist focus is not on the will or good graces of an external God but on the power of the individual to transform her own consciousness and purify her *karma* in order to achieve either personal or collective liberation from suffering. In terms of blind faith, the Buddha is said to have discouraged his followers from accepting without question even his teachings, encouraging aspirants to rely instead on their own direct experience, especially the insights accumulated through meditation. Such insights form the basis for a kind of faith or deep inner knowing.

A NEW WAY OF THINKING

While there do exist people whose religious faith compels them to look forward to—or even help orchestrate—an apocalyptic Rapture or Final Judgment scenario, most of us share the hope that we might somehow overcome our current global crisis, or at least avert the most disastrous consequences. We may have specific hopes that a certain amount of wilderness remains intact, that a certain number of life forms be preserved, or that our own species survives. At the very least, we all share a desire that we and our loved ones be spared from acute, long-term suffering, however severe the global crisis becomes.

Although it is becoming increasingly difficult to look on the bright side of the present situation, many people nevertheless remain optimistic about the future, believing that humanity possesses the collective intelligence and resourcefulness needed to solve the problems it has created. Too often, however, such optimism rests on the conviction that Nature will be saved by technology—new methods of generating energy, purifying water, maximizing agricultural output, etc. While innovations like these may prove important in buying crucial time, the limitations of this kind of reasoning have been duly noted: "The significant problems we face cannot be solved at the same level of thinking with which we created them." In this famous quote, uncertainly attributed to Albert Einstein,[2] the word "thinking" is sometimes replaced with either "consciousness" or "awareness," the general idea being that what is required more than any short-term technological fix is a profound transformation in the collective psyche.

Indeed this book rests on the belief that a fundamental change in human consciousness is vital to overcoming the current global crisis. Just as the path of Buddhism requires a transformation of individual awareness, our present challenge requires nothing less than a collective shift in perspective. Granted, such a profound transition will undoubtedly take time, as did former seismic shifts like the agricultural, scientific, and industrial revolutions, all of which occurred over many generations. Our current transition is certainly comparable to these in magnitude, with one major difference and that is the urgency

150

of our situation: there may not be many generations left. In this sense, I am not optimistic but realistic in accepting that the crisis is likely to get a good deal worse before it gets better. The number of species will certainly continue to decline as the number of increasingly consumptive humans continues to rise, and much of the natural beauty and diversity we all hope to preserve will be lost forever. Meanwhile, the human community will undoubtedly face its own unprecedented challenges and changes.

Still, this book is itself a testament of hope that a catastrophic ecological tipping point can be avoided, and that the shift in consciousness that is already underway will reach its own tipping point, after which a critical mass of humanity will achieve full global citizenship. As has been mentioned, there are a number of prehistoric precedents for the kind of evolutionary quantum jump that seems to be required, and on good days my hopefulness manifests as a faith that the universe in its own innate wisdom would not strive for 14 billion years to achieve self-reflective awareness in the human, only to stumble backward into the relatively primitive consciousness of a bacterium or cockroach. It would seem (again, on good days) that humanity is cosmically destined to survive, although our resultant quantities and qualities remain completely uncertain.

At the end of the day, it is the uncertainty of our situation with which we all must finally make our peace. Behind the hope, optimism, and faith lies a deeper realization that the future must always remain unknown. Just as none of us can predict what the immediate future holds for our own individual lives—we may get sick, win the lottery, crash the car, fall in love—neither can anybody be sure about the fate of humanity and of life on Earth. Recognizing and coming to terms with the radical uncertainty lurking beneath the veneer of existence is in itself a profound spiritual challenge, one that promises great rewards, including a sense of inner peace and the freedom to act more selflessly, without having to worry about praise or blame, success or failure. This is the kind of non-attachment cultivated by the Bodhisattva who vows to liberate all beings from suffering, despite the apparent impossibility of such a task. The intention is what truly matters.

THE GREAT TRANSITION

The wisdom of remaining detached from expectation yet passionately and compassionately engaged is exemplified by Joanna Macy, who speaks of the Great Turning towards a more sustainable way of life. Concurrent with this huge and hopeful shift is the Great Unraveling, involving the disappearance of much of what we modern humans have long taken for granted: ways of thinking and being in the world as well as many aspects of the natural world itself. Having already investigated many of the tangible, biological unravelings and some of the historical, philosophical causes behind them, we now return to the present moment and to a few of the more abstract global changes occurring during this dramatic and decisive Third Act.

Eschatons

Our transition out of an old worldview that no longer serves humanity and is in fact detrimental to many other species is just one of several endings or eschatons (from the Greek *eschatos*, meaning "last") that are either occurring presently or will be occurring in the near future. The most major of these eschatons involves the 65-million-year Cenozoic era, which began with the Cretaceous-Tertiary extinction event that decimated the dinosaurs and is now closing with another mass extinction event. Given that the primary evolutionary

152

	SIX CURRENT ESCHATONS	Duration (approx.)
1.	Cenozoic Era	65 million years
2.	Age of Empire/History	5,000 years
3.	Piscean Age	2,000 years
4.	Age of Colonialism	500 years
5.	Period of American Supremacy	100 years
6.	Period of Cheap Oil	100 years

force is now the human, renowned biologist E.O. Wilson has dubbed the emerging era the "Anthropocene," while cosmologists Thomas Berry and Brian Swimme have given it a much more hopeful name: the "Ecozoic" era.

Another eschaton is that of the 5,000-year era of human history, inasmuch as history has been defined by wars of conquest, competing ideologies, and Empire. Although we earthlings may never overcome our martian nature, competition and conflict are fast becoming more about survival than anything else. Winning out over communism and tyranny, capitalism and democratic ideals have emerged as the dominant global forces, and wars of the future are likely to be fought instead over dwindling natural resources. Of course, the end of history does not mean that events stop occurring.

Also ending is the 2,000-year age of Pisces, which began several hundred years before the birth of Jesus and has been dominated by Christianity in particular and religion in general. Astrological ages like the Piscean can be demarcated because of the precession of the equinoxes, a phenomenon in which the Sun, when viewed at the same time on the same day of the year (the vernal equinox), appears to precess or move backward from year to year through the constellations of the zodiac. Caused by the slow wobble of the spinning Earth, a full precession (known as a Great Year or Platonic Year) takes about 26,000 years, while a single age lasts about one-twelfth of that, or 2,160 years. Since there are no definitive cusps between ages, it is uncertain as to whether we will soon enter or have already entered the New Age: the Age of Aquarius, characterized not by Christ-like hair but by the increased role of technology and democracy.

We are also currently witnessing the finale of a 500-year era of colonialism, at least as that embarrassing word is traditionally understood. With the establishment of the United Nations and the ratification of international agreements, the ideas of national sovereignty and self-determination have prevailed over cold-blooded imperialism, illegal invasion, and genocide (at least in theory, these things are decidedly immoral and forbidden). Also drawing to a close are the 100-year era of American global dominance and the era of cheap oil, the latter of which has in large part fueled the former.

With the exception of the mass extinction marking the end of the Cenozoic era, each of these eschatons is neither distinctly positive nor negative. While each may introduce a certain amount of disruption in the status quo, each also brings with it the hopeful promise of a new and more enlightened era. On the darker side of eschatology is the formulation of various doomsday scenarios, such as those suggested by Stephen Petranek, former editor of *Discover* magazine. The "Ten Ways the World Could End" are as follows: asteroid impact, encounter with a rogue black hole, global epidemic, giant solar flares, reversal of Earth's magnetic field, biotech disaster, particle accelerator mishap, ecosystem collapse, alien invasion, and a worldwide epidemic of depression.[3] Others add the possibility of a cosmic gamma ray burst, increased volcanic activity, the destruction of humans by robots or nanotechnology gone awry, and global thermonuclear war. Clearly, many of these scenarios are outside our collective control and are therefore outside the purview of this book, my concern being with that which we can control, namely our ways of thinking and acting in relation to the Earth and its inhabitants.

Arenas of Change

The Great Unraveling and the Great Turning can be compared to death and rebirth, respectively, with both happening simultaneously. In the midst of this challenging process, we may vacillate between joy and sadness, optimism and despair. Perhaps our mania reflects a deep ambivalence towards our own actual death, thoughts of which can either bring up anxiety and fear of a grim finality, or elicit feelings of hope, optimism, or faith in a glorious afterlife or a favorable rebirth. In either case, the strength of our dis-ease depends on our degree of attachment to what we fear losing or what we hope to gain. Our Great Challenge is to stay centered no matter how dire—or promising—the circumstances.

According to Macy, the Great Turning is occurring in three different, interrelated arenas: holding actions, structural change, and shift in consciousness. The first of these is what is usually called "activism," whether political, social, or environmental, and involves all

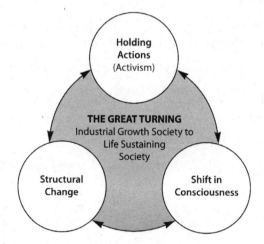

attempts to curtail the destruction wrought by the literal and figurative machinery of the industrial growth society as we move towards a more desirable life-sustaining society. The second dimension, structural change, relates to the creation of new and more sustainable systems, such as renewable energy and green technologies, food cooperatives, farmers' markets, local currency exchanges, eco-villages and intentional communities, land trusts and conservancies, etc. Third is the shift in consciousness that can be seen in the emergence of integral cosmology, deep ecology, Gaia theory, eco-feminism, eco-psychology, eco-philosophy, and other schools of thought dedicated to redefining and enriching humanity's relationship to the Earth and the Cosmos.

Although this book and this chapter are concerned primarily with the shift in consciousness, the other dimensions of change are not to be thought of as less important. Indeed a successful transition to a more sustainable world will require substantial, simultaneous, and prolonged effort in all three areas. Just as it would be dangerous to rely solely on some sort of short-term technological fix to our large-scale problems, it would surely be unwise to believe that consciousness alone could save the planet from further degradation and dis-ease. Clearly the other dimensions of change are crucial, for they make possible the preservation of life and thus the evolution of the collective psyche. Like everything else in the universe, the three arenas of change are intimately interdependent.

Initiation and Individuation

When viewed through a wide lens, our current global situation can be framed as a kind of initiation process for humanity, similar to that faced by the archetypal hero. In many of the world's myths, the hero is forced to confront some dangerous challenge, endure some difficult ordeal, or complete some seemingly impossible task, after which he usually emerges triumphant and transformed. Often the initiation involves dismemberment and death, followed by a re-membering and rebirth into a more fully integrated form in which the hero realizes his true calling or higher purpose. Typically the hero experiences a diminishment of his own ego-based identity and a connection with the larger collective to which he belongs.

The process of initiation, which appears not only in myths but in shamanic rituals and so-called mystery cults of the ancient Near East, seems to hold symbolic significance for the modern human. Certainly the current global crisis represents the greatest challenge our species has ever faced, with stakes that could hardly be higher. The very structures that support life—the only known life in the universe—are being rapidly dismantled, and our daunting challenge is to come together as a human family in order to engage our collective wisdom, compassion, and creativity to preserve as much life as possible. This would seem to require an authentic, heroic humility; a softening of the rigidified ego structure; and a recognition of an intimate interconnectedness and interdependence with everything.

Not coincidentally, a softening of individual ego that allows for a deeper communion with other beings lies at the heart of Buddhist practice. Whether conceived as detachment from ego or an expansion of the self to include the whole world or even the entire Cosmos, the process involves a transformation of one's usual identity as a "skin-encapsulated ego," to borrow a phrase from philosopher Alan Watts. The degree to which one can break free—if even temporarily—from this self-imposed limitation is the degree to which inter-subjective communion can occur and compassion can manifest.

From a psychological perspective, one's ability to transcend ego may depend, somewhat paradoxically, on the strength and stability of one's sense of self. A secure foundation must first be established before it can be surmounted. In thinking about this apparent conundrum of spiritual progress, we might consider the egolessness of an infant: as much as we might envy her beautifully open-hearted expressiveness and spontaneity, hers is not a wise, serene, and selfless state to which we should aspire but a naive, volatile, and selfish one out of which we have grown (but may of course revisit on occasion, whether intentionally or not). This conflation of trans-egoic consciousness with pre-egoic consciousness is what Ken Wilber calls the "pre-trans fallacy," a kind of false romanticism that is often extended not only to young children but to prehistoric and traditional cultures.

Humanity's initiation can be regarded as a culmination of the collective individuation process that has unfolded over the course of human history. Having evolved into self-consciousness at the birth of civilization, self-knowledge during the Axial Age, and greater independence and self-security throughout history, *Homo sapiens* is now being called to greater self-transcendence and selflessness involving a compassionate regard for all forms of life and the Earth as a whole. Again, what our situation asks is not a reversion to some imaginary Eden of yesteryear, but an advance towards what has been dubbed *Homo universalis,* a new stage of evolution that, in Wilber's terms, both "transcends and includes" all previous stages.

Through the Hourglass

It should be noted that the term "individuation" was popularized by Jung, who also coined the terms "collective unconscious" and "archetypes," all of which are relevant to the discussion at hand. During his life-long investigation into the unconscious, Jung discovered that this deep psychic well—from which emerge dreams, slips of the tongue, irrational behaviors, nervous tics, etc.—has not only a personal but a collective component, as evidenced by certain myths and symbols that appear across different cultures and times. To these universal forms Jung originally assigned the term "primordial images," later calling them archetypes, from the Greek *arche*, meaning "first principle." As basic structures of both the personal and collective unconscious, archetypes play a role in all life's major moments.

Jung also coined the term "synchronicity," defined as an "acausal connecting principle" between the unconscious mind and the physical world. In one example among many documented by Jung, he was once speaking with a client about her powerful dream of a golden scarab when suddenly a real beetle with gold wings—quite uncommon in that region—flew into the room, surprising the woman and erasing her skepticism. By taking seriously such inexplicable yet undeniably potent experiences, Jung transformed not just psychology but philosophy and sociology, while his work with archetypes helped the modern mind recontextualize mythology not as something make-believe and distant but as a real and vital part of human existence.

In terms of the death/rebirth process, the world's leading expert would have to be Stanislav Grof, a Czech-born psychologist who has witnessed, facilitated, and undergone thousands of such experiences over the course of his long career. Working initially with mind-altering substances and eventually with a special breathing technique (dubbed "holotropic"—towards wholeness), Grof has plumbed the depths of the human psyche and expanded the map of consciousness well beyond the limits set by his predecessors. While Freud highlighted the importance of early childhood experience and Jung emphasized the collective unconscious and its archetypes, Grof found a vital link between the personal and transpersonal realms in the birth process, which he separates into four stages. Each of these four "basic perinatal matrixes" (BPMs) is characterized by particular archetypes and images that may be experienced during holotropic states, especially if connected with trauma. The idea is that by consciously confronting such normally repressed, unconscious material, a person may achieve greater psychological integration, balance, and wholeness.

Grof's expanded model of the psyche can be depicted as an hourglass, with the bottom half encompassing the personal, biographical realm and the top half outlining the transpersonal, archetypal realm. Between these lies the narrow canal of death and rebirth, through which passes both the fetus on its way to "personhood" and the disembodied psyche on its way to "transpersonhood." One may also pass through this bottleneck during non-ordinary states or during what Grof calls "spiritual emergencies," both of which involve a dissolution of ego boundaries. Depending on how complete or rapid is

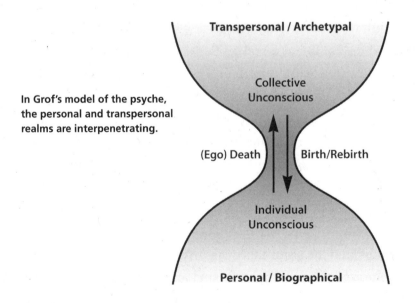

Transpersonal / Archetypal

Collective Unconscious

In Grof's model of the psyche, the personal and transpersonal realms are interpenetrating.

(Ego) Death   **Birth/Rebirth**

Individual Unconscious

Personal / Biographical

DARK NIGHT, EARLY DAWN

Not only have Stan Grof's theories transformed the field of psychology, his therapeutic methods have transformed the lives of countless individuals. Notable among Grof's devotees is Christopher Bache, a professor of religious studies who for almost thirty years underwent a program of psychedelic therapy, fearlessly confronting his personal demons while gaining deep insight into the transpersonal realms and what he calls the "species mind." In his book *Dark Night, Early Dawn,* Bache writes:

> I saw humanity climbing out of a valley and just ahead . . . beyond our present sight, was a brilliant, sun-drenched world that was about to break over us. The time frame was enormous. After millions of years of struggle and ascent, we were poised on the brink of a sunrise that would forever change the conditions of life on this planet. All current structures would quickly become irrelevant. All truths . . . rendered passé. Truly a new epoch was dawning. The lives of everyone living on the edge of this pivotal time . . . had been helping to bring about this global shift.[4]

Alas, not all was bright and beautiful. Bache also saw foresaw a "dark night of the species-soul" brought about by a worsening global ecological crisis, a "superheated pressure cooker" that will put the species mind through great distress. Yet like myself, Bache sees this collective crisis as potentially unifying:

> At one level, this cultural death will involve the death of certain deeply held ways of viewing the world . . . At a deeper level, I think this death will involve a deep shift in how we collectively feel about each other and the world at large . . . In place of [our] sense of separation might arise a new feeling for the inherent wholeness of life, with circles of compassion rippling through life's web.[5]

(continued)

Speaking optimistically about this shift, Bache draws upon the insights of chaos theory, describing the current state of global affairs as a "far-from-equilibrium" system in which "nonlinear behavior replaces linear behavior; systems phase-lock in unpredictable ways to allow previously separate systems to act as one."[6] When driven into far-from-equilibrium conditions, "some systems do not just break down; they generate new structures that pull higher forms of order out of the surrounding chaos."[7] Extending these dynamics beyond the material realm, Bache suggests that:

> . . . the global eco-crisis may push the field of the species mind so far that it too may draw forth new structures from itself . . . If this were to happen, synergistic tendencies that are latent within the species mind may become manifest, exerting a coordinating influence within seemingly disparate human activities. Synchronicities may increase. Realities that are unconscious to all but a few may become available to many.[8]

Delving further into chaos theory, Bache explains that if a system goes far enough into disequilibrium, it reaches a fork in its destiny called a bifurcation point—"a moment of truth in which a system must 'choose' which one of several evolutionary paths it must follow."[9] When a system approaches a bifurcation point, it becomes extremely sensitive to influence.

> In the highly unstable, supercharged morphic field of tomorrow, those persons who have already made the transition individually that humanity is trying to make collectively, who have begun to think and act as ecologically responsible global citizens, who have truly lifted from their hearts the divisions of race, religion, class, gender, nation, and so on, may function as seed crystals working in conjunction with these strange attractors to catalyze new patterns in human awareness. In this setting, each of our individual efforts . . . may have far-reaching consequences.[10]

this personal death/transpersonal rebirth, it may be experienced as either terrifying or liberating.

As for humanity as a whole, it seems that we are currently in the midst of BPM-3, the birthing process, which involves an intense struggle for survival that is usually experienced as simultaneously pleasant and unpleasant. This matrix (which combines elements of BPM-2 and BPM-4, dominated by feelings of fear and joy, respectively) is commonly associated with images of military and revolutionary battles, boxing matches, treacherous airplane, boat, and car rides, wild parties, and carnivals. In these scenarios, in BPM-3 in general, and in our current global crisis there is a clear and present danger accompanied by a heightened awareness, as well as a hopeful sense that the threat can ultimately be vanquished.

INTEGRAL CONSCIOUSNESS AND COSMOLOGY

By now most readers may well be wondering: what is this new form of consciousness into which humanity is being initiated? One way to address that question is to recall Jean Gebser's structures of consciousness—the archaic, magic, mythic, mental, and integral. It is the last of these that remains to be fully developed, both within these pages and in the collective psyche. The term was first used not by Gebser but by the Indian philosopher-mystic Sri Aurobindo, who developed an "integral yoga" that fuses the traditional *karma, bhakti,* and *jnana* paths as well as the Hindu systems of Tantra and Vedanta, while also synthesizing Eastern and Western philosophy.

As its name implies, the integral structure incorporates all the other, more fundamental structures, adding to it a number of new insights about the nature of reality. One such insight is that reality is far more complex and mysterious than previously understood by the rational mind, which for hundreds of years has operated on the assumption that everything could be understood and explained solely by means of reason, logic, and mathematics. This delusion has rested in large part on the belief in an ontologically objective world existing as radically separate from consciousness, some stuff "out there" that could be measured, poked, prodded, and coaxed into revealing its innermost secrets. To study the great machine of the universe, one usually studied an individual part in artificial isolation from the whole.

By contrast, integral consciousness understands the world as "a communion of subjects, not a collection of objects,"[11] as Thomas Berry once wrote. For this reason, true comprehension involves not just rationality but imagination, intuition, and an acknowledgment of a certain subjectivity on the part of the "object" of study. Surely one cannot fully know another person just by observing her external features, measuring her height, weight, and inseam, or looking up her address and phone number; there must occur an inter-subjective dialogue, an intimate encounter, a dance through which more and more—but perhaps never everything—may be divulged and discovered. An important new insight is that the same rules of engagement apply to the world at large. Although butterflies, seashells, and protons may not possess a subjectivity to which we can readily relate, they nevertheless reveal themselves more fully in mutual exchange. In recognition of this fact, the late Austrian philosopher Martin Buber emphasized the value of "I-Thou" relationships over the shallow and isolating "I-It" orientation of the modern human.

Integral consciousness recognizes and values multiple ways of knowing, each of which may inform or enrich but not negate another. For example, a mythic engagement with a giant redwood as a source of wisdom is not to be considered inferior to a rational engagement with its photosynthetic processes; each reveals something completely different but equally true about the tree. Indeed truth is substantially redefined. Since what Gebser calls "verition" can be approached from various perspectives (or quadrants, in Wilber's model), the integral structure is sometimes called "aperspectival." No particular perspective is completely true, or completely false, and each contributes to a fuller description of reality. This is not to deny the existence of objective truth, a tendency of the extreme postmodernist who invites alienation instead of communion and must defend the Truth that Truth does not exist. Rather, integralism favors the inclusiveness of both/and statements over the divisiveness of either/or proclamations, while avoiding the absolutism of "only this." It embraces a reality in which multiple truths are harmoniously coexistent and mutually supportive.

In this spirit, integral consciousness does not dismiss the importance of the rational structure from which it is emerging, but transcends and includes it. Without a doubt, the analytical, empirical mind has been crucial in bringing about the many technological and medical breakthroughs that have enabled humans to live long and prosper, and it has produced the many scientific discoveries that have deepened our understanding of the universe. Indeed, it was *through* the rational structure that many new-paradigm discoveries were made, particularly in the fields of physics and astronomy. Some of these microscopic and macroscopic insights were mentioned in the previous chapter, and they bear reviewing because of their central importance to a new and more sophisticated conception of the Cosmos.

Microcosmic Insights

As with other mental structures, integral consciousness has its own way of perceiving time and space. In the old paradigm, time was conceived of as regular and linear, with clear divisions between past, present, and future, as represented by clocks and calendars that need only occasional adjustments during daylight savings time and leap years. While acknowledging the practical utility of categorizing and measuring time, integral consciousness recognizes time as an indivisible whole. Gebser describes the integral experience of time as a "consciousness encompassing all time and embracing both man's distant past and his approaching future as a living present."[12]

Like time, space has been conceived by the rational mind as regular and homogenous, with each cubic foot being exactly alike except in its contents. In the old mechanistic model, the universe was regarded as something like an exceptionally big box, within which events occurred in accordance with well-defined and immutable scientific laws. Objects within the cosmic container were thought to move about and bump into each other in predictable ways, politely obeying the laws of gravity and thermodynamics and never exceeding the speed of light. Objects themselves were believed to be composed of other objects: tiny, indestructible particles with a tendency to stick together and also obey universal laws. Consciousness, meanwhile, existed nowhere but in the human brain, having been placed there by God or perhaps appearing there suddenly during the course of human evolution.

Known as the Newtonian-Cartesian paradigm after Newton and Descartes, this conception of the cosmos should sound familiar as the one most of us were taught in school. It should also sound perfectly reasonable, as it works pretty well in explaining events on the earthly, human scale. But when examined carefully through powerful microscopes and telescopes, the cozy blanket of the old paradigm appears to be frayed at the edges and full of black holes that reveal a mysterious dark matter beneath. During the twentieth century, physicists discovered that space and time are woven together into the elastic fabric of space-time, which curves in the vicinity of dense objects; that energy is interchangeable with matter, which consists almost entirely of empty space; that the position and velocity of two subatomic particles cannot be measured simultaneously or precisely, indicating a fundamental uncertainty in the universe; that certain quarks demonstrate "non-local entanglement" in which they seem to communicate instantaneously over great distances, thus defying causality; that light acts as both wave and particle, defying logic; and that the vast majority of the universe is likely composed of invisible, non-material "dark matter." Clearly, we're not in Kansas anymore.

In fact, when we peek behind the Newtonian-Cartesian curtain, we see that the Wizard of Oz looks a lot like us. One of the more profound revelations of quantum physics is that, at the subatomic level at least, any observation reveals as much about the subject (viewer) as it does about the object; that in a very real way the observer determines the outcome of her observations. Not that the observer creates her own reality, but that reality is collaborative and participatory. Mind and matter are intimately intertwined, and there is no privileged vantage point from which to view the world objectively. As astrophysicist James Jeans wrote in the 1930s: "The universe is more like a great thought than like a great machine."[13]

Although gained through careful empiricism and rationality, the paradigm-busting insights of twentieth-century astrophysicists might at first seem irrational, illogical, counterintuitive, or even mystical. The emerging worldview seems to require a yogic flexibility of the mind, a more "oriental" orientation potentially *dis*orienting to the occidental psyche. Indeed the parallels between modern physics and Eastern mysticism have been duly noted by various authors such as Fritjof Capra *(The Tao of Physics, The Turning Point, The Hidden Connections, The Web of Life)*, Gary Zukav *(The Dancing Wu Li Masters)*, and Deepak Chopra (*Quantum Healing* and many others). While some of these works have been criticized as "New-Agey" and unscientific, the fact remains that many great physicists of the modern West have leaned towards the ancient East philosophically and perhaps even spiritually. According to Einstein himself, "the finest emotion of which we are capable is the mystic emotion. Herein lies the germ of all art and all true science."[14]

A New Map of the Cosmos

These insights into the small-scale structure and dynamics of the universe have been accompanied by revelations about its large-scale structure and potential origin. Over the course of the last century, our map of the heavens has continued to expand exponentially as our instruments have enabled us to peer ever deeper into space. What we have learned about the incomprehensible vastness of the Cosmos is by itself enough to boggle the mind and rouse it from its old-paradigm slumber. As philosophers, poets, sages, and sociologists have continued to tackle the question of *who* we are, modern astronomers have been arriving at an ever-clearer picture of *where* we are in the universe.

Our very first maps, drawn in the dirt with sticks or carved into clay, depicted relatively small geographic regions, perhaps not much bigger than could be traversed on foot or horseback within a day or two. The ancient Greek cartographer Hecataeus was among the first to draw a map of the world, which included Europe, North Africa, and East Asia, with Greece at the center. By the time of Aristotle it was widely accepted that the Earth was spherical, and a few centuries later Ptolemy figured out various methods of projecting his 3-D world map (the most extensive, detailed, and accurate that had yet been conceived) onto a 2-D piece of paper. It was also Ptolemy who offered a temporary solution to the problem of the wandering planets by constructing a more elaborate model of the *kosmos*, understood by most of his predecessors as consisting of the Earth; the secondary sphere of the Sun, Moon, and planets; and the sphere of the fixed stars, beyond which lay the divine realm.

Due to Copernicus and the first telescopes, our Sun became one of many in a vast sea of stars, the dimensions of which nevertheless remained unknown. Galileo confirmed the suspicions of ancient astronomers that the Milky Way is indeed composed of countless stars, and the notion that our galaxy is likewise one among many was first proposed the following century by Kant and finally confirmed in the early 1920s by Edwin Hubble and his powerful telescope.

Thanks to Hubble and other modern astronomers, we now know the following about our place in the universe:

- The Sun is an average-sized star some 865,000 miles in diameter that lies about 93 million miles from Earth (or 8 light-minutes, the speed of light being roughly 186,000 miles per second).
- The Sun accounts for 99.85 percent of the mass of the solar system, the diameter of which is anywhere from 8.5 light-hours (using Pluto's orbit) to 22 light-hours (using the bubble of solar wind called the termination shock) to 2 light-years (using the Oort cloud, from which emerge comets that are influenced by the Sun).
- The nearest star apart from the Sun is Proxima Centauri, invisible to the naked eye at about 4.2 light-years away. Other visible neighbors include Sirius (8.6 light-years), 61 Cygni (11.4 LY), and Epsilon Indi (11.8 LY).
- Our galaxy, the Milky Way, is a barred spiral galaxy some 100,000 light-years in diameter and 1,000 light-years thick on average,

comprised of 200–400 billion stars. Our solar system, situated within the galaxy's Orion arm, lies some 26,000 light-years from the galactic center, where there likely lurks a super-massive black hole (as may well be the case with all galaxies).

- Our closest galactic neighbor is Andromeda, located approximately 2.5 million light-years away. These two large galaxies orbit around each other, and are in turn orbited by about 35 smaller galaxies that comprise the "Local Group."

- The Local Group, itself roughly 10 million light-years in diameter, is being drawn towards the Virgo Cluster, located 53 million light-years away. The Virgo cluster contains somewhere between 1,000 and 2,000 galaxies.

- The Virgo Cluster is part of our Local Supercluster, comprised of some 100 galactic groups and clusters and measuring about 200 million light-years in diameter.

- The Local Supercluster (also called the Virgo Supercluster because of the dominance of the Virgo Cluster) has as its nearest neighbors the Hydra and Centaurus superclusters, all three of which are being drawn towards a gravitational anomaly known as "The Great Attractor."

- The universe contains millions of superclusters.

A Growing, Fecund Universe

Given the difficulty of comprehending even a single light-year, this description and map of the observable universe is humbling, to say the least. As if such astronomical distances weren't overwhelming enough, we must also try to wrap our head around another modern discovery: that the universe is expanding at an extremely rapid rate. Even Einstein, who came across the theoretical possibility while working on general relativity in 1917, was so unnerved by the idea that he added to his equations a fudge factor called the "cosmological constant" in order to preserve the Newtonian model of a steady-state, box-like universe. Over a decade later, after squinting through Hubble's telescope at receding, red-shifted galaxies, Einstein conceded his cosmological cover-up as the biggest blunder of his career.

In addition to forcing us to think outside the Newtonian box, the concept of an expanding universe has profound implications, most notably the notion that if all the galaxies are currently moving apart from each other, they once must have been much closer together if not in the same place. The notion that at one point the universe was one point was first proposed in 1927 by Belgian Catholic priest and Einstein fan Georges Lemaître, whose "hypothesis of the primeval atom" was later expanded (and contracted) by Russian cosmologist George Gamow into the Big Bang Theory. Gamow's model predicted that the energetic remnants of the primordial fireball should be detectable at the very edges of the universe, and indeed this cosmic microwave background radiation was inadvertently discovered in 1965 by Arno Penzias and Robert Wilson, thus helping to establish the dominance of Gamow's explosive theory.

One of the more mind-blowing aspects of this new cosmology is that space is not a static fixture of the universe but is being created at every moment of its existence. In a very real sense the Big Bang is still occurring, as the edges of the universe continue to unfurl—not *into* space but *as* space—while space is also being added between galaxies, effectively pushing them apart. As it turns out, there is nothing static about the universe at all; it is forever emerging, growing, and evolving. Indeed it is more accurate to describe the universe not as a *place* but as a *process,* a phenomenon, or an event, a revelation with profound implications for humans, as pointed out by Brian Swimme:

"Within a static universe, your activities have to fit into an existing order. We don't live in a set, existing order; we live in an order that is emerging."[15]

Based partly on analysis of the background radiation first detected by Penzias and Wilson, astronomers have calculated that the process we call the universe has been occurring for somewhere around 13.73 billion years, give or take 120 million years. So, what happened before that? The question is a natural one, and also a meaningless one, given that space-time was created by the Big Bang. Thus it makes no sense to speak of a "before," and even the term "beginning" is a little clumsy. Still, astronomers have had to use limited human conceptions of time—based on the rotation and revolution of the Earth, clearly meaningless elsewhere in the universe—in order to "turn back the clock" to the first instants after the Big Bang began, when the fundamental forces and elementary particles were born and the universe came into existence.

Did the universe arise out of nothing? Another good question, also problematic in that "nothing" is difficult to comprehend. We might imagine a vacuum, a space completely devoid of matter, air, visible light, invisible light, and radiation, as if such a space exists anywhere in the universe. The space between galactic stars often contains dust, gas, and photons, while intergalactic space is filled with invisible filaments of super-heated hydrogen and oxygen, not to mention non-visible particles of antimatter and dark matter. Meanwhile on Earth, modern physicists have discovered that even in a near-perfect vacuum, elementary particles simply pop into existence, seemingly out of nowhere, out of "nothing." This discovery has been revolutionary and revelatory, for it means that the universe, at its very foundation, seethes with creativity; that the ground of existence is a "fecund emptiness" that physicists call "quantum foam" or "space-time foam." Swimme, who speaks of the ground of being as an "all-nourishing abyss," writes:

> The foundational reality of the universe is this unseen ocean of potentiality. If all the individual things of the universe were to evaporate, one would be left with an infinity of pure generative power.[16]

Again, things are starting to sound a bit mystical. The quantum foam at the base of reality calls to mind the Buddhist concept of emptiness or *shunyata*. Contrary to the notion that emptiness implies nihilism (the belief that existence is meaningless), Buddhist emptiness is also, paradoxically, a fullness, reflected in the famous teaching that "emptiness is form, form is emptiness." While the comparison between quantum foam and Buddhist emptiness may be thought-provoking, it would surely be a stretch to conflate the two, as the latter pertains not only to the metaphysical ground of being but to everyday objects, which are said to be "empty" in the sense of lacking inherent existence. In the case of a chair, for example, there really is no chair apart from its function, its components, the wood from which it is made, etc. This conception of reality is pretty much the opposite of Plato's Idealism, which posits some universal template for all chairs, a transcendental "chairness" of which all chairs partake.

Apparently Aristotle was right to affirm that "nature abhors a vacuum," while Democritus and Leucippus were a little off the mark. Their idea of matter being comprised of solid, indestructible units fails to capture the ongoing creation and destruction occurring on the subatomic level, and misses the fact that atoms are less solid than empty, in the literal sense. Still, the atomic model was not only revolutionary in its day—who would have thought that rocks and elephants were made of the same stuff?—it has served as a relatively solid basis for the scientific enterprise, as it works well enough on the scale of gadgets and widgets. The major drawback to considering atoms as foundational is that matter itself becomes primary, leading to materialism, consumerism, and their attendant problems. If reality is basically a collection of tiny objects, then objects themselves appear all the more valuable and worthy of collecting, whereas quantum foam and Buddhist emptiness both highlight the interdependent, constantly arising, and transitory nature of all things.

In the new cosmology, matter and energy are interchangeable, a concept first expressed by Einstein in his famous equation $E=mc^2$, in which energy equals the mass of an object multiplied by the speed of light squared. On the quantum level, particles exist only in relationship to other particles and only as mathematical possibilities or potentials that manifest only when observed. Matter can thus be considered "empty" in the sense of lacking inherent, independent existence. Indeed, according to Neils Bohr, "an independent reality in the ordinary sense can be ascribed neither to the phenomena nor the agencies of observation."[17]

An Omnicentric Universe

One of the more flabbergasting aspects of the expanding universe is that it seems to be doing so in all directions, at an equal rate. Where one might expect to find some variation in the rate of expansion in a certain hemisphere of the sky (perhaps suggesting a center of the universe from which the Big Bang originated), one finds that from every point on Earth, everything appears to be moving away from us at a uniform velocity, with nearer galaxies moving half as fast as those located twice as far away.

Based on such observations, one might be tempted to conclude, then, that the Earth is actually the center of the universe, and in a sense this conclusion is correct. But only partially so, for the evidence seems to indicate that a uniform expansion would also be detected from the Andromeda galaxy, the Virgo cluster, or from any point in the universe. To get a sense of this, imagine the universe as a giant loaf of raisin bread, with each galaxy a raisin. As the loaf expands, the raisins move further apart while themselves remaining more or less the same size. From the vantage point of, say, a yeast on one of the raisins, all the other raisins would appear to be moving away at equal speeds as the bread expanded in volume. Like a loaf of baking bread, the universe is expanding as the space between galaxies grows.

Thus our understanding of the universe has evolved from a geo-centric model to a heliocentric model to an *omnicentric* model, in which the center is everywhere. Or perhaps it is more accurate to say that the center of the universe is wherever the observer happens to be located, which in humanity's case happens to be planet Earth, and in the individual's case happens to be right where you are sitting at this moment. In keeping with the integral perspective, the other models are not discarded as useless but honored as partially true, while the

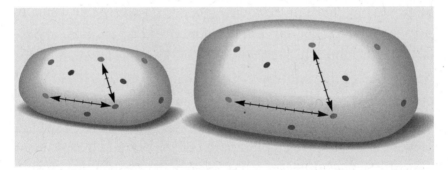

The expanding universe has been likened to a baking loaf of raisin bread, with each raisin representing a galaxy. As the dough expands, each raisin moves away from each of the others at a uniform rate. Meanwhile, the galaxies themselves are expanding, albeit at a much slower rate than the universe at large.

emerging model has the benefit of being both scientifically accurate and spiritually relevant, for in an omnicentric universe, each moment of life can rightly be regarded as a cosmic event.

This aspect of the new cosmology is not intended to reinforce the delusion of the megalomaniac that the world revolves around him, but to counter the equally strong delusion of the modern human that the Cosmos is something "far out" or alien, something from which he is somehow disconnected. The twentieth-century English philosopher Alfred North Whitehead described each moment as a cosmic "concrescence" of all previous moments, an eruption into being as momentous as the Big Bang. This idea is related to the Buddhist concept of "dependent arising" in which everything depends upon the magical confluence of specific causes and conditions, and can be related to the *dharma* of *karma,* in which each moment of existence represents the blossoming of seeds planted in the past.

Consider, for example, the act of eating an apple. While it may seem relatively mundane, it actually involves a good deal more than one usually considers, including your acquisition of the apple (which involves your own personal history of going to the store, earning money to buy the apple, getting a job, going to school, learning to read, being born, the survival of your ancestors, etc.), the apple's arrival at the store (involving among other things the invention of the combustion engine and the efforts of many people, each with their own necessary history and genealogy), and the growth of the apple (involving the evolution of apple trees and of life on Earth, not to mention the existence and formation of the Sun, itself dependent upon the birth of galaxies...). In actuality the chain of connections involved in the simple act of eating an apple extends so far and wide as to include the entire universe in its 14-billion-year existence, with each step along the way being a mind-boggling miracle in itself.

Of course, the chain also extends into the future: the energy from the Sun, captured and stored in the apple, becomes stored in your cells, waiting to be converted into push-ups or poetry.

It is just this kind of shift in perspective—from the commonplace to the cosmic, from the mundane to the miraculous—that is being invited by the new worldview and supported by the new cosmology. While the subatomic world may seem counter-intuitive and perhaps confusing in its indeterminacy, it also contains a certain fluidity, creativity, and openness not found in the old deterministic model. Likewise, learning about the large-scale structure of the universe may be deflating or disorienting at first, but it can also foster humility and bring home an appreciation for the uniqueness and beauty of planet Earth, the preciousness and fragility of life, and the sacred import of one's own existence.

Even outside of Eden, the eating of an apple can be considered a cosmic act.

A Synthesis of Sacred and Secular

The idea that the human race and each of its members are woven into the story of creation has been central to almost every culture in history. Through countless myths and rituals, humans have celebrated their intimate and mystical engagement with the Earth and the Cosmos. To the modern industrialized human, by contrast, Nature is merely a clump of trees to visit on vacation and perhaps cut down during the work week, while the universe seems a vast and vacant place forever threatening to annihilate his individuality and about which he prefers not to think too much. The old paradigm has taught him that he and his fellow humans are ultimately alone in a world whose meaning lies primarily in its monetary value.

Fortunately, the new story of the creation and evolution of the universe has recaptured or highlighted some of its latent mystery. Among the many findings of twentieth-century science is that the universe could have unfolded in an infinite number of ways, yet it did so in an extremely particular way that allowed for the birth of galaxies, the seeding of stars, the formation of the Sun and Earth, the evolution of life, and the emergence of self-reflective consciousness in the human. At each stage of the journey, the circumstances had to have been *just so*, with only minor variations resulting in a completely different scenario, a totally different universe.

Consider gravity, for example, one of the four fundamental forces of the universe that are believed to have emerged within the first second after the Big Bang. If the force of gravity were weaker by even the most infinitesimal degree, the first elements would have scattered off into space, never to form galaxies or stars, resulting in a cold and lifeless universe. Similarly, the slightest variation in the strengths of the weak and strong nuclear forces that hold together atoms and their nuclei would have prohibited the formation of hydrogen and helium necessary for galaxies and stars, which in turn needed a particular gravity to have coalesced at all. Of course, the well-researched, poorly understood, and seldom-celebrated force of gravity also lovingly prevents the Earth from being sucked into the Sun and keeps each of Earth's creatures from flying off into space.

A reasonable if not unavoidable conclusion is that the fundamental forces of the universe, as well as their evolutionary roles, were all present within the tiny singularity from which everything burst forth. In a sense, all the galaxies, suns, planets, dolphins, and DNA strands were already contained within that tiny seed, each waiting for its eventual emergence onto the cosmic stage. One could easily extend this logic to humans, the implication being that each of us, as a manifestation of the universe, has a particular cosmic destiny to fulfill, even if unknown or unknowable by us. Perhaps our collective destiny, as conscious components of the Earth, is to participate in our planet's destiny, which is necessarily bound up with that of humanity and perhaps of the Cosmos as a whole.

The controversial idea that the fundamental forces of the universe have been in some way pre-arranged or fine-tuned in order to bring about intelligent life represents the "strong anthropic principle" or SAP, while the weak version, WAP, relies more on statistical probabilities based on the age and size of the universe. From one perspective, the anthropic principle is not controversial but self-evident: the only universe we can observe is one that supports our existence; it could be no other way. Although a simple truism, it suggests the more mystical possibility that the universe, like a subatomic particle, needs an observer in order to "really" exist. Yet another possibility is that our universe is one among many, each with its own fundamental laws, and that our universe just happens to possess the conditions necessary for the existence of life. In this case, we simply lucked out.

What many rational scientists dismiss is the concept of "intelligent design"—that the process of cosmic evolution is being guided by some unseen, divine hand. It seems to me that both the aversion *and* the attraction to this idea are rooted in a dualistic, old-paradigm conception of the universe, in which matter is thought to lack intelligence or subjectivity while spirit or divinity is regarded as being separate and transcendent, like the old cosmic watchmaker. Call me a SAP, but my suggestion, and that of what might be called integral or deep cosmology, is that the universe is in itself intelligent, creative, and spiritual, forever evolving towards greater complexity, diversity, beauty, and self-realization. Evidence of extinctions and geologic upheavals indicates that the process is hardly smooth and linear, but it does seem to have a *telos*—a direction and purpose.

As I see it, the primary problem with intelligent design lies not with "intelligence"—if understood as being immanent in matter or intrinsic in the universe—but with "design"—usually understood as necessitating a wholly transcendent, all-powerful Designer with a perfect plan. Clearly, the plan is not quite perfect; but neither is it haphazard or random. Just as the intelligent person might fumble or falter on her way towards a goal, so too does the intelligent universe strive imperfectly towards an unknown future, postulated by Pierre Teilhard de Chardin as universal God-consciousness or enlightenment. Whether or not the universe ever reaches this "Omega Point," the exciting implication is that each one of us, as intelligent components of an intelligent Cosmos, has a potential role to play in the continually unfolding story of evolution.

In the cosmic drama that is being written every moment, we are not "merely players" as Shakespeare wrote, we are also the audience and the co-writers. But as participants in the cosmic drama, we must be careful to avoid stealing the spotlight, for the *anthropic* universe can too easily become the *anthropocentric* or human-centered universe in which all other species are merely supporting actors. In the new epic of the universe, humans are understood to be intimately connected to other forms of life, not because of their utility or even their necessity for our survival but because of their own intelligence, beauty, and co-participation in the cosmic adventure, in which our role is no longer that of the ruthless and greedy king but the benevolent steward.

By combining a universal teleology with the discoveries of astrophysics, deep cosmology helps to reconcile the age-old debate between spirituality and science. In keeping with the integral perspective, neither system is rejected—instead each is honored for containing its own truth. When we understand evolution as a sacred process and matter as intelligent, we are able to transcend dualistic, either/or thinking and arrive at a both/and conception of the universe in which science and religion are not antagonistic but mutually supportive. In the spirit of Aquinas, both serve to illumine the mystery and meaning of existence.

Of course, creationists who believe the Earth to be about 6,000 years old may never be open to the possibility of an emerging, evolving, 14-billion-year-old Cosmos. An evolutionary cosmology is, however, becoming increasingly popular among mainstream Christians, due in part to the efforts of "evolutionary evangelists" like Michael Dowd. Through countless speaking engagements, radio interviews, and the promotion of his 2007 book *Thank God for Evolution,* Dowd has been preaching what he considers the gospel of our time, building bridges between the scientific and religious communities. His "evolutionary theology" has received praise from religious leaders of many traditions and from Nobel laureates, including molecular biologist Craig Mello, who has optimistically declared that "the science vs. religion debate is over!"[18]

EVIDENCE OF EVOLUTION

Although Mello's declaration of a truce between age-old rivals might seem a tad premature, there is good reason to believe that things are headed in that direction, as many disparate groups within the human community awaken to the fact that they share common ground in a very literal sense. This section will highlight some of the more promising developments taking place on the world stage, each contributing to the hope that our species is in fact rising up from its slumber and wising up to a worldview that is more in harmony with both the natural world and the universal order.

The World's Largest Movement

Even among traditional New Earth creationists, the concept of planetary stewardship is gaining wider appeal. The old conception of the world as either a place of battle between the forces of good and evil or an unholy purgatory is giving way to an awareness that the Earth is a life-giving expression of divine creativity that needs to be preserved for future generations. As E.O. Wilson explains in his book *The Future of Life*, even the dictate of Genesis 1:28 that mankind "rule over . . . all living creatures that move upon the earth" is being reinterpreted as a call to environmental protection. Pope John Paul II declared the ecological crisis to be a moral issue, and in 2008 the Vatican added polluting to its list of deadly sins (other additions were genetic engineering, being obscenely rich, drug dealing, abortion, pedophilia, and causing social injustice).[19] Bartholemew I, leader to 250 million Orthodox Christians, has said:

> For humans to cause species to become extinct and to destroy the biological diversity of God's creation, for humans to degrade the integrity of the earth by causing changes in its climate, by stripping the earth of its natural forests, or destroying its wetlands, for humans to contaminate the earth's waters, its land, its air, and its life with poisonous substances, these are sins.[20]

Protestants too are joining the environmental movement, as indicated by the statement of Reverend Stan LeQuire, head of the Evangelical Environmental Network:

We evangelicals are recognizing more and more that environmental issues are not Republican or Democrat, that they really come from the most wonderful teachings that we have in Scripture, which command us to honor God by caring for creation.[21]

Like myself, Wilson is optimistic about, well, the future of life. He insists that the Earth is still productive enough and that humans are creative enough to feed the world now *and* to raise the standard of living of the global population projected to the middle of the twenty-first century at least; and that meanwhile the great majority of the world's surviving species and ecosystems can be preserved. Wilson's plan—presented as a challenge—includes salvaging the world's most endangered and biologically rich habitats such as tropical rainforests and arid scrublands; keeping intact the remaining frontier forests of the Amazon, the Guianas, the Congo, New Guinea, Canada, Alaska, Russia, Finland, and Scandinavia; ceasing all logging of old-growth native forests by converting to environmentally and economically sustainable tree farming; concentrating on the conservation of freshwater lakes and rivers; defining and preserving marine hotspots and coral reefs; completing the mapping of the world's species; finding ways to make conservation more profitable than poaching; initiating restoration projects to increase the share of the Earth allotted to nature (currently about 10 percent; Wilson suggests 50 percent); increasing the capacity of zoos and botanical gardens to protect, breed, clone, and otherwise preserve endangered species; and supporting human population planning.

Wilson estimates that such global conservation measures would cost around $30 billion (in 2001 dollars), a mere one-thousandth of the global domestic product or one-hundredth of the annual U.S. military budget. Even if Wilson's price tag is adjusted for inflation, the comparisons remain roughly the same, the point being that the resources are available if the social and political will can be mustered. According to Wilson, implementation will require a sustained and coordinated effort among society's three sectors: government, the private sector, and science and technology, all of which have begun, to varying degrees, to take sustainability seriously. Most promising is the sharp rise in the popularity and influence of nongovernmental organizations (NGOs) such as the World Wildlife Fund, the Nature Conservancy, the National Wildlife Federation, the Sierra Club, and the National Audubon Society, all of which have seen their memberships and budgets soar in recent years. Still, as of 2000, the combined global investments of governments and NGOs in environmental initiatives amounted to only $6 billion, or one-fifth of Wilson's goal. One can only hope that this number will grow as awareness grows, that a change in consciousness will bring about a change in priorities.

Meanwhile, the growth experienced by national and international NGOs is being accompanied by a proliferation of smaller grassroots organizations dedicated to ecological sustainability and social justice. In his book *Blessed Unrest,* eco-activist Paul Hawken describes the emergence and evolution of such groups as part of "the world's largest movement"—commonly called environmentalism and less commonly understood as the transition of humanity into an era of global awareness. Hawken himself likens the growing movement to a global immune response system and considers the number and diversity of its organizations (many catalogued at www.wiserearth.org) as advantageous to its survival and growth. Hawken writes:

> This is a movement away from the maximization of anything that is not conducive to life. It will continue to take myriad forms. It will

not rest . . . no words can encompass it, because the movement is the breathing, sentient, testament of the living world. The movement is an outgrowth of apostasies and it is now self-generating. The first cells that assembled and metabolized under the most difficult of circumstances deep in the ocean nearly 40 million centuries ago are in our bodies now, and we are, in Mary Oliver's words, determined, as they were then, to save the only life they can.[22]

Fortunately, the world's largest movement is occurring not only from the ground up but from the skyscraper down, with a growing number of corporations investing in green technology and renewable energy while attempting to reduce their own (often massive) environmental footprints, sometimes even setting internal standards and goals beyond those required by law. While one could argue that corporations are typically if not necessarily less interested in going green than in making green (hence the term "greenwashing"), I believe that these changes, however small and incremental, should be encouraged and celebrated. Given the unlikelihood of stopping the roaring machine of economic progress, perhaps it can at least be steered gradually in the direction of ecological responsibility.

The course of the juggernaut is largely determined by the consumer, whose purchasing power translates into an imperative to make wise and skillful choices about which companies to buy from and what products. For better or worse, the market is now awash with eco-friendly offerings of every sort, while putting your nest-egg where your values are has been made easier by the creation of socially responsible investing schemes that allow for the screening out of companies with poor environmental or labor records, thus enabling the investor to "do well while doing good." Ideally, wiser consumption patterns will also result in lower consumption rates.

As national governments drag their feet in the proverbial mud, many local governments are taking the initiative by joining the "green cities movement," which is comprised of practices such as lowering vehicle emissions, running public transportation on alternative fuels, conserving and creating green spaces, and requiring new buildings to be green-certified. Many cities have set goals of operating within regional carrying capacities by using only renewable resources, recycling 100 percent of all non-renewables, and not producing more waste than can be absorbed locally. At the time of this writing, the greenest cities in the world are Copenhagen, Portland (Oregon), Montreal, London, Reykjavik (capital of Iceland), Curitba (Brazil), Malmo (Sweden), Vienna, Vancouver, and Tokyo.[23]

Smaller in scale but no less inspiring is the "transition town" movement, which began in Kinsale, Ireland, and Totnes, England, and has since grown to include almost four hundred communities worldwide. Inspired by the twin challenges of dwindling oil and climate change, the movement aims to establish local resiliency and energy independence within villages and smaller cities by encouraging community gardening, building strong social networks, minimizing waste, and sometimes using local currency. While each transition town may employ different methods or adopt its own unique "energy descent plan," the movement is united not by a fear of scarcity but a belief that life in the post-oil world will in fact be richer and more fulfilling, with more time available for learning, leisure, and the arts.

In both urban and rural areas, the Earth's carrying capacity and productivity are being preserved and maximized by more sustainable agricultural methods, particularly organic gardening and permaculture. The latter term, a portmanteau of "permanent agriculture" or "permanent culture," was coined in the 1970s by Australians Bill Mollison and David Holmgren to describe a practical and eco-

Rooftop gardens like this one in Toronto, Canada, are not only beautiful but functional, providing food as well as insulation.

friendly way of growing food, as well as engaging holistically with the natural world. Permaculture design principles are based on those of Nature herself, utilizing mutually supportive relationships among flora, fauna, and humans and emphasizing sustainability and self-sufficiency. The antithesis of permaculture is large-scale monoculture, the practice of planting huge crops of a single species, which must be protected from comprehensive infestation and disease by synthetic chemicals, which must in turn be imported from off-site and which degrade the quality of both the food and the environment. In the case of dent corn, for example, the yield is not consumed locally but often transported long distances, usually to be fed to animals that also consume vast amounts of water and produce their own greenhouse gases.

Most cities now contain at least one community garden, many of them employing organic methods and permaculture principles. These green and growing spaces yield not only healthy produce but happier humans, often serving as local gathering spots for adults and hands-on learning environments for children, many of whom have never interacted with Nature or yet considered the source of their food. For many individuals and communities, gardening can be rewarding and empowering, fostering what has been called "biophilia"—love of life.

Declarations of Interdependence

Considering the continued resistance to international environmental agreements like the Kyoto protocol—particularly by powerful and polluting nations—it seems increasingly unlikely that the drastic, large-scale changes required to mitigate climate change and other ecological crises will come from the top down. Still, recent political developments provide further proof that a meaningful, albeit incremental, shift in priorities is indeed taking place in the collective human psyche.

In 2008, Ecuador became the first country on Earth to grant rights to Nature, known in that part of the world as Pachamama. In support of indigenous beliefs, the Constitution declares that nature "has the right to exist, persist, maintain, and regenerate its vital cycles" and requires the state to "apply precaution and restriction measures in all the activities that can lead to the extinction of species, the destruction of the ecosystems, or the permanent alteration of the natural cycles." The Constitution prohibits the cultivation of transgenic seeds and the patenting of "collective knowledge" associated with biodiversity.[24] Whether or not other countries will follow Ecuador's example remains to be seen, as does the effectiveness of its new laws. In late 2010, a lawsuit was filed against British Petroleum (BP) in Ecuador for damages related to the massive oil spill that occurred earlier that year in the Gulf of Mexico (according to the plaintiffs, the rights of Nature extend across the globe).

Less recent but no less monumental is the Earth Charter, an international declaration designed to create a more just, sustainable, and peaceful global society. Although initially conceived of in 1987, the document was officially launched in 2000, after a six-year worldwide consultation process organized by Mikhail Gorbachev and Maurice Strong. The charter is arranged in four sections or "pillars"—Respect and Care for the Community of Life; Ecological Integrity; Social and Economic Justice; and Democracy, Nonviolence, and Peace—each of which contains four principles (making sixteen main principles, many of which put forth a number of supporting principles). One of the charter's most powerful insights is the recognition that environmental health, sustainable development, human rights, and global peace are interdependent and indivisible; none of these areas can continue to ignore any other area if genuine progress is to be made.

Worldwide, the Earth Charter has been endorsed by more than two hundred and fifty universities, several global organizations like UNESCO and the International Union for the Conservation of Nature, various international religious organizations, a growing number of youth groups, and a smattering of cities, particularly in the U.S. and UK. Ideally, support will continue for this ground-breaking document, which begins with a poignant preamble:

> We stand at a critical moment in Earth's history, a time when humanity must choose its future. As the world becomes increasingly interdependent and fragile, the future at once holds great peril and great promise. To move forward we must recognize that in the midst of a magnificent diversity of cultures and life forms we are one human family and one Earth community with a common destiny . . . it is imperative that we, the peoples of Earth, declare our responsibility to one another, to the greater community of life, and to future generations.[25]

New Monetary Models

For dozens of years, national well-being has been measured solely in economic terms, most often using Gross Domestic Product as a reflection of a country's living standards. Unfortunately, GDP considers only the market value of all the goods and services exchanged within a given area and time frame; it disregards that which cannot be assigned a price tag (such as volunteer work, bartering, and open-source products) and likewise pays no attention to *what* is being produced (war, auto accidents, and disease contribute to GDP despite their obvious undesirability). Furthermore, GDP fails to account for the inequity between rich and poor (clearly connected to national mood) and, perhaps most significantly, ignores the results or "externalities" of industry such as pollution and other forms of ecological degradation. As proof that GDP is an unreliable indicator of human well-being, consider that happiness has remained more or less constant in the last fifty years, despite the fact that global GDP has risen steadily, while income has doubled in places like the U.S., UK, and Japan.[26]

Because of its serious limitations, GDP is now being modified or replaced altogether by other metrics that assess economic progress in a more accurate and holistic way. The GPI or "genuine progress indicator," for example, makes adjustments to GDP for its oversights and externalities while distinguishing between beneficial growth and harmful effects. In an attempt to add psychological factors into the equation, the government of Bhutan, a Buddhist country in Southeast Asia, has developed a "Gross National Happiness" index that has been used in other countries. More recently, the New Economics Foundation has been advancing a "Happy Planet Index" that weighs a country's ecological footprint against its subjective satisfaction.

Even more encouraging is the emergence of new economic models that eschew unlimited growth as a guiding principle. Although it should have been apparent centuries ago that the "more is better" mindset is incompatible with the finite resources of a spherical planet, the problems of unrestrained profit-making were brought to public attention only in the last few decades, largely through landmark books like *Silent Spring* (1962), *Limits to Growth* (1972), *Small Is Beautiful* (1973), and *Steady-State Economics* (1977). As awareness continues to increase, so does the field of ecological economics, which emphasizes sustainability and rightly considers the economy as a subsystem of the environment. On the grassroots level, recent years have seen the proliferation of alternative methods of exchange such as local currency programs, bartering and sharing systems, consumer cooperatives, open-source networks, gift economies, and the "freecycling" of unwanted items.

A Spiritual Renaissance

In every culture and every era, there have existed small numbers of revolutionary thinkers, avant-garde artists, iconoclastic writers, bohemian poets, and spiritual seekers. There also seem to be recurring periods (corresponding with Uranus-Neptune alignments, for those who know astrology) during which larger portions of the population undergo transformative spiritual experiences. One such "great awakening" began in the late 1960s, when there occurred an unprecedented explosion of interest among Westerners in alternative spiritual philosophies and practices, particularly those of the East. Meditation, yoga, Zen, Tantra, and other mystically oriented systems became popular among the counterculture beatniks and hippies and have been slowly and surely trickling into the mainstream ever since.

The surge in spirituality that began in the '60s intensified during the '80s and '90s, manifesting in part in the latest phase of the New Age movement, with its wide embrace of holistic health, consciousness studies, parapsychology, motivational psychology, indigenous spirituality and shamanism, goddess worship, and Western esotericism including astrology, numerology, Tarot, Theosophy, and Gnosticism. Something of a second wave of awakening, this movement was fueled by countless books as well as the concurrent growth of the Internet, which allowed for quick and easy access to information about a staggering variety of religious and spiritual traditions from throughout the world. For the first time in history, millions of people were suddenly able to tap into a rich reservoir of human knowledge and wisdom, resulting in a widespread spiritual eclecticism that was both celebrated for its breadth and criticized for its relative lack of depth. Doubtless, however, the Internet and the movement it helped spawn has served as a means of spiritual inspiration, growth, and emancipation for many earnest seekers.

More recently, the esotericism and eclecticism of previous decades has been gaining wider appeal in the popular psyche, thanks in part to certain spiritually oriented mega-stars like Madonna and Oprah Winfrey, the latter of whom hosts a "Soul Series" on XM radio, among her many other public appearances and activities. Oprah's book club has showcased several spiritually themed books such as Eckhart Tolle's *A New Earth*, while an episode of her television show was devoted to *The Secret*, a book that speaks of a universal "law of attraction" governing human achievement and happiness. While *The Secret* could easily be criticized for focusing on monetary and material gain and for being overly simplistic in regard to *karma*, it has served to introduce millions of people to the powers of intention and attention, and to the importance of taking responsibility for one's own happiness. Moreover, the widespread appeal of these kinds of books and programs demonstrates just how many people are hungry for meaning and thirsty for an authentic and engaged spirituality.

Practices like yoga and meditation, once considered far-out and fringe, are entering the corporate environment as more and more CEOs recognize the importance of establishing a low-stress workplace and maintaining the health and happiness of their employees. True, in many cases the focus is less on spiritual growth than economic well-being and practical output, but the fact remains that spiritual practice is being integrated into the lives of more and more working-class folks. At the same time, spirituality is entering the academic environment, as seen in the growing number of colleges offering degrees in alternative medicine, transpersonal psychology, integral studies, deep ecology, and other emerging fields that fuse the sacred and the secular. Indeed this kind of integration can be seen not only in new degree programs but entire institutions of higher learning such as the Naropa Institute, Ken Wilber's Integral Institute, the Institute of Transpersonal Psychology, and the California Institute of Integral Studies.

North Meets South

In many parts of South and Central America the elders speak of a time of great tribulation when many species will disappear from the Earth. During this dark period, the reigning eagle of the North, which has been flying alone for centuries, will be joined by the condor of the South. The common interpretation of this prophecy is that the eagle represents the scientific knowledge and technology of the developed countries (perhaps the U.S. in particular, the national symbol of which is the eagle), while the condor represents the wisdom of the indigenous traditions: their sacred rituals, powerful myths, and healing arts. The confluence of these two systems can be thought of abstractly as an integration of left-brain rationality with right-brain creativity, an important characteristic of integral thinking.

A similar synthesis is found in the image of Quetzalcoatl, the winged serpent of ancient Mesoamerican culture. Author Daniel Pinchbeck, whose experiences of this powerful archetype are presented in his book *2012: The Return of Quetzalcoatl,* writes that the feathered serpent "symbolizes the meeting of bird and snake, or Heaven and Earth ... the integration of rational, empirical thought with shamanic, intuitive, and esoteric knowledge."[27] We will return to a brief discussion of 2012 prophecies in the next chapter.

The integration suggested by the figure of Quetzalcoatl, as well as by the eagle and condor prophecy, can be seen in the burgeoning interest of Americans and Europeans in the beliefs and practices of the indigenous cultures of Mesoamerica and South America. Along with a sharp rise in ecotourism in places like the Guatemalan highlands and the rainforest of the upper Amazon, the last decades have seen the formation of a movement known as "neo-shamanism" in which Americans and Europeans have been training and working with traditional shamans in order to bring indigenous wisdom and healing practices to the North. Thus the exchange between North and South is happening in both directions.

Contemporary interest in shamanism was certainly fueled by Carlos Castaneda's *The Teachings of Don Juan: A Yaqui Way of Knowledge,* the first in a series of books published in the late '60s describing the author's supposed shamanic training (much of which is now considered fictitious). The initial spark, however, was probably the 1951 publication (and 1964 reprinting by Princeton University Press) of Mircea Eliade's *Shamanism: Archaic Techniques of Ecstasy,* in which an attempt is made to determine the underlying themes of shamanism that extend across cultures and time periods. Primary among these is the belief that the world is pervaded by both good and evil spirits with which the shaman is able to communicate, usually for healing purposes and usually by entering a non-ordinary state of consciousness. No doubt influenced by Eliade and also trained in South America, anthropologist Michael Harner has since 1978 been teaching what he calls "core shamanism," a distillation of various traditions into a few effective, legal, ecumenical techniques for reaching ecstatic states.

The word "ecstasy," although used commonly to describe joy or euphoria, is derived from the Greek *ex-stasis*, meaning "to stand or be outside of one's self, to be removed," indicating that such states often involve an element of ego loss or dissolution. Given its emphasis on ecstatic states produced in part by hypnotic electronic music, the rave scene that flourished during the '90s could also be considered neo-shamanic in character, as could the increasingly popular practice of "ecstatic dance," which uses music of various rhythms to guide the participant through a deep, embodied, meditative journey. Prolonged dancing, ecstatic states, and neo-shamanic/tribal culture are also important aspects of the Burning Man festival, an annual week-long art and counterculture event that takes place in a temporary city in the Nevada desert and operates on the basis of a gift economy.

Like any such movement, neo-shamanism undoubtedly attracts its share of quacks and charlatans (sometimes called "plastic shamans"), and it risks becoming another form of cultural appropriation. Still, like the many other examples of spiritual revolution outlined above, it does hold a certain promise of psycho-spiritual transformation and healing, of reconnection to the Earth, and of a reawakening of the modern psyche to the sacred dimension of existence.

Bit by bit, the integral structure of consciousness is being built as East meets West, North meets South, matter meets mind, science meets religion, tradition meets technology, economy meets ecology, and humanity meets its destiny as compassionate caretaker of the Earth and wide-eyed child of the Cosmos. The pressing question is whether the creation of this new structure will happen faster than the destruction of the vital structures upon which we depend; whether the Great Turning will prevail over the Great Unraveling; whether we will be able to push through the narrow straits of the hourglass before the last of the sand trickles out.

Pessimists are encouraged to recall how far we have come in a short period. Within the last century alone—a blink of an eye in terms of human evolution—we have seen many positive changes: the increasing establishment of democracy and universal suffrage, the formation of the United Nations, the ratification of the Universal Declaration of Human Rights and other international treaties, the civil rights movement, the women's movement, the LGBTQ movement, the environmental movement, greater sensitivity towards the disenfranchised and developmentally challenged, and other awakenings mentioned in the previous section. In just the last couple of decades, we have witnessed the emergence of the Internet, a kind of collective psyche that may prove instrumental in bringing about the kind of large-scale psychic revolution that seems required to avert ecological and societal collapse.

Many people like Christopher Bache who are deeply concerned with the evolution of consciousness have observed that potent ideas tend to spread very rapidly, often reaching a point of critical mass in the popular psyche within a relatively short time. Just as the realization of one or two students in a classroom may trigger an understanding among the entire group, powerful ideas seem to crop up simultaneously yet independently at different places on the globe, as evidenced by Axial Age developments and by many subsequent examples of concurrent scientific discoveries and inventions. It is as if the greater mind is a vast network of branches upon which grow fruits that eventually ripen and fall to Earth.

If the noosphere is a giant tree of life, then we are certainly responsible for its fertilization. Ultimately, the question of whether humanity will survive this trying period lies with how we choose to engage with the world. As long as we continue to regard the Earth as an existential trap, a moral battleground, or simply a collection of resources waiting to be exploited, we will almost certainly continue our downward spiral. But if, as Joanna Macy suggests, the world is regarded as a lover or an extension of the self—something sacred and precious—and if we can transform this collective love for the world from grief surrounding its loss into action for its longevity, then hope exists that we may overcome the considerable challenges we face.

Of course, a change in the collective psyche depends in turn upon the transformation of each of us as individuals. It is not enough to hope and pray for a better world; we must each take responsibility to think and act in accordance with our highest principles. While our involvement in the Great Turning may take many forms, the focus of this book and of the next chapter lies with a psycho-spiritual trans-formation brought about through individual action, which naturally feeds one's community and ultimately serves the greater collective. The path ahead may seem long, steep, and treacherous, but as the Taoist sage Lao Tzu once said: The journey of a thousand miles begins with a single step.

FOUR
THE ROAD TO RECOVERY

A human being is a part of the whole, called by us "Universe," a part limited in time and space. He experiences himself, his thoughts and feelings as something separate from the rest—a kind of optical delusion of his consciousness. The striving to free oneself from this delusion is the one issue of true religion. Not to nourish it but to try to overcome it is the way to reach the attainable measure of peace of mind.

—Albert Einstein[1]

A WAY FORWARD

After disclosing the truth of suffering, the truth of the cause of suffering, and the truth of the end of suffering, the Buddha, a being of both compassion and action, laid out a plan—a method of getting from here to there, from suffering to liberation. The term he used was *margha*, usually translated as "path" but also meaning "vehicle," an apparent conundrum that can be resolved by using the English words "way" or "means." This is *how*, the Buddha told his followers, to move beyond constriction and dis-ease to spaciousness and freedom.

199

The Buddha's plan was both concrete and specific, containing eight interrelated components. The Noble Eight-fold Path is not to be thought of as a series of steps but perhaps more like a set of interlocking puzzle pieces that when gradually assembled begin to present a clearer and clearer picture of reality. A more traditional symbol is that of the eight-spoked wheel (see page 208), with each spoke being crucial to movement along the path. In turn, each of the eight spokes or components relates to one of three areas of development: wisdom, ethical conduct, and mental development, all of which are understood as essential for spiritual progress.

Those readers who have heard of the Eight-fold Path are probably aware that each component is usually presented in terms of "right," as in "right speech" or "right livelihood." Here the word has the connotation of wise, skillful, or beneficial. It is not to be thought of in strict moralistic terms, as though certain ways of thinking and acting are right while others are wrong in an absolute sense. As mentioned earlier, "right" can be understood as the opposite of "left," as when describing direction and orientation. While moving through life, one must make choices about which way to go, the idea being that certain paths lead to increased dis-ease while others lead to greater ease and well-being. Thus right speech, for example, is understood as the kind which leads to decreased suffering for one's self and others, and it is left to the individual to look within for the wisdom to speak skillfully.

Practicing right speech is different from obeying stern rules against bearing false witness or taking the Lord's name in vain. Such commandments assume an absolute, God-given morality, whereas the Buddhist traditions regard morality as being somewhat flexible. Not that Buddhism subscribes to a moral relativism in which anything goes; rather it views morality as being situationally determined. To cite an oft-used example: Most people would consider it wrong for someone to stab someone else, unless of course the knife-wielder is a surgeon. The vital difference lies with intention, which in the case of an assailant is malevolent and in the case of a doctor is benevolent. As we shall see, the Buddha considered intention important enough to warrant its own mention in the Eight-fold Path.

As noted, however, the Buddhist "roadmap to recovery" covers not only morality but also wisdom and mental development, and in this way it differs from a set of strict dictums. Rather than simply forbidding particular behaviors, the Eight-fold Path encourages and inspires certain beneficial actions, practices, thoughts, and attitudes. The difference lies not with its reliance on positive injunctions rather than negative ones, but with its focus on the holistic development of body, mind, and heart. The Eight-fold Path can be thought of as a kind of "user's guide" for the human vehicle as it travels along the path to greater freedom and peace of mind.

THE BUDDHA'S NOBLE EIGHT-FOLD PATH

The Eight-fold Path is best understood as a set of practices. Just as nobody expects an amateur pianist to play Rachmaninoff flawlessly, it is not expected that the Buddhist practitioner will always think and act in perfect harmony with the *dharma*. In fact, each mistake offers another chance to extend forgiveness to one's self, a highly beneficial practice in its own right.

Right View

Considered an aspect of wisdom practice, right view pertains to one's understanding of the *dharma*, defined as the teachings of the Buddha as presented in the Four Noble Truths and elsewhere.

(continued)

A person with "right view" has a firm grasp of the suffering caused by clinging to that which is impermanent and empty of essence, and she possesses the increasing ability to see things as they really are.

Right Intention

Although related to volition rather than cognition, intention is also considered an aspect of wisdom practice, the idea being that such energy stems from the heart-mind or *citta.* Here the focus is on the development of *bodhicitta,* the altruistic intention to alleviate the suffering of all beings. In the Buddhist traditions, the path to *nirvana* is paved with right intention.

Right Speech

The Buddha understood quite clearly the power of words to help and to harm, and for this reason he attributed particular importance to this part of the path. An aspect of ethical conduct, right speech involves refraining from lying, gossip, and malicious speech while practicing kind and gentle communication. Given the human tendency to engage in meaningless small talk, a good deal of emphasis is placed on the value of silence: If you know of something untrue and hurtful, don't speak; if you know of something true and hurtful, don't speak; if you know of something untrue and helpful, don't speak; if you know of something true and helpful, wait for the right opportunity to speak with clarity and benevolence.

Right Action

This second aspect of ethical conduct relates to behavior, which of course has a strong influence on one's state of mind. First, do no harm, either to one's self or others. Second, take only that which is freely given, which rules out stealing as well as "lesser" offenses such as fudging the books or borrowing a friend's belongings without asking. Third, avoid engaging in sexual behavior that could be harmful to your own or someone else's health or peace of mind. Stated simply and affirmatively: Treat yourself and others with loving-kindness, honesty, and respect.

Right Livelihood

Given that we all must make a living, the injunction is to do so ethically, skillfully, and peacefully, avoiding occupations that might be harmful to others. The Buddha spoke of four particularly unwholesome jobs: selling weapons, dealing in living beings (which includes slavery, prostitution, and raising animals for slaughter), slaughtering animals, and selling substances that harm the body and cloud the mind. While it may be more difficult than ever to make a life-sustaining living, such is the challenge presented by right livelihood.

Right Effort

This and the remaining components of the Eight-fold Path relate to mental development, which is often what people think of when considering Buddhist practice. In a sense, all parts of the path rest on right effort, which is the application of mental energy (or will) to spiritual progress. It relates to self-discipline and diligence and underscores four particularly noteworthy endeavors: preventing the arising of unwholesome states (such as anger), abandoning unwholesome states that have already arisen, arousing wholesome states (like loving-kindness), and maintaining and perfecting wholesome states that have already arisen.

Right Mindfulness

Right mindfulness is grounded in clear perception, particularly of one's own physical, mental, and emotional states. A mindful person maintains an awareness of the present moment without getting swept away by daydreams, elaborate mental constructs, or stories; she observes sensations, thoughts, and emotions as they arise and

(continued)

handles them skillfully. This is, of course, much easier said than done, and for this reason the Buddha taught a form of meditation based on mindfulness of one's immediate experience, which will be discussed in greater detail later in the chapter.

Right Concentration

A final aspect of mental development is practicing sustained and focused awareness, a.k.a. concentration. In many forms of meditation, including Vipassana, the practitioner directs her attention to a specific aspect of experience such as the breath and attempts to hone this one-pointed focus of mind. Ideally, the concentration developed during formal meditation carries over into other activities so that one remains continually focused on wholesome thoughts and skillful behavior. Of course, distractions are inevitable and even important, as they provide chances to awaken to one's wanderings and to practice returning to focus with gentleness and compassion.

TRANSFORMATION AND TRANSLATION

The obvious implication of the Eight-fold Path is that some action must be taken, some effort must be expended in order to achieve enlightenment. It is not enough to adopt a certain set of beliefs, don a special garment or amulet, memorize a few prayers, or receive a magical blessing from a powerful saint. If one seeks full liberation, she must undergo a profound change in consciousness, a radical realignment of her heart-mind that leads to an entirely new outlook. Although she may read scriptures, recite mantras, or wear robes, such trappings and practices may have to be abandoned at some point along the way as her relationship with reality is fundamentally altered.

In describing this approach to spirituality, Ken Wilber uses the term "transformational," which stands in contrast to the "translational" approach of mainstream religion. The former can be conceived of as having the vertical orientation of a ladder, while the latter is concerned primarily with the horizontal plane of Earthly existence, where one prays for health, wealth, and progeny. It should be noted that all major religions contain both a translational or mainstream aspect and a transformational or esoteric aspect: Islam has Sufism, Judaism has Kabbalism, Christianity has Gnosticism and contemplative practices, and many Eastern traditions have Tantra, to cite the most well-known examples. In each of these mystically oriented branches, the aspirant foregoes the intercession of a priest, mullah, rabbi, or guru in order to commune directly with the Divine.

Likewise the Buddhist path can be described as mystical in orientation, as it requires no special intermediary through whom one attains enlightenment. Although one may sometimes rely on the wise guidance of someone who has been on the path long enough to know its twists, turns, peaks, and pitfalls, it is understood that the responsibility lies squarely with the practitioner. It is her dedication and diligence that will determine the degree of her realization, not some religious or spiritual authority. One famous saying goes: "If you meet the Buddha on the path, kill him," which is a blunt way of saying that salvation is not bound up with any external person or thing. This is a bit like the commandment "Thou shalt not have false gods before me," the difference being that such authority comes from an all-powerful, external source rather than from within.

In terms of the global ecological crisis, there are certainly those who anticipate some sort of divine or extraterrestrial intervention. Unfortunately, the book of Revelation indicates that heaven can only accommodate 144,000 souls, while seating aboard alien spacecraft is probably likewise limited. In either case, the overwhelming majority of humanity will be left to fend for itself here on Earth. Clearly, the responsibility is ours and ours alone, on both the individual and collective levels, to transform our worldview and heal our world. In the words of Barack Obama (apparently inspired by a widely circulated Hopi poem): "Change will not come if we wait for some other person, or if we wait for some other time. We are the ones we have been waiting for. We are the change that we seek."[2]

THINKING UNIVERSALLY, ACTING PERSONALLY

The change sought by the Buddhist practitioner is a change in individual consciousness. The change sought by this author (who happens to be a Buddhist practitioner) is a change in the collective consciousness, and to that end I have been trying to describe the dynamics of this monumental psychic shift and to outline the characteristics of a wiser worldview. In this chapter I will present a more substantial plan—a pathway of sorts—for the establishment and maintenance of a more integral and sustainable way of thinking about humanity's role in the world and our place in the Cosmos.

Being concerned primarily with a change in consciousness, I offer no detailed, practical plan for saving the planet. As much as I wish I had The Answer, I recognize that I hold only a tiny portion of the solution and a big responsibility to do my part. Indeed we are all being called upon to pool our unique talents and gifts in the service of life, to put our heart-minds together in order to become not individual superhumans but a collective super-humanity whose greatest liability—our numbers—is also our greatest potential strength.

Of course, like any ecologically minded person, I would advocate making practical personal changes towards sustainability: drive less and bike or walk more; practice voluntary simplicity; spend less money and more time; eat out less; grow a garden; buy local organic produce from farmers' markets or participate in community-supported agriculture; shop in locally owned stores; go solar; go vegetarian; compost and recycle; buy carbon credits; use compact fluorescent light bulbs, efficient appliances, ceiling fans, and power strips to minimize electrical waste; conserve water by taking short showers, using greywater, or building a rain-catchment system; stay politically, socially, and physically active; practice yoga and meditate; and perhaps most importantly, be grateful and joyful for the short, precious life you have been given.

Chances are, many readers are already doing the kinds of environmentally responsible and psychologically rewarding things mentioned here. Like a spiritual practice, greening one's life is an ongoing process that may never reach a dramatic grand finale, although it does offer appreciable benefits along the way. In striving to live in closer harmony with Nature, one is likely to feel more physically healthy and emotionally alive, perhaps even more spiritually fulfilled, provided that the ego does not intervene and insist on taking credit for "selflessly" saving the planet. For although each of us deserves kudos for making changes and sacrifices that might be challenging, the greater challenge, it seems, is to avoid falling into a greener-than-thou attitude. Instead, we must all humbly acknowledge that on the road to global sustainability, we all have a long way to go.

To provide some practical perspective: dividing the 2009 "gross global product" ($58–70 trillion, depending on the method of calculation[3]) by the current global population results in a figure between $7,000 and $10,000. In terms of average annual income, that's the global mean, meaning that *statistically* half the world makes less than that amount while half makes more (in actuality, roughly half the world lives on less than $2 per day). Thus for those truly interested in an equitable distribution of global wealth, the goal is about $8,000 to $9,000 for annual income. Now for the kicker: that standard of living is already unsustainably high for the Earth.

Those of us with first-world purchasing power cannot afford to rest on our laurels. We must continue to think globally and act locally, which means curbing consumption and making lifestyle changes like those mentioned above. Meanwhile, we can effectively downsize desire by changing our heart-mind. A wider, wiser worldview will enable us to think not only globally but universally, and to act not just locally but personally. What might this mean?

To think universally and act personally is to recognize ourselves as creative extensions of a creative Cosmos. We are its eyes and ears and dexterous hands, striving to bring into being something not yet seen, heard, or grasped. As unique expressions of a 14-billion-year-old evolutionary impulse towards greater depth, complexity, and beauty, each of us has a priceless opportunity to participate in the further enrichment and evolution of the universe. If this seems too daunting a challenge, we need only remember the invitation to act personally, which was expressed so well by Joseph Campbell: "Follow your bliss." For in pursuing our deepest aspirations and doing what most enlivens us, we honor the aspirations of the universe and of life itself.

IN SEARCH OF
☻ WISE RELATION ☻

In an inter-subjective universe, it makes sense to use relational language, and therefore the eight components of this path are all defined in terms of "wise relation," which can be interpreted as balanced, healthy, or beneficial to life. My intention is not to carve into stone a rigid set of dictums or beliefs, but simply to present a number of ideas designed to encourage some soul-searching on the part of the reader about "wise relation"—what it might mean and how it might feel, both personally and collectively. I myself do not pretend to have easy access to such wisdom, although I know that it lies within the core of my being.

Although based on the Eight-fold Path, this plan is not to be thought of as an alternative to, or a vain attempt to improve upon, the profound and timeless teachings of the Buddha. The similarity between these two systems lies merely in their structure, just as this book as a whole uses the elegant framework of the Four Noble Truths to address dis-ease on a global rather than a personal scale.

1.
WISE RELATION
WITH SELF

Thus far I have been using the terms "self" and "ego" as if they are interchangeable, which I realize may require an overdue explanation. In the West, those who are not philosophers or psychologists rarely speak of "the self (or Self)" as an impersonal thing; rather the word is almost always connected to a pronoun, as in "herself" or "myself." The generic "self" is more common in the East, where it has traditionally been used in a philosophical sense to signify something that underlies experience, independent of bodily sensations, thoughts, emotions, memories, etc. In Hindu traditions, the subjective version of the true self is called *atman,* usually translated as "soul," while the universal, underlying Self is called Brahman. In the end, say the Vedantic sages, *atman* and *brahman* are unified, as captured in the famous phrase *tat tvam asi,* meaning "thou art that."

The Buddha broke with the Hindu tradition by denying the existence of *atman* and asserting that the underlying reality, both subjectively and universally, is emptiness. All things, taught the Buddha, lack inherent or intrinsic existence. Nothing exists in a wholly independent way, an assertion that is meant to be verified by looking deeply into experience. Through careful and unbiased investigation, the Buddha found that all things change and are without intrinsic existence or self, and our failure to bear this in mind is the cause of our attachment. The more we believe things to be eternal and fixed, the more we suffer.

My aim here is not simply to reaffirm the Buddha's thoughts about the self and presumably wrap up this section of the book, as in "wise relation to the self is that there is no self." Clearly, the situation is much more complex than that. We all speak of "me, myself, and I" in everyday conversation, with pretty near universal agreement as to what those words mean, and most of us have some vague but persistent sense that in terms of our experiences, the whole is greater than the sum of its parts. While our language and our sense of continuity may simply indicate the depth of our delusion, they do indicate that the self does exist in a conventional sense at least, so we must regard it as "real enough" and thus find and maintain a healthy relationship with it. .

EGO AND THEN SOME

While the self may be a philosophical construct, the ego is, in theory, a psychological structure, conceived by Freud as that part of consciousness that interprets, organizes, rationalizes, remembers, decides, and mediates among the impulsive and instinctive Id, the moralistic Super-Ego, and the external world. The word "ego" is lifted from the Latin personal pronoun, "I myself," while Freud actually used the German term *Das Ich*, meaning "the I" (the Id being *Das Es*, "the It," and the Super-Ego being *Über-Ich*, the "Over-I"). Generally speaking, the ego is what we reference in everyday experience when we talk about ourselves. It is also in this conventional sense that I have been using the word "self" (as opposed to the Hindu *atman* or the Abrahamic soul), although in this section I will be taking liberties to include not just the personality but the body as well.

Since Freud's time, ego has come to mean not simply a sense of self but an inflated self-concept, as in having a "big ego" or being an "egomaniac." These terms, and the attribute they describe, seem to be most common, traditionally at least, in the West, where individuality is highly valued. But nobody in any culture likes a person who thinks and talks only about himself while ignoring or dismissing the thoughts and feelings of others. Everyone has encountered such people, and we could probably all agree that this is not wise relation with self—not only because of the way such behavior affects others, but because we all recognize intuitively that beneath the self-centered bravado lies insecurity and unhappiness.

The opposite of selfishness is selflessness, which I define not as "non-self" but as possessing a strong tendency to value the welfare of others—clearly more skillful than egocentrism or "big ego." The reasonable assumption might be that "small ego" is the ideal, yet if

we look at some of the figures most closely associated with selflessness, such as Gandhi, Martin
Luther King, Jr., and the Dalai Lama, we see
people with distinct personalities and healthy
egos. In fact, it is often the undeniable charisma
of such people that attracts attention and inspires
emulation. Each of these three examples represents a different religious tradition, indicating that
spiritual progress does not necessitate becoming
a faceless nobody with no personality; indeed it
often produces an influential somebody with a
strong sense of self and an equally strong sense
of service—a big mind and a big heart.

Many psychologists and philosophers believe
that the ego must be firmly established in order
to be transcended. It was Ken Wilber, for example, who developed the "pre-trans fallacy" which
implies that the pre-egoic consciousness of a child
is not the same as the trans-egoic consciousness
of a saint. Similarly, Wilber's idea of "transcend
and include" means that the saint is not "less
than ego" but "ego and then some." In Wilber's
words, "we do not 'get rid' of the small ego, but
rather, we inhabit it fully, live it with verve, use

**Selfless somebodies:
Mohatma Gandhi,
Tenzin Gyatso (the
14th Dalai Lama),
and the Reverend
Doctor Martin
Luther King, Jr.**

it as the necessary vehicle through which higher
truths are communicated." Referencing the Great Nest of Being, he
continues: "Soul and Spirit include body, emotions, and mind; they
do not erase them."[4]

Almost all spiritual traditions consider the ego as the central
obstacle to spiritual progress and universal love. But the suggestion

made here and elsewhere is that the ego or the "I" should not be regarded as an enemy that needs to be eliminated but as an important yet limited part of one's being. As Jung writes: "The greatest limitation of man is the 'self'; it is manifested in the experience: 'I am *only* that!'"[5] The problem is not with *having* an ego but *being* one, for if we identify strongly and exclusively with the self we become selfish, insecure, impatient, and unkind. To me, our personalities can be likened to clothing that we can learn to take off and put on at will—and isn't a costume always more enjoyable for everyone than a uniform?

THE BODY

When most of us think about ourselves, we usually consider not just our psychological ego but also our physical body, as captured by Alan Watts' term "skin-encapsulated ego." The body seems to occupy a unique and ambiguous place in our mind; it is both self and other while not being completely either—a mysterious, in-between thing. In a sense (in five senses, actually) our body serves as a link between the inner and outer worlds—between psyche and matter—while itself partaking of both.

Most of us would say "I *have* a body" rather than "I *am* a body," yet our relationship to this form that we seem to possess is clearly an ambivalent one. On one extreme are those who overvalue or even worship the body, always preening, posing, and obsessing about appearance, while on the other extreme are those who undervalue or reject the body and allow it to fall into ill health. The rest of us tend to vacillate between these poles, enduring a love-hate relationship with the body that manifests in periodic "health kicks" alternating with stints of overindulgence and neglect. A variation on this theme can be seen in the widespread practice of trying a variety of fad diets, most of which end with a pint of chocolate ice cream.

This ambivalence towards the body can be understood philosophically as a reflection of humanity's ambivalence towards the physical world. Generally speaking, the world's most popular religions have tended to emphasize the spiritual realm and de-emphasize the material realm and the body by extension, as well as sexuality by further extension. As discussed, the Western worldview has been greatly influenced by Judaism and Christianity and their general disregard of the earthly, while the situation is hardly much better among Eastern traditions, Buddhism included. Indeed certain Buddhist scriptures, in order to discourage attachment to the body, describe it as nothing more than a putrid sack of blood, pus, mucus, and other bodily fluids.

Despite such unflattering descriptions, I believe that Buddhism approaches a "wise relation" to the body. After all, the Buddha himself rejected the body-denying practices and ascetic attitudes of his Hindu teachers in favor of a Middle Way that balances the material and spiritual realms. As with the ego, the problem is not with the body itself but with attitudes of clinging and aversion, caused by an essential unwillingness to admit that nothing is unchanging or fixed. In the case of the body, impermanence becomes all too obvious as we age and begin to experience wrinkled skin, gray hair, stiff joints, failing faculties, and other inevitable forms of physical deterioration. Like all things, the body is subject to change and eventual passing away, and a full appreciation of this reality encourages nonattachment—an attitude that is neither a clinging to the body nor an aversion, rather a wise view that fosters balance and equanimity.

The path of Tantra, which has both Indian and Tibetan branches, regards the body as essential for spiritual transformation and uses certain yogic and meditative practices to direct the energy of the

body towards spiritual growth. These
practices often capitalize on the power
of an instinctual, libidinal energy called
kundalini, channeling it upward through
the spine and the *chakras* or energy centers of the body. In the East, sexual yoga
is respected as an advanced form of spiritual practice that requires an exceptional
degree of focus and non-attachment,
while in the West, this kind of practice is
usually viewed with either deep mistrust or shallow fascination. This
dualistic reaction is representative of Western attitudes towards sexuality in general; it is both condemned and celebrated in the extreme.
Such mania is a far cry from the balance and equanimity being advocated here.

The seven chakras.

Readers may recall the Great Chain of Being and its hierarchy
of matter, body, mind, soul, and spirit. In this scheme, the self would
be located by most of us in the lower two regions of body and mind,
while the individual soul and universal spirit remain the subject of
speculation and controversy. Rather than try to definitively settle such
disputes, I wish simply to point out that the body and the mind can be
both transcended and included. As one makes spiritual progress, the
body, like the ego, naturally remains intact and effective, ideally even
more so. It is not rejected but respected as a vehicle for more subtle
energies, a temple that deserves to be treated with care and kindness,
given proper exercise and ample rest, nutritious food, and a moderate
amount of sensual pleasure. Of particular value in this regard are
the practices of yoga and meditation, which balance and strengthen
mind and body, as well as the transformative power of dance, which,
like sex, has the potential to integrate all aspects of one's being.

215

Alas, eventually death overtakes the body, at which point it must finally be abandoned as another reality is encountered. For the Bodhisattva, however, this life is simply followed by another incarnation into bodily form, which again emphasizes the sacredness of this mortal coil and also points to what might be called "ideal relation" with self. To transcend the personal is not to take flight from the world of suffering but to face it with a spacious mind and embrace it with a boundless heart. Such *bodhicitta* may seem somewhat lofty if not unattainable, yet a right relation to these ideals can serve to awaken and inspire us along the path.

Meanwhile, each of us can practice compassion for the self. This may seem a strange idea in the West, where people have long understood narcissism but have only recently begun to practice self-love, perhaps as a way to counteract the prevalence of guilt and low self-esteem. As the story goes, when the current Dalai Lama was first introduced to the term "self-hatred," he had a difficult time understanding what it meant, perhaps because he had grown up in a culture that both de-emphasizes and extends compassion to the self. Fortunately for all of us, there exists a particular form of meditation geared towards the generation of loving-kindness for self (as well as other beings), which will be presented in the following section on "Wise Relation with Others." Loving-kindness practice can be considered a counterpart to the wisdom practice that follows.

MINDFULNESS MEDITATION

To aid in the cultivation of peace, equanimity, and non-attachment, the Buddha prescribed a form of meditation called Vipassana, also called insight or mindfulness meditation. Presented in the *Satipatthana Sutta,* this technique is based upon the "four foundations" of mindfulness that are meant to cover all types of experience. Although usually presented in the order that follows, the four foundations are not linear steps but categories into which a given experience may fall. An important point is that one is not looking for any particular experience or striving for a particular state, as such an attitude is counterproductive to developing non-attachment. Rather, the instruction is to devote "bare attention" to whatever is happening, gently noting any expectations or judgments that do arise.

To begin, find a comfortable and quiet space and assume a comfortable posture that allows your back to be straight but not rigid. If seated, it is best to avoid leaning against the back of the chair; keep the feet flat on the ground and the hands resting on the knees or in the lap. If you are seated on the ground, your legs can be folded in half-lotus or "Indian style," with the butt and hips elevated above the knees with the help of a cushion. Though it might feel slightly odd or uncomfortable at first, keeping your back straight will enable you to sit longer and to breathe more freely. Gently closing the eyes eliminates visual distraction.

Like some other forms of meditation, Vipassana uses the breath as an object of concentration. This phase of the practice starts by bringing attention to the breath, noticing whether it is fast or slow, deep or shallow, without trying to change or control it. Notice too where in the body that you feel the breath most strongly and center your focus there, a common suggestion being the area just below the nostrils where you will likely feel warm air flowing out and cool

(continued)

air flowing in. Try to remain connected to these sensations for as many cycles of the breath as possible, noticing when your attention strays, as it will naturally do. Each time this happens, rather than chide yourself, practice returning to the breath with gentleness, self-love, and gratitude that you have woken up to your distraction.

After just a few minutes of one-pointed concentration, distractions will begin to diminish in frequency and intensity. Thoughts will begin to settle down, the breath will usually slow, and the mind will become increasingly calm and spacious. As concentration continues to deepen, the body will begin to relax, giving rise to a sense of peace and well-being. While this state, which may take anywhere from fifteen minutes to an hour or more to establish, is highly beneficial in itself, it is considered to be the starting point of mindfulness meditation. At this point in this practice, one-pointed concentration is abandoned in favor of a more open field of awareness that can accommodate all experience, as categorized by the four foundations.

The first of these is awareness of the body, i.e., bodily sensations. A common technique is that of slowly scanning the body from the top of the head to the tips of the toes, noticing the sensations present at each point, perhaps making a gentle note with words like pressure, warmth, cold, tickling, tingling, pulsing, etc. In this context at least, these are not "your sensations" but are simply expressions of physiological processes that are naturally arising and passing away, as they always do. Experiences of pain are particularly instructive, as they are often accompanied by strong expressions of ownership and perhaps thoughts about the pain's cause, concerns about its long-term effects, fears about the hospital bills, etc. Notice when such mental activity arises and return to the actual sensation, which may be nothing more than heat or pressure that will eventually change or cease. (As far as I know, meditation has never resulted in injury.)

The second foundation is awareness of feeling tone, used not in the usual sense of "feeling" but as a reaction to an experience, namely pleasant, unpleasant, or indeterminate. This concept is simple yet crucial, for it is on the basis of "feeling tone" that we cultivate desire and aversion and separate the world into good and bad. This strengthens the ego and its attachments and also closes the heart, since *what* we like and dislike often affects *who* we like and dislike. To catch this persistent habit of the mind in action can be extremely enlightening.

Third is an awareness of thoughts and feelings. The Buddha used the term *citta,* which applies to both the mind and the heart, and the activities thereof. In the context of mindfulness meditation, the connection between thoughts and feelings can be observed directly, as thoughts may give rise to emotions, emotions may influence thoughts, or thoughts and emotions may arise together. In our usual state of mental crowdedness, these connections go unnoticed, but they become clearer when the mind is calm and attentive. In this regard, it may again be helpful to use the technique of noting particular kinds of mental and emotional activity such as planning, worrying, sadness, anger, or joy, while labeling thoughts "about the future" or "about the past" can also help bring attention back to the present. One of the more common mental activities is the telling of stories in which the ego always plays the starring role, whether as the good guy who plans to save the world with his newfound spiritual powers or the bad guy who never does anything right.

The fourth and final foundation is awareness of *dharma(s),* understood in this particular context as something like "the mechanics of the mind." In the *Satipatthana Sutta,* the Buddha lays out an array of lists, such as the Five Aggregates, the Six Senses (in Buddhism, the mind is counted as a sense organ), and the Seven Enlightenment Factors, all of which lie beyond the scope of this

(continued)

basic tutorial. Most relevant here are the Five Hindrances, each of which any practitioner will eventually experience and ideally befriend: desire, aversion, restlessness, sloth and torpor (fatigue), and doubt. Desire and aversion in this context refer to a general inclination and a disinclination, respectively, a prevailing attitude that all experiences are either rosy or rotten. The next pair relate to one's energy level, either too much in the case of restlessness or too little in the case of sloth and torpor. Finally, doubt describes a mindset in which urgent questions loom: Am I doing this right? What's the point anyway? Does the self really exist?

More often than not, such doubts and other hindrances will naturally fade away if simply observed for what they are. The normal tendency of the mind is to compound suffering by turning direct experience into personal narrative, as in "I can't stop thinking about french fries. I need to concentrate!" or "I shouldn't be tired while meditating. I shouldn't have stayed up so late last night!" instead of simply noting desire or fatigue and their physical manifestations. Of course, it is difficult to pay attention to such details when one is tired, and for this reason the Buddha prescribed certain antidotes such as taking deep breaths, pulling on the ears or hair, or standing up while meditating (taking a nap is also an option). In the case of doubt, a reasonable response is to finish the meditation and then seek an answer to any pragmatic or philosophical questions.

Alas, some doubts cannot be resolved, particularly those connected with the ego and its insistence that things should or should not be a certain way. But with practice, one begins to recognize this restless inner voice when it speaks and to form a wise relationship with it. One of the most beneficial aspects of meditation is the gradual emergence of a space or distance between what is called "the witness" and the ego, as well as an increased objectivity towards sensations, reactions, thoughts, emotions, and mind-moods. Without this distance—which is not cold detachment but wise engagement—one is always subject to being controlled by the limited agenda of the ego, the ever-changing passions of the Id, and the entrenched biases of the Super-Ego.

The spaciousness and non-attachment cultivated during meditation bring freedom, which allows us to make skillful choices in everyday life. Breaking free from mental conditioning also means being able to live more fully, in service of one's higher being. The ego becomes the vehicle rather than the driver, and one is able to navigate more easily towards one's true purpose and potential.

2.
WISE RELATION WITH OTHERS

Our relationship to self naturally affects how we relate to others, which for the time being will be confined to a consideration of other human beings. The main reason for this ultimately arbitrary division is that except for the odd hermit, everyone's primary experience in this life is with other people, and it is people with whom we generally form the deepest connections and strongest attachments. Our lives are intimately enmeshed with those of our families, friends, lovers, partners, and colleagues, and in a less immediate and obvious way, the lives of people in our respective communities, cities, countries, and in our world. Without these connections with others, none of us would be who we are; indeed we would not exist at all.

Each one of us was created through an intimate connection between our parents. They and perhaps other relatives gave us nurturing, food, clothing, shelter, protection, and ideally other forms of love and support. They taught us how to walk, talk, count, identify shapes and colors, tie our shoes, and tell the time. Other people taught us how to read, write, manipulate numbers, solve problems, and if we're fortunate, to think critically. They helped us to understand the sun, moon, and stars, clouds, oceans, rocks, continents, countries, plants, animals, atoms, cells, DNA, dinosaurs, pharoahs, kings, presidents, and so much more. Friends have given support, encouragement, companionship, consolation, praise, forgiveness, levity, and laughter. Lovers have extended affection, intimacy, and tenderness, given pleasure and joy, and have taught us—whether consciously or not—how to love more deeply and fully.

Except perhaps on special occasions, most of us take for granted the amount of love and kindness that has been extended to us during our lives. Even more rarely do we think about our important connections with people we may never meet: those who make our clothes, cars, houses, medicines, and other things upon which we depend. In an increasingly fast-paced world, fewer and fewer people say grace before meals, and among those who do, gratitude is not usually extended to the people who planted, harvested, transported, packaged, or sold the food. Of course, each of these people depend in turn upon countless others, meaning that all of us are involved in a network of interconnectivity that ultimately spans the entire globe.

As we enlarge our frame of reference, we see that we are dependent not only on countless other humans throughout the world, but also on people who have lived before us. Our very existence—and that of everyone we are connected to—depends of course on the existence and survival of our parents, grandparents, great-grandparents, and their ancestors, back to the very first members of our species. Naturally, our species evolved from species that came before, back to the earliest forms of life, which depended upon organic molecules, water, Earth, Sun, stars, and galaxies. Our interdependence extends not only through space but through time.

In Buddhist thought, this interconnectivity is called "dependent origination," a concept related to that of emptiness, positing that nothing does or could exist in a completely autonomous or isolated way. Although usually taken for granted, interdependence is relatively apparent on the human or biological levels, especially when considering our common needs for food, shelter, and intimacy. When applied to inanimate objects, dependent origination seems more ambiguous until one understands how a chair, for example, needs its individual parts, the floor upon which it rests, the space in which it exists, and a confluence of other factors in order to exist as a chair. As we have seen, the atoms, subatomic particles, and quarks that comprise the chair also owe their existence to a certain set of conditions. If this seems difficult to grasp, remember that from the Buddhist perspective, a true apprehension of interdependence constitutes enlightenment.

WHEN IT ALL COMES DOWN

As modern humans, we like to think of ourselves as independent rather than interdependent, and by and large we do enjoy greater freedom and autonomy than in the past, particularly in the West. But as soon as something goes wrong, we are on the cell phone with a loved one, and heaven forbid the network goes down. How much more disorienting and disturbing if the crash were to affect the entire infrastructure upon which we depend, preventing us from communicating electronically, withdrawing money from the bank, buying food from the store and gas from the pump, and even driving on the roads. All of these systems are of course maintained and repaired by people, and in the event of a systemic collapse, all of us would suddenly become painfully aware of our interdependence. The question is: would we panic and lapse into a chaotic, every-man-for-himself mentality, or would we be able to capitalize on our connectivity and compassion by pooling our resources, skills, and talents?

To imagine and prepare for a large-scale systemic collapse is actually an interesting exercise, particularly if done with a group of people who agree to take it seriously. Having engaged in a few such activities, each in a different setting, I have been impressed by the creativity and organizational skills of the other participants and have also been struck by the sense of fear that often arises. In every instance there has surfaced a discussion about the sharing of resources outside the camp, with certain people insisting on a closed container—perhaps even maintained through the use of violence—and others calling for an open boundary or even the establishment of search and rescue teams. This tension between self-preservation and altruism has seemed to me a reflection of the internal dynamics of the ego as applied to a larger group context, the question in either case being, in essence, when to fearfully contract and when to lovingly expand. In most cases there was an agreement among the group that generosity could be extended to outsiders only when internal needs had been covered and stabilized, which finds a parallel in the idea that the ego must be healthy and secure before it can be transcended (and included).

Some people might consider large-scale infrastructure collapse to be too much in the realm of science fiction to really worry about, while others might regard it as a real possibility that deserves serious consideration. From one perspective, systems collapse is already happening in the natural world, most apparently in the form of rapid species loss and increasingly erratic and destructive weather. Granted, the process has been happening more gradually than suddenly and therefore might best be described as a systems decline rather than a collapse. Still, the latter does remain a possibility, albeit one that I dearly hope can be avoided.

My aim in highlighting the global crisis here and elsewhere is not to instill a counterproductive fear but to encourage universal love, which I see as crucial in our collective passage through the figurative hourglass. Just as it is possible to transcend and include the ego, I believe we can rise above our attachments to state, country, culture, race, and religion—while still allowing them to be a source of personal strength and collective enrichment—in order to become true members of a global community. This appears to be our challenge, and I believe that our evolutionary journey has brought us to a level of collective self-knowledge, psychological security, and emotional maturity that will enable us to take the next step.

The Dalai Lama speaks of our situation in a similar way:

> Because of the profoundly interconnected reality of today's world, we need to relate to the challenges we face as a single human family rather than as members of specific nationalities, ethnicities, or religions. In other words, a necessary principle is a spirit of oneness of the entire human species. Some might object that this is unrealistic. But what other option do we have?[6]

UNIVERSAL AND UNCONDITIONAL LOVE

The Stoics of ancient Greece considered each human soul to be a fragment of the universal, divine force and thus regarded all of humanity as a family, as "one body as partaking in reason," with no difference "between Greek and barbarian, between male and female, and bond and free."[7] They spoke of an ideal universal city or Cosmopolis in which all citizens exist for the benefit of one another,

225

always striving towards the common good. While this may sound like a utopian fantasy, Cosmopolis is fast becoming a practical reality as more and more humans migrate to urban areas. For the first time in history, more than half of the world's population now lives in cities, a percentage that is expected to keep rising. Given that most cities are highly diverse or "cosmopolitan," this trend translates into increased interaction among people of different ethnic and religious backgrounds, which ideally translates into greater understanding, tolerance, respect, and universal love.

Even for those not living in cities, there exists more exposure than ever to disparate lifestyles and ways of being in the world, particularly through television and the Internet. Such technology is in effect shrinking the planet, making it all the more possible to wrap one's *citta* around it. Regarding our increasing interconnectivity and its effects, Daniel Pinchbeck writes:

> The new communication tools soften and diffuse the boundaries of the ego. Increasingly, with our networked lifestyles, we experience our identity as contextual, fluid, and relational, rather than a separate entity that is fixed and permanent. Academics have long argued that identity is a social construct, but this phenomenological shift makes it explicit.[8]

Pinchbeck's description of identity should sound familiar, being essentially consonant with that of Buddhism. Meanwhile, the ideal of universal love put forward by the Stoics is similar to the Buddhist ideal, with one notable difference being that although Stoics promoted a deep respect for Nature, their universal love was not usually extended to other species, perhaps because they were thought to lack a soul. Another apparent difference is that while the Stoics did practice meditation to calm the mind, as far as I know they offered no particular method for opening the heart, whereas the Buddhist tradition prescribes a number of practices for this purpose, one of which will be presented below.

To be fair, almost all religions and ethical systems emphasize brotherly love, as reflected in Christ's commandment to "love thy neighbor as thyself" and in the more secular and universal Golden Rule to "do unto others as you would have them do unto you." Almost everyone is familiar with the injunction to love others, yet how often do we actually extend love to people outside our circle of friends and family or perhaps our community? We may occasionally be inspired to give money to charity or disaster relief, but generally our circle falls short of a full embrace of the human race, and too often it explicitly excludes certain ethnic groups, certain religions, certain types of people, and specific individuals.

And if we tend to feel inadequate regard or even disregard for people outside our sphere of immediate influence, we tend to become overly attached to people on the inside. To love fully and passionately is of course a beautiful thing, although it might not seem so when a loss of love brings about acute misery—an emotional low that represents a direct inverse of the high once provided or symbolized by that person. Particularly in the case of romantic partners, our sorrow and anguish represent our attachment to what is gone, while the emotional turbulence we feel while in the midst of relationship indicates the conditional nature of our love. We might think that we truly love so-and-so, until he or she does or says something we don't like; indeed our supposed true love can turn quickly into hatred if our partner develops an affection for someone else.

In my experience, it is rare to find a relationship characterized by unconditional love. The love between parent and child certainly comes close, although even this can easily become corrupted as the

227

child grows and begins to defy the parent's wishes or deeply held expectations, the latter usually based on the projection of the parent's unfulfilled dreams onto the child. The love shared between or among siblings often approaches unconditionality, although it is certainly not uncommon to find love-hate relationships or outright rivalry. The love between friends can also approach unconditionality, yet as we all know too well, a true and lasting friendship is difficult to find. Perhaps rarest of all is true love of the romantic variety, which almost by definition is characterized by attachment and based on certain implicit or explicit conditions, particularly that of fidelity.

Of course, not all romantic relationships are founded on the traditional premise of exclusivity or monogamy. The practice of polyamory ("many loves") is based on the untraditional idea—radical or even unspeakable to some—that a person's sensual or sexual being is not meant to be confined to one person. While there are certainly those who use this model as an excuse for irresponsible promiscuity or a protection against deep intimacy, polyamory can also be approached as a spiritual practice that requires an ability to communicate honestly, a willingness to confront difficult feelings of jealousy, and a desire to work through deep-seated issues of attachment, ideally all in the service of unconditional love.

My intent is not to uphold polyamory as the wisest path but to present it as a valid one and to suggest what non-attachment might look like in the context of romantic relationships. In a monogamous situation, an act of unfaithfulness usually marks the end of the relationship and the beginning of ill will, whereas in a so-called open relationship, extracurricular intimacy offers the chance to practice what Buddhism calls "sympathetic joy," brought about by an awareness of someone else's good fortune. If the affectionate or sensual engagement in question brought joy to Jane, why shouldn't it bring joy to Jane's partner, who loves Jane and wants her to be happy and free? Of course, this degree of open-heartedness is rare to find and difficult to achieve, and most of us might find a more suitable ideal in a Middle Way that balances freedom with stability and encourages a kind of "unattached attachment" in romantic relationships.

In Buddhist philosophy, sympathetic joy or *mudita* is considered one of the Four Immeasurables or *Brahma Viharas*, the other three being compassion or *karuna* (an underlying theme of this book), loving-kindness or *metta* (which will be discussed below), and equanimity or *upekkha* (a balanced concern for the welfare of all beings, not only those close to us). Each of these wholesome emotions has its "far enemy" and its "near enemy"—an opposite and an "evil twin" for which it is often confused. In the case of sympathetic joy, the far enemy is jealousy or resentment (being displeased by someone else's good fortune) while its near enemy is exuberance or over-excitement. The far enemy of compassion is cruelty (being pleased by someone else's suffering), and its near enemy is pity. Loving-kindness finds its far enemy in ill will and its near enemy in selfish affection; and as for equanimity, its far enemy is clinging or attachment while its near enemy is simple indifference.

Through the avoidance of all the near and far enemies and the cultivation of each of the Four Immeasurables, one is said to be guaranteed happiness. As the translation might imply, these emotions are meant to be applied not selectively to a small group of loved ones at

THE FOUR IMMEASURABLES	Near Enemy	Far Enemy
Compassion (*karuna*)	Pity	Cruelty
Loving-kindness (*metta*)	Selfish affection	Hatred
Sympathetic joy (*mudita*)	Overexcitement	Jealousy
Equanimity (*upekkha*)	Indifference	Attachment

certain times only, but universally and unconditionally, to all beings at all times. A key factor in the cultivation of these "divine emotions" is mindfulness, for being aware of the arising of the near and far enemies means being aware of the limits of one's love. Bearing in mind that we're all human yet possess a divine nature, an awareness of our limitations and contractions can be considered a gift—an opportunity to extend loving-kindness to one's self and ideally to open one's heart ever wider to others. Fortunately, there exists a practice designed to accomplish both of these objectives.

LOVING-KINDNESS MEDITATION

This practice is based on a central Buddhist belief that all sentient beings share a common desire to be happy. Even though certain people seem to be searching for happiness in all the wrong ways and perhaps even causing great suffering in the process, behind their confusion and delusion lies a simple motivation that is essentially the same as anyone else's pursuit of happiness. When taken seriously, this idea inspires a deep kinship with others and a sense of compassion for our common plight, an open-heartedness that is the foundation for *metta,* which means loving-friendliness or loving-kindness.

In theory, this practice is simple, while in practice it is often difficult and always rewarding. One begins by assuming a comfortable and balanced seated posture as in mindfulness meditation, with the option of holding the hands in front of the heart, either in prayer position or against the chest, if comfortable. These postures help keep the attention focused on the heart center so that one may be aware of its contractions and expansions. Meanwhile, the mind is kept focused on the repetition of various "resolves" for the well-being and happiness of various individuals or groups.

Traditionally, the first recipient of *metta* is one's self. With your eyes closed, bring to mind an image of yourself, perhaps at a time of vulnerability or innocence. While maintaining this picture in your mind, begin quietly or silently repeating a series of resolves, such as: "May I be healthy and strong . . . May I be happy . . . May I be peaceful and at ease . . . May I be free from suffering." While these are among the most traditional resolves, any kind-hearted variation is permissible, such as "May I have good fortune . . . May I be fulfilled," etc. Most important is that the resolves not become dull and repetitive but remain alive and "juicy," and that the mind remain focused on the resolves as well as on the object of loving-kindness. As with concentration on the breath, be aware when the mind wanders and gently bring it back to focus without engaging in self-criticism, which would be especially counterproductive in this context.

While mindfully cycling through the resolves, allowing a few seconds between each, you may begin to notice a change in your emotional state. The heart may begin to feel soft or warm, and you may notice the arising of joy or sorrow, perhaps strong enough to elicit tears. This is perfectly natural, although it is also perfectly natural to feel painful contraction or perhaps nothing at all. As with mindfulness meditation, achieving a particular state is less important than simply being aware of what's happening in the moment. Whatever the emotion present, continue holding an image of yourself in your mind's eye while repeating sincere wishes for your own health, happiness, peace, and liberation.

After a few minutes, or whenever you choose, you may switch your object of concentration to someone you love dearly, whether a friend, relative, partner, or teacher. Bring to mind an image of this person and again begin repeating various resolves, such as "May you be well . . . may you be happy," noticing any emotions that arise. Also note any thoughts of conditionality or selfishness,

(continued)

like: "If you were happy, then I would be happy," bearing in mind that person's own deep desire to be happy. If extending *metta* to yourself felt awkward or challenging, then opening your heart to a loved one or a benefactor may prove much easier.

Next, direct your attention and loving-kindness to a larger group of friends or family members, maybe imagining them all sitting quietly in the same room while you express your wishes that they be well and happy, peaceful, and so forth. After repeating a series of resolves, you may enlarge your circle of loving-kindness to include your community or city, perhaps bringing to mind a much larger room or an amphitheater with you at the podium, offering your sincere wishes for everyone's comprehensive well-being. Continuing to widen your circle of *metta,* you might recite your resolves while picturing a map of your country or perhaps imagining yourself speaking on national television. Finally, your bubble of love can be expanded to include everyone on Earth.

In this practice, nobody gets left out. In the spirit of universal and unconditional love, even those for whom we typically feel aversion and hatred—enemies and evildoers—are considered worthwhile recipients of loving-kindness. Indeed these personal, political, or pathological villains would seem to be even more lacking in well-being, happiness, and peace than the average person, while from the opposite perspective they provide the invaluable service of showing us the limits of our love. My own recommendation would be to choose just such a person or group as a specific focus of *metta,* bearing in mind their desire to be happy while offering sincere wishes that they achieve such happiness. In my own experience, this practice is as difficult as it is transformative, and I can say without reservation that the injunction to "love thine enemy" is the most radical and powerful teaching I have yet to encounter.

3.
WISE RELATION WITH OTHER SPECIES

As you may have gathered, *metta* need not be confined to humans. Indeed ultimately, each of the four *Brahma Viharas*—compassion, sympathetic joy, loving-kindness, and equanimity—is meant to be extended to all sentient beings; that is, all beings with awareness. The understanding is that all conscious beings, at least those within the wheel of cyclic existence called *samsara*, are subject to suffering and therefore share the desire to be happy and free from such affliction.

Largely for ethical reasons, a primary distinction is made in the Buddhist traditions between sentient and non-sentient beings, with humans and animals belonging to the former camp and plants to the latter. In my understanding, however, the line between sentience and non-sentience is vague and somewhat mysterious in Buddhism, just as it is in the world of science. Among empiricists, consciousness itself is something of a phantom, yet a line is usually drawn between the sophisticated, self-reflective awareness of humans and the comparatively simple awareness of animals, while plants are thought to be completely oblivious.

In the previous section, I may have seemed to display a similar anthropocentrism by devoting special attention to humans, although I hope to make it clear that the separations being made here are more practical than they are philosophical or ethical. In regard to consciousness, I do not view it as something amenable to the strict categorization of self-aware and not-self-aware, or sentient and non-sentient; rather, I see it as a spectrum of increasing complexity and awareness that begins at the subatomic level and extends to human consciousness and beyond. In this conception, consciousness and

233

matter both emerge from the same source of creative energy—the quantum foam, the "implicate order" of physicist David Bohm, or the metaphysical ground of existence, a.k.a. God—and are inter-twined at every level of complexity. Thus electrons are in a sense intelligent, as are bacteria and trees; in animals, intelligence begins to manifest as awareness; and humans are not only self-aware but capable of transpersonal awareness.

Although divisions along the spectrum of consciousness may always be somewhat arbitrary, such distinctions have certainly been made by many philosophers and scientists over the years. Perhaps the most comprehensive system is that of Ken Wilber, whose model incorporates and integrates dozens of others, including that of Jean Gebser. Along with the structures already discussed—archaic, magic, mythic, mental, and integral—Wilber's model includes a number of pre-human stages such as the uroboric, locomotive, vegetative, and protoplasmic stages. Buddhism, as mentioned, divides sentience from non-sentience, while science distinguishes rational from non-rational and life from non-life.

In this section I part ways with both science and Buddhism by considering animals and plants together while also acknowledging different degrees of awareness between kangaroos and coconut palms. My primary aim is not to make definitive claims about consciousness but to encourage respect and reverence for all forms of life. In this sense I am betraying my biophilia and perhaps aligning myself with the Swiss government's Ethics Committee on Non-Human Biotechnology (ECNH), which in early 2008 issued what has been called a Bill of Rights for Plants. Actually entitled "The Dignity of Living Beings with Regard to Plants," this document examines the question of whether living beings have intrinsic worth (apart from their value to humans, which is undisputed) and concludes that "living organisms should be considered morally for their own sake because they are alive."[9]

According to the ECNH, there are a number of ways to consider the worth of living things: "theocentrism" asserts that organisms have value because of their relation to God; "ratiocentrism" maintains that organisms matter because of their ability to reason (the dominant position in the largely anthropocentric West); "pathocentrism" judges the value of living things relative to their ability to suffer or distinguish between favorable and unfavorable stimuli (the position of Buddhism); while "biocentrism" assigns intrinsic value to all living things (the position of the ECNH and my own).

Based on its biocentric stance, the ECNH document asserts that humans cannot claim "absolute ownership" over plants and that "we may not use them just as we please, even if the plant community is not in danger, or if our actions do not endanger the species, or if we are not acting arbitrarily." According to the ECNH, humans should exercise restraint towards plants, in particular refraining from damaging them for no rational reason, as in the senseless decapitation of flowers. The document in question also states that humans should be restrained in handling plants, "because we may influence or even destroy other players of the natural world, and so alter their relationships."[10]

In attempting to define the term "harm," the ECNH considered the question of sentience in plants, noting that they undergo complex interactions with their environment, are capable of complex adaptations, exhibit "plasticity of behavior," and react to stress, touch, and other stimuli. (Many fascinating examples of apparent sentience are presented in *The Secret Life of Plants* by Peter Tompkins and Christopher Bird.) Although divided on the question of plant sentience, the ECNH concluded that the possibility could not be ruled out.

But regardless of whether a plant is sentient, the committee argued, it can be harmed through an interference with its *telos*—its natural propensity for growth, development, and reproduction.

JAINS AND CARNIVORES

To seriously consider the ethical treatment of plants might seem ridiculous to some and revolutionary to others. In one sense the ECNH document could be seen as a trivialization of more gross forms of suffering, while on the other hand it might represent the culmination of a natural moral progression that began with the 1948 Universal Declaration of Human Rights, the 1959 Declaration on the Rights of the Child, the Swiss government's own 1998 document on the Rights of Animals, and the animal rights movement in general. In any case, the status of non-human organisms actually has been the subject of serious consideration for eons, most notably among Jains.

A product of the Axial Age, Jainism is an ascetic religion that has had an appreciable influence on the spiritual and cultural milieu of India. Jains share a reverence for a group of enlightened teachers called *Jinas* ("conquerors") and a deep respect for life. Based on their belief that every living being possesses a soul, Jains practice universal nonviolence and refrain from eating meat as well as any foods that take the life of a plant, such as root vegetables, potatoes, onions, and garlic. More devout Jains will eat only fruit that has fallen from trees, walk only on ground that has been swept free of insects, and breathe only through cloth so as to prevent inhaling airborne microbes. The Jain ideal of nonviolence was adopted by Gandhi, whose mother was a Jain.

Jainism has also had an effect on Buddhism (and virtue-versa), particularly in regard to nonviolence and vegetarianism, although

Buddhism does not support the existence of an eternal soul. Also, Buddhism is not as ascetic or strict and assigns more importance to the role of intention with respect to violence. The act of killing, for example, is believed to generate considerable negative *karma* if done out of malice or anger, and very little to none if done unintentionally and with regret, as would presumably be the case with stepping on insects. In terms of vegetarianism, while certain branches of Mahayana Buddhism abstain from eating meat, others such as Tibetan Buddhism do not, the reasoning being that the *karma* presumably belongs to the butcher and the person who raised the animal for slaughter.

Symbol of Jainism: a hand representing a vow of nonviolence or *ahimsa* (central text).

Here I will make a controversial move of challenging this particular religious position by pointing out the basic economic law of supply and demand. Whether or not one buys into the idea that killing an animal is immoral, literally buying into the system surely means being implicated in the act. The second controversial move is to make a heartfelt plea for a substantial reduction in meat eating, for the benefit of the entire Earth community. One does not have to be a devout Jain or a Swiss floraphile in order to appreciate the detrimental effects of livestock production on the environment. According to a 2006 United Nations report, raising animals for food:

> ... contributes on a massive scale to air and water pollution, land degradation, climate change, and loss of biodiversity, [and] emerges as one of the top two or three most significant contributors to the most serious environmental problems, at every scale from local to global.[11]

The report, which was supported by the UN Food and Agriculture Organization, the World Bank, the European Union, the International Fund for Agricultural Development, the U.S. Agency for International Development, and the international ministries of France, Germany, and the UK, states that in terms of greenhouse gases, "the livestock sector is a major player, responsible for 18 percent of greenhouse gas emissions measured in CO_2 equivalent. This is a higher share than transport."[12] A more recent study claims that the percentage of greenhouse gases attributable to livestock products is actually an astonishing 51 percent.[13]

Rather than wading through all the saddening statistics about how much pollution and deforestation are caused by livestock production, how much more fresh water is needed to produce a pound of beef versus a pound of grain, how much grain is fed to livestock instead of people, and how many people could be adequately fed if farmland were used more wisely, let's look on the positive side. According to researcher Marianne Thieme, if everyone in the U.S. refrained from eating meat for just *one day a week*, the effect would be equivalent to removing more than 19 million cars from the roads for a full year, or eliminating 46 million round-trip flights between New York and Los Angeles. If all Americans abstained from meat for *three* days per week, it would be like replacing every U.S. car with a Prius, while *seven* meatless days would be like clearing all U.S. roads entirely.[14] Now imagine if these dietary changes were not confined to a single country but extended across the globe. It would not be too much to say that many of the ecological threats we currently face would be quickly reduced if not eliminated, as would world hunger. To describe such a change as "revolutionary" would be an understatement; it would be an *evolutionary* shift.

As crucial as it is to examine the consequences of livestock production on environmental and human health,* it is also important to consider the treatment of the animals themselves, which is particularly bad on large industrial farms. Here, cows are routinely injected with growth hormones, antibiotics, and other chemicals (which are eventually ingested by humans); calves raised for veal are separated from their mothers at birth and often forced to live in total darkness in pens designed to prevent movement; chickens, territorial by nature, are often crammed into overcrowded cages, which normally leads to aggression and necessitates the cruel practice of de-beaking; and all farm animals eventually meet a violent and unceremonious death. Increased sensitivity to these issues has created greater demand for organic beef and free-range poultry and eggs, which, while slightly more healthy and humane on the whole than large-scale factory-farm products, are nevertheless unsustainable and detrimental to global health.

Most of the world's hens are raised in so-called battery cages in which movement is severely restricted. The EU has issued a ban on such cages, effective in 2012.

THE FOOD CHAIN AND THE WEB OF LIFE

Vegetarians and vegans, having heard much of the information presented above, are probably nodding in agreement, while everyone else is probably feeling a certain amount of dis-ease relative to their degree of attachment to steak and hamburgers. Surely even some

---

*Numerous studies have linked red meat consumption with high cholesterol, heart disease, and colon cancer, and carnivores are also susceptible to *E. coli*, salmonella, and mad cow disease.

Buddhists would be quick to point out that the Buddha himself, although an advocate of nonviolence or *ahimsa,* never enforced a strictly vegetarian diet, mainly because of the monastic tradition of alms begging in which any food offered was to be accepted with gratitude. Furthermore, the argument goes, all acts of consumption are linked with the destruction of life, as earth is disturbed and many organisms killed in the extraction of resources, the clearing of land for homes and buildings, and indeed in the farming of vegetables. Even breathing, as Jains acknowledge, is potentially fatal for certain organisms. Life requires the taking of life; welcome to planet Earth.

I am sympathetic to such arguments, and do understand how difficult it can be to change something so fundamental as one's eating habits. In my mind, however, the reality of life taking life can be seen as a spectrum, along which we must all orient ourselves. At one end might be the most conscientious Jain who eats only fallen nuts and berries, while on the other we can imagine a hardcore carnivore with the most lavish consumption habits. Just as we can make a legal distinction between petty theft and grand larceny, it seems reasonable to make ethical evaluations not in terms of right vs. wrong but in terms of harmful vs. less harmful. It should be emphasized that the spectrum of which I speak is meant to apply to particular *behaviors* rather than to judge individual *persons.*

As illustrated by the information above, our dietary choices alone have effects that extend from the health of our own body to the well-being of animals to the welfare of humanity and finally to the health of the planet as a whole. The case for reduced consumption of meat, which could have been made in any of the sections dedicated to self, others, other species, or the Earth (next section), becomes especially urgent at a time when the human population is straining the limits of the biosphere. Even more pressing is the fact that population growth is occurring most rapidly in large developing countries such as China and India where eating meat is widely regarded as a symbol of status and affluence. If only that high-income marker were heart- and eco-friendly menu items.

Most of us can probably recall learning about the food pyramid, which recommends meat and dairy as part of a healthy diet. As has been pointed out by Tom Robbins and others, the food pyramid and the four "food groups" were developed not by nutritionists but by the U.S. Department of Agriculture, which faced pressure from the meat and dairy industries to emphasize these foods. Fortunately, the pyramid has undergone some revision in recent years and is sometimes presented in the form of a unilateral, multicolored table. Readers might also recall the traditional food chain, with large carnivores at the top and tiny organisms and plants at the bottom, a hierarchical scheme that is also being abandoned in favor of a food web that highlights the complex network of interactions among living beings. The changes mentioned here reflect both a more sophisticated understanding of Nature and a more integral view of reality.

Many people who remain unconcerned about species loss find comfort in the prospect of cloning, perhaps imagining a futuristic Noah's ark scenario. Unfortunately, this kind of optimism relies on an old-paradigm way of thinking in which living beings are regarded as entirely independent and self-sufficient. In reality, each of the species on Earth has evolved in relation to other species and to the environment, meaning that even if humans could somehow harvest the DNA of every extant species on Earth, their survival in some kind of eco-bubble is certainly far from guaranteed. As understood by the ecologist and taken to heart by the Bodhisattva, every living thing—indeed every thing—exists as part of an integrated system, and to affect any part of the system is to affect the whole.

An understanding of interdependence raises questions about genetic manipulation in general. While this field of endeavor certainly holds promise for the curing of disease and the production of a more robust agriculture, its long-term effects on the gene pool, on human health, on biological diversity, and on the trajectory of life on Earth are far from clear. What is clear is that biotechnology, and science in general, must be approached with due caution and ethical consideration. With specific regard to plants, the Swiss ECNH states that "sound and appropriate justification is necessary if plants are to be instrumentalised so that they lose their ability to reproduce and adapt."[15] If this perspective seems limited or extreme, we might find inspiration in another quote from the Dalai Lama:

> We must begin by putting faith in the basic goodness of human nature, and we need to anchor this faith in some fundamental and universal ethical principles. These include a recognition of the preciousness of life . . . and—above all—the need to ensure that we hold compassion as the key motivation for all our endeavors and that it is combined with a clear awareness of the wider perspective, including long-term consequences.[16]

4.
WISE RELATION WITH
THE EARTH

When considering planet Earth, most people tend to think of a huge chunk of rock floating in space. Granted, there is a widespread recognition that Earth occupies a unique position relative to the Sun and happens to possess a special kind of atmosphere that supports carbon-based life forms—ideas that are commonly learned in grade school. But alas, few people have the chance to develop their conception of our precious planet beyond the elementary scientific one, and thus for the majority of modern humans the Earth remains an impersonal "third stone," capable of supporting life but lifeless in itself. This limited conception seems to explain a good deal about the current state of affairs.

The Gaia hypothesis of James Lovelock and Lynn Margulis was developed as an attempt to explain the Earth's homeostatic and self-regulatory processes. In its mildest form, the hypothesis states that terrestrial organisms have altered the composition of the Earth as a whole, while a stronger version proposes that the Earth and its creatures collaborate in maintaining the appropriate conditions for the existence and advancement of life itself. Stronger yet is the claim that all forms of life are something like cells in a larger planetary life form, named Gaia after the Greek goddess of the Earth. As influential as Lovelock's conception has been, it has predecessors in traditional Native American and shamanic mythology, and in the ideas of Johannes Kepler, Pierre Teilhard de Chardin, and Buckminster Fuller.

Perhaps the most radical interpretation of Gaia philosophy is that the Earth is in some way consciously coordinating its own internal dynamics in order to create and sustain life, perhaps even in the service of some greater evolutionary purpose. In the mind of biologist Rupert Sheldrake, the Earth, like all living things, is surrounded by a "morphogenetic field" that might behave something like a group mind from which all organisms receive information. While these ideas may rest more on spiritual faith than scientific provability, there is one sense in which the Earth is undeniably sentient and intelligent: through the minds of the sentient and intelligent creatures it has nurtured. Having evolved from the Earth's constituent components, humans in particular can be regarded as the consciousness of the

Earth, finally turning to face itself for the first time in 4.5 billion years. *Ecce "eco sapiens"*—behold knowing Earth.

If few modern humans conceive of the Earth as having a mind, then surely even fewer regard the Earth as having a soul. Such a notion was not so radical among the ancient Greeks, who spoke of the *anima mundi* or "world soul," first described by Plato in his treatise *Timaeus:* "... this world is indeed a living being endowed with a soul and intelligence ... a single visible entity containing all other entities, which by their nature are all related."[17] Recall that in ancient Greece, the "world" usually referred to all of nature and the *kosmos,* which was believed to extend only a few miles above the Earth, itself thought to be stationary, central in position, and relatively small in size.

Since the time of Plato, our understanding of the structure and scale of the Cosmos has undergone considerable revision, and in the process the Earth has lost its central status as well as its numinous essence. Fortunately, after millennia of dormancy, the soul of the Earth is taking rebirth in the modern cosmology of people like Thomas Berry and Brian Swimme, who consider the Earth a "biospiritual" planet. In his *Canticle to the Cosmos* series, Swimme describes the Earth as numinous, stating: "If any human in history is numinous or spiritual, it is only because the Earth in the primordial sense is numinous and spiritual."[18]

A BRIEF TOUR OF SOLAR SYSTEM AND PSYCHE

The notion that the Earth has a consciousness or a soul might find wider acceptance among those who believe that other bodies in the solar system possess their own characteristic energies. Such is the basis of astrology, which has also enjoyed something of a rebirth in recent decades, although its application seldom extends beyond the generic, Sun-sign horoscopes printed in the back of the daily paper and the weekly tabloids. In the ancient world, where spirituality and astrology had yet to diverge from science and astronomy, the study of the stars was considered quite a serious and lofty pursuit that required great depth of both intellect and intuition.

Although most commonly associated with the twelve signs of the zodiac, astrology can also be approached through the ten planetary archetypes: Sun, Moon, Mercury, Venus, Mars, Jupiter, and Saturn are known as the "personal" planets; Uranus, Neptune, and Pluto are the "transpersonal" planets. Notice that the Sun and Moon are considered planets and that the Earth is left out of this sequence, since it is regarded as the stationary focus or audience of the players on the cosmic stage. Each member of this revolving cast of characters can be understood as an archetype, an energy constellation that has both cosmic and psychic dimensions, as reflected in the ancient esoteric maxim "As above, so below." If one accepts the potency of these archetypes as well as the interpenetration of interior and exterior (or mind and matter), then it is easy to understand how the planets and the psyche might be involved in an intimate and synchronistic relationship in a universe in which all things dance together.

Like many people, I began my astrological investigation as a skeptic, although I was apparently open enough to receive what could only be called a revelation. I had been studying the planetary archetypes, each in isolation, when it dawned on me rather dramatically how they work together to form an intimate whole, a cohesive map of both cosmos and psyche. Their traditional astrological sequence can be seen to represent the evolution of consciousness, along at least four different but interrelated lines: intrauterine development; postnatal spiritual development; holotropic or shamanic experiences; and the death-rebirth experience, as outlined in many myths and traditional "books of the dead." Along with the realization of the evolution of consciousness on an individual level came an affirmation that the collective psyche does seem to be evolving in this same manner. The sequential discovery of the outer "spiritual" planets (Uranus in 1781, Neptune in 1846, and Pluto in 1930) speaks to the fact that astrology itself, while rooted in ancient principles, is a dynamic, unfolding, living system, much like the Cosmos with which it corresponds.

Both the evolution of consciousness and the planetary archetypes themselves can perhaps best be communicated through the story of a journey. This journey begins at the Sun, representing pure and radiant consciousness, from which emerges a sunbeam—the self, the rational ego. Venturing forth, our luminous hero meets the Moon— the physical and emotional form of the feminine, of the mother, of Nature herself. In encountering an "other," our hero realizes a need to communicate, calling upon Mercury, the mindful mediator and quick messenger. With Mercury's help, a harmonic connection manifests in the beautiful form of Venus, our hero's first romance. When disconnected from this love, our hero takes on the willful and aggressive nature of Mars. Boldly asserting himself in the world, he first meets the exuberant Jupiter, who generously offers support and encouragement, followed by the stingy and strict Saturn, who sternly reminds him of his limits and his mortality. Not to be deterred, our hero calls upon the rebellious and creative Uranus, who inspires him to push beyond the boundaries of the "real world" and venture fearlessly into new territory. Now independent and liberated, our hero emerges into the far-out dream world of Neptune, a place of shifting shapes, ephemeral spirits, and immortal gods and goddesses. The atmosphere is comfortable but confusing, and after what seems like an eternity, our hero finally encounters the tempestuous and demonic

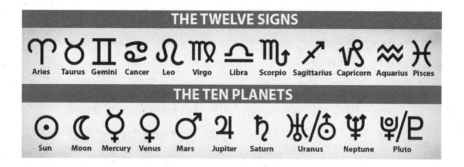

Pluto, who offers passage through a gateway of fire beyond which lies either a chaotic hell or a rebirth into the heavenly heart of the Sun.

It is interesting to consider that the two outer planets, Neptune and Pluto, sometimes switch position due to their highly elliptical orbits. In this scenario, our hero leaves the fiery fierceness of Pluto to encounter the watery wistfulness of Neptune. Also worth pondering is the recently discovered tenth planet (named Eris after the Greek goddess of war and strife), which is tentatively believed to represent chaos. If we imagine our hero's journey as an evolution of the collective consciousness of humanity, it appears that we are in the midst of a monumental transition between two of the outer planets, having already established our personality through our encounters with the inner planets. But where are we in our spiritual journey? Surely we can see Saturn in the limits of the biosphere and the breakdown of structures in the "real world," while Uranus strives to break free from old habits and outdated ways of thinking. But as we pass through Pluto's frightening canal, will we encounter the hellish chaos of Eris or be reborn into a new and higher form of solar consciousness?

While I hope it is informative and thought-provoking, this digression into astrology is primarily intended to illustrate that the Earth belongs to a larger family, namely the solar system. Just as each one of us is part of a larger holon called humanity, to which we strive to relate in meaningful ways, and as humanity is part of the Earth, which our species needs to relate to meaningfully, so the Earth relates to its closest neighbors in a meaningful way. The secondary purpose of this cosmic detour is to enter into a discussion of various possibilities for the future of our planet, with an understanding that astrology is far more suggestive than predictive, and an acknowledgment that ultimately the future must always remain uncertain. With those caveats in mind, let us resume our speculative voyage.

WORLD TRANSITS AND AGES

While many people understand astrology in terms of the personal horoscope or the natal chart, which depicts the position of the planets at the time of one's birth, astrology also has relevance for humanity at large. The position of the planets relative to the Earth and to each other, called "transits," can be assessed with respect to either the individual chart (personal transits) or the planet as a whole (world transits). At any given moment, each planet occupies a particular place in the heavens, and the angular relationships or "aspects" between and among these celestial bodies determine the energies at work. Of particular importance are conjunctions (when two or more planets occupy roughly the same position in the sky), oppositions (two planets at 180 degrees from one another), squares (angular relationships of 90 degrees), and trines (120 degree relationships). The more

MAJOR ASPECTS	Angular Relationship	Symbol	Type
Conjunction	0°	☌	Hard/dynamic
Sextile	60°	⚹	Soft/confluent
Square	90°	□	Hard/dynamic
Trine	120°	△	Soft/confluent
Opposition	180°	☍	Hard/dynamic

mathematically precise the aspect, the more powerful the effect. Also worth noting is that transits involving the faster-moving inner planets last only days, while those involving the slowly cycling outer planets may last for years or even decades. A few examples will help provide a clearer understanding of transits.

In terms of world transits, the Earth began experiencing in September 2007 a Saturn-Uranus opposition that will last until July of 2012. With Saturn representing breakdown and Uranus representing breakthrough, we can see the template for our current situation: the Great Turning occurring in the midst of the Great Unraveling, as well as a heightened tension between the forces of change and the status quo. (This opposition was exact on election day of 2008, when the younger, progressive, Uranian Obama faced off against the older, conservative, Saturnian McCain.) From 2009 through 2011, Saturn will also form a square with Pluto, a planetoid associated with powerful, deeply buried forces of transformation. The Saturn-Pluto combination is often linked with devastating events such as earthquakes (consider Haiti, Chile, and Japan) and with either a disruption or further entrenchment (Saturn) of power (Pluto).

From 2009 to 2020, Uranus will be squaring Pluto. During this period we can expect to see a certain resurgence of the tumultuous and revolutionary energy that manifested during the previous Uranus-Pluto transit of the 1960s through the early '70s. The emancipatory, inventive, and rebellious nature of Uranus—often associated with Prometheus, the fire-bringer—is likely to be amplified by the dynamism of Pluto, just as the unconscious, instinctual, and sexual energies of Pluto will likely be liberated by Uranus.

In his book *Cosmos and Psyche*, Richard Tarnas also makes note of a significant and prolonged relationship between Pluto and the second most distant planet, Neptune: a 60° aspect or "sextile" that began in the middle of the twentieth century and will continue until the middle of the twenty-first. Since Neptune is associated with altered consciousness and Pluto with raw energy, the hopeful expectation is that this archetypal combination will help initiate a new world-view. Given that the last Neptune-Pluto aspect took place during the eighteenth century and culminated in the Enlightenment and the American and French revolutions, we can at least expect "a more confluent relationship between nature and spirit, between evolutionary and instinctual forces, and the spiritual resources and idealistic aspirations of the pervading cultural vision."[19]

The current Neptune-Pluto sextile is also significant in that it marks the beginning of a new cycle:

> We are living today at the moment when ... the largest planetary cycles known to us have just completed their conjunctions in succession, marking the full initiation of the corresponding archetypal dynamics for the next several centuries ... Our present moment in history is most comparable, astronomically, to the period exactly five hundred years ago ... that brought forth the birth of the modern self during the decades surrounding the year 1500.[20]

As mentioned earlier and announced by the Fifth Dimension, the Earth is also making a transition out of the roughly two-thousand-year age of Pisces into the age of Aquarius. The Piscean age is widely believed to have been ushered in by Jesus, who spoke in the New Testament of the age after his, telling his disciples, "a man will meet you carrying an earthen pitcher of water; follow him into the house where he goes in" (Luke 22:10). According to some New Age thinkers, the water of Aquarius represents a quenching spiritual essence, while from an astrological perspective the water bearer himself is often described as visionary, creative, independent, individualistic,

RECENT, CURRENT, AND UPCOMING WORLD TRANSITS	
Saturn-Uranus opposition	2007–2012
Saturn-Pluto square	2009–2011
Uranus-Pluto square	2007–2020
Uranus-Pluto-Saturn T-square	2009–2010
Neptune-Pluto sextile	Mid-20th–Mid-21st centuries

intelligent, idealistic, intuitive, and sociable. Other Aquarian traits include universal tolerance and humanitarianism, as well as stubbornness and practicality. (Aquarius is a fixed sign that was ruled by Saturn until the discovery of Uranus.)

Also believed to be ending is the Kali Yuga, the last and darkest of the Hindu ages, which supposedly started around 3102 BCE. This age is associated with density, degeneration, and discord, and with the foul-smelling, apocalyptic male demon Kali. It is interesting to note that 3100 BCE was also right about the time at which the building of Stonehenge is believed to have begun, and is only a few years after the beginning of the current Mayan Long Count calendar, which began on August 11, 3114, and is scheduled to end on December 21, 2012.

2012 AND BEYOND

Surely no discussion of Earth cycles would be complete without mention of the ancient Maya and their calendar system, perhaps the most sophisticated and accurate ever devised. Before their rapid and mysterious decline in the ninth century, the Maya were expert astronomers who, without the aid of telescopes, calculated the length of the lunar month to within 34 seconds and were aware of both the precession of the equinoxes and of an energy source at the center of the Milky Way (believed by the ancient Maya to be the cosmic womb, now thought to be a black hole). To measure time, the Maya used as many as twenty different but interrelated calendars, based primarily on the numbers 20 and 13, which correspond to the number of digits and the number of major joints on the body. By multiplying these two numbers, the Maya developed a 260-day calendar that corresponds roughly to the human gestation period (260 is also the number of annual risings of Venus, whose cycle was well understood by the Maya).

The Mayan year or *tun* consists of 360 days, with 5.25 "nameless days" devoted to ceremony, while 400 Mayan *tun* (about 395 Gregorian years) comprise a *baktun*, thirteen of which comprise a "Sun" of 5,125 years. According to Mayan scholars, the thirteenth *baktun* and the Long Count calendar will terminate on the winter solstice of 2012, which also marks the end of a longer, 26,000-year Age consisting of five Suns, each ruled by a different element (as is the case with the four ages of the Hindus and of the ancient Greeks). On that fateful date, it is believed, the Sun will be perfectly aligned with the dark rift at the center of the Milky Way galaxy for the first time since the beginning of the previous precession cycle roughly 26,000 years ago, thus ending another great epoch in history.

MAYAN DIVISIONS OF TIME	Gregorian Equivalent (approx.)
1 *Kin*	1 day
1 *Winal* (20 *Kin*)	20 days
1 *Tun* (18 *Winal*)	360 days
1 *Katun* (20 *Tun*)	7,200 days (19.7 years)
1 *Baktun* (20 *Katun*)	395 years
1 Sun (13 *Baktun*)	5,125 years
1 Age (5 Suns)	25,625 years

For many, 2012 simply marks the end of one arbitrary cycle and the beginning of another, with no appreciable difference between the two. Others anticipate a dramatic and monumental transition into a brave New Age characterized by peace, prosperity, and universal enlightenment. Those who believe we have nothing to fear and everything to look forward to often describe the galactic center as a source of divine energy, something like a cosmic third eye, which by opening on December 21 of 2012 will facilitate the spiritual rebirth of humanity.

Another camp regards 2012 as a time of sudden global cataclysm or apocalypse, pointing to a number of apparently convergent prophecies of the Egyptian, Essene, Dogon, Aborigine, Hopi, Apache, Navajo, Cherokee, and Iroquois cultures, and the deeply considered concepts of scholars and authors like José Argüelles and Terence McKenna. Certain proponents of this view also find support in scientific data indicating that the Earth is due for some major changes such as: global climate shift, a deterioration and eventual reversal of the Earth's magnetic field, a period of intense and catastrophic solar activity, a collision of the solar system with an intergalactic energy cloud, increased volcanic and geothermal activity including the eruption of the Yellowstone supervolcano, and a devastating comet or asteroid impact.

While the scientific evidence for these doomsday scenarios is often quite compelling, all but perhaps climate shift remain speculative (especially in terms of time frame), or else outside human control and therefore beyond the reach of this book. Just as the Buddhist traditions focus on the pragmatic question of what can be done here and now to alleviate suffering, my concern lies primarily with the reality of the current global crisis, even if a fair amount of peripheral information has been offered up as food for thought. This chapter in

This image of the Milky Way highlights the so-called dark rift (also called the Cygnus Rift because of its proximity to that constellation), which is actually a cluster of giant dust clouds obscuring the stars in this portion of the galaxy. The Maya called this dark area Xibalba Be, the Road to the Underworld. The winter solstice sunrise has been aligned with this rift since the late 1990s, as it will be until about 2016.

particular is devoted to the idea that the cessation of global dis-ease is something that remains under the collective control of humanity rather than some extraterrestrial or metaphysical force.

With regard to the Mayan calendar, I believe that 2012 may indeed be an important and perhaps pivotal year, although I think it very unlikely that either global catastrophe or universal enlightenment will manifest on that exact date. While both breakdown and breakthrough are already in progress, it seems to me that investing in either one as an ultimate outcome is not only intellectually questionable but ecologically dangerous, as both rely heavily on extra-personal forces and fates, and thus discourage the taking of responsibility. If the future is in some way predestined for either ultimate good or bad, the rationale goes, then striving towards a healthier world is basically pointless, a conclusion that will surely result in further environmental ruin—a self-fulfilling prophecy in the case of the doomsday crowd. My own conviction is that the future will be determined by each one of us in the choices we make and the steps we take, and that our pathway is one that balances the possibility of ecological collapse with the promise of spiritual transformation.

5.
WISE RELATION WITH THE FEMININE

One of the attributes of the Kali Yuga is that it will be dominated by aggressive energy. As with the final age of classical mythology, the metal associated with this fourth age is iron, connected with the warrior god Mars and the planet named after him. In astrology, the symbol for Mars is the simplified sword and shield that has also come to represent the male gender. Having just emerged from the most violent and militaristic century in human history, and finding ourselves in a world defined by masculine, Martian energy, it is easy to see why our age is considered to be the last one before the *mahayuga* or "great cycle" begins anew.

Another traditional characteristic of the Kali Yuga that can be seen manifesting in our times is that the degenerate powers of the age will try to dismiss spiritual matters as old and outdated while attempting to convince everyone that materialism is the one and only reality. As noted, the Cartesian-Newtonian worldview that has prevailed for the last several hundred years seems to encourage the kind of materialism and consumerism being championed by economic powers such as the World Bank, the IMF, the G8, and other proponents of globalization, a movement that in turn contributes to militarism and the destruction of Nature. Unfortunately, both materialistic science and capitalist economics, while certainly not "degenerate" in themselves, are too often ruled by the ethic of progress at any cost, which could hardly be considered an ethic at all.

As the Hindu sages might point out, it hasn't always been this way. In earlier ages of humankind, the feminine played a larger role in the world, and indeed there was a period in human history when the feminine prevailed over the masculine. As suggested by archaeological evidence including Paleolithic cave paintings depicting female genitalia and the large-breasted figurines of the Mediterranean region, the earliest known cultures were often centered on a fertile mother goddess sometimes called the Great Mother. Given the default connection of early humans with natural cycles including menstruation and childbirth, it is easy to see how the primary creative force in the universe could be regarded as feminine.

During this period in prehistory there seems to have been very little warfare, evidently none on a large, organized scale. Although rivalries must have existed between neighboring clans, an absence of evidence such as fractured skulls, mass graves, or obvious weapons supports the idea that any inter-tribal disputes were usually settled peacefully. Given the low population density, the lack of permanent settlements, and the relatively equal access to resources, a common way to avoid conflict may have been to retreat or simply leave the area. Among our Paleolithic ancestors, a live-and-let-live approach seems to have prevailed.

After the Agricultural Revolution, the feminine was gradually supplanted by the masculine. While it might be tempting to blame a particular group such as the war-like and equestrian Aryan culture that is believed to have migrated southward from near the Caspian Sea, most historians suggest that the decreased status of the feminine was a result of the increased importance of physically demanding labor such as the ploughing of fields, and perhaps a greater emphasis on annual solar cycles over monthly lunar ones. Another possibility is that as the population grew and resources became scarcer, men and women decided mutually upon a division of labor and assumed roles that only in retrospect seem unequal, a scenario which, as Wilber points out, makes men appear less like oppressive pigs and women less like passive sheep.

Whatever the causes, the primary image of creativity and sustenance became masculine, as did popular conceptions of the Divine. Gods became more important and abundant than goddesses, and eventually many gods morphed into one God, with multiplicity itself becoming associated with the feminine. During the Roman Empire, paganism was expressly forbidden, and during the subsequent Christian era, female images of the Divine all but disappeared in the Western world. Certainly gone were the days when women held important spiritual positions as high priestesses, shamanic drummers, and magical healers; indeed such practices eventually came to be considered forms of witchcraft, which was regarded as evil and punishable by death. Even states of mystical rapture such as those experienced by Teresa of Avila or Joan of Arc were deemed questionable if not diabolical by the Christian church.

Although she was eventually canonized, Joan of Arc was persecuted during her life because of her mystical experiences.

Although women do hold more positions of power in the modern world, the sacred feminine is still generally viewed with suspicion by the mainstream, while on the margins paganism, Wicca, female shamanism, goddess worship, and natural healing have all seen a resurgence in recent decades. Ideally this largely underground movement will find a firmer foothold in the popular psyche and help counteract its widespread fear of the feminine, its general disregard for Nature, and its disconnection from her creative rhythms and regenerative cycles. Though we cannot return to the relatively peaceful, prehistoric epoch of the Great Mother, we can surely strive to find a greater harmony and balance in our overly Martian world and our overtly masculine worldview.

INTEGRATING THE ANIMA

In Chapter Two, I spoke of our current crisis as being rooted in various imbalances in the collective psyche, particularly in the West: increasing individualism and isolation leading to the loss of inter-subjectivity, the disenchantment of Nature and the Cosmos, the devaluation of the feminine, imbalance and antagonism between religion and science, and an increasing constriction of time and space. While each of these causes of global suffering is significant in its own right, they all can be seen as manifestations of an increasingly imbalanced relationship to femininity in general. For this reason the pathway being presented in this chapter emphasizes "wise relation" in an attempt to help create a more fundamentally feminine worldview.

The extreme individualism that pervades the modern world finds its origins in the birth of civilization itself and the rise of city-states, associated in this book with the birth of the solar, rational, and masculine ego, which has grown in strength and influence throughout "his story." The ideals of personal achievement, heroism, fame, and financial success have all but eclipsed a more feminine understanding that humans are fundamentally relational beings and that Nature and reality are characterized more by interconnection and interdependence than by autonomy and isolation. This is certainly not to say that women are incapable of being willful, assertive, and independent; rather, I am suggesting that this type of ego-driven energy is "masculine" in essence and overemphasized in the world at large.

When considering time, it seems apparent that in the Western worldview at least, a linear conception of time—as conveyed in phrases like "the arrow of time" and "the march of progress"—has replaced a more feminine understanding of time as rhythmic and cyclical. This will be discussed in greater detail in the section devoted to time, but for now I would like to point out that Western notions of time were quite literally born from the feminine. The Greek word *metre* (from which are derived the words "matter," "mother," and "measure") originally meant "uterus," suggesting that the original marker of time may have been the female cycle. A reasonable conclusion would be that as menstruation came to be regarded as unclean and even unholy, so did a cyclical understanding of time fall from favor, and with it fell humanity from a graceful state of living in harmony with the recurring movements of Nature.

The decline of the feminine has occurred more or less in tandem with a desacralization of the natural world and of matter, this largely due to the near-universality of the Mother Nature archetype. If the material world is understood as feminine, then anything non-material—consciousness, mind, psyche, or spirit—automatically becomes masculine, and a hierarchy is established, usually reflecting the one present in society at large. In many world religions, the material world is regarded as a trap from which the presumably masculine

259

Psyche is an ancient Greek goddess whose lover is Cupid (Eros to the Romans).

soul must escape or at least become disentangled, which indicates an underlying mistrust of the feminine and of carnality.

While it might seem somewhat logical or perhaps even unavoidable to assign a masculinity to psyche/consciousness and a femininity to matter/body, these attributions are ultimately arbitrary. For example, the ancient Greeks and Romans gave female attributes to Psyche, while her lover, as presented by Lucius Apuleius in his second-century novel *The Golden Ass*, was the god of love and sexuality known as Cupid to the Greeks and Eros to the Romans. Similarly, the Latin term *anima*, which means either "soul" or "mind," describes a feminine essence, with *animus* being its masculine counterpart (tellingly, in English this word means "hostility").

The terms *anima* and *animus* (both of which likely stem from the proto-Indo-European root word *ane*, meaning "to breathe") were used by Jung to describe the unconscious inner self in its feminine and masculine forms. According to Jung, it is the task of each male and each female to come to fully conscious terms with their *anima* and *animus* respectively, or else be controlled by them and doomed to form romantic attachments with others based largely on projection. In Jung's scheme, a healthy relationship with one's "other side," whether masculine or feminine, translates into healthier relationships with other people as well as an increased capacity for creativity and love. Such is the kind of integration and balance that needs to be established in the collective consciousness, in which we currently find an overabundance of masculine energy and *animosity*.

If a worldview can be understood as representing a collective psyche, it seems clear that the task of the modern mind is to encounter and embrace the *anima* from which it has become estranged. In describing this process of integration, Jung spoke of four different levels of *anima* development, each named after a different feminine archetype. During the first stage, the immature hero confronts the first woman, Eve, seen as an object of desire who is nevertheless regarded as evil and powerless—an image of the female usually presented in pornography. In the second phase, the hero meets Helen (of Greek mythology), who is seen as externally competent, self-reliant, and intelligent but nevertheless lacking in virtues such as faith and imagination. Third, the hero perceives the *anima* as the virtuous Mary (the mother of Jesus), and in the fourth stage, the hero regards the feminine as Sophia (the Greek goddess of wisdom). At this final stage, a man is developed enough to see women not as stereotypes but as individuals who possess both negative and positive attributes.

In describing a female's integration of her *animus*, Jung also divided the process into four phases, each corresponding to a different type of person: the athlete (embodying physical power), the planner (embodying the capacity for independent decision-making and action), the professor or cleric (embodying a philosophical stance), and the guide (embodying a wise, mediating force). To Jung, the *animus* was more multifaceted than the relatively monolithic *anima*. In

THE BUSINESS OF BIRTH[*]

Although the birth described above is symbolic, there is much to be said about the literal birth process, which has been dramatically altered by modern medicine. Over the last century, the age-old practice of what is now called "home birthing" has become increasingly rare, particularly in wealthier countries (in the U.S., UK, and Japan, the percentage has dropped to about 1 percent).[22] For the first time in history, most babies are delivered in an impersonal hospital environment, usually by men, for whose convenience mothers are made to lie on their back during labor rather than in a more comfortable and natural squat. The resulting restriction contributes to the liberal use of anaesthesia, epidurals, and other interventions that compromise and even sever the vital connection between mother and child during the birth process, which Grof considers the most definitive of shared initiations. Perhaps most disturbing is the growing popularity of induced labor and elective C-sections, which, while convenient and lucrative for doctors, introduce unnecessary risks and violence to both mother and child.

Meanwhile, the psychological effects of circumventing *the* archetypal rite of passage remain uncertain and worrisome. If we hope to establish a wiser relation with the feminine and restore trust in the wisdom of the body and of Nature, it would seem crucial that we reexamine our attitudes and actions surrounding the most fundamental human experience.

---

[*]The title of this section, and much of its content, are inspired by a 2008 documentary entitled *The Business of Being Born.*

terms of the latter, Jung understood the process of integration as a gradual opening of the male to his own emotional core, a process that enables him to form a new worldview incorporating intuition, creativity, imagination, psychic sensitivity, and unitive spirituality.

THE SACRED MARRIAGE AND ITS CHILD

When considering the development of a more balanced and integrated worldview, it should be emphasized that the feminine attributes just mentioned are not to be thought of as contents of the collective psyche but as descriptions of its character. In other words, the new paradigm is less about *what* we think than *how* we think, and therein lies the revolution. An integral worldview will embrace a more comprehensive epistemology in which knowledge and wisdom are accessible not solely through rationality but through a variety of modalities including physical, emotional, intuitive, psychic, and mystical.

Again, the key lies in balance, in this case between a left-brain, linear, solar, analytical way of thinking and a right-brain, cyclical, lunar, intuitive way of knowing. Just as it would be unwise and impossible to return to an Eden of the past, or to simply replace a Western outlook with an Eastern one, it would be unskillful to abandon the masculine in favor of the feminine. Despite the detrimental effects of a patriarchal paradigm, it has been a necessary part of our evolutionary process, without which we would have remained in a pre-rational, pre-egoic consciousness rather than being poised for a transcendence of this limited way of understanding and relating to the world. To quote a lengthy passage from the epilogue of *The Passion of the Western Mind:*

As Jung prophesied, an epochal shift is taking place in the collective psyche, a reconciliation between the two great polarities, a union of opposites; a *hieros gamos* (sacred marriage) between the long-dominant but now alienated masculine and the long-suppressed but now ascending feminine. . . .

For the deepest passion of the Western mind has been to reunite with the sacred ground of its own being . . . And that reunion can now occur on a new and profoundly different level from that of the primordial consciousness unity, for the long evolution of human consciousness has prepared it to be capable at last of embracing its own ground and matrix freely and consciously . . . And this is the great challenge of our time . . . to choose to enter into a fundamentally new relationship of mutuality with the feminine in all its forms. . . .

We seem to be witnessing, suffering, the birth labor of a new reality, a new form of human existence, a "child" that would be the fruit of this archetypal marriage, and that would bear within itself all its antecedents in a new form . . . Each perspective, masculine and feminine, is here both affirmed and transcended, recognized as part of a larger whole; for each polarity requires the other for its fulfillment. And their synthesis leads to something beyond itself: It brings an unexpected opening to a larger reality that cannot be grasped before it arrives. . . .[21]

6.
WISE RELATION WITH SPACE

Throughout this book, the Pali term *dukkha* has been rendered as "dis-ease," a variation on its usual translation as "suffering." Being composed of the root word *kha* (space) and the negative prefix *du*, its deeper meaning is that of a crowded or chaotic space. One might imagine a small, single-screen movie theater on the opening night of a long-awaited blockbuster, with hundreds of overly enthusiastic patrons attempting to squeeze through the front doors. Everyone is shoving and shouting, each insisting that they are the biggest fan or were the first in line and therefore deserve the best seat in the house. So it is in the theater of the mind, where every thought clamors to be front and center, screaming "Me me me!" while the manager tries to maintain order and civility. Her task is a tough one, made all the more so by her own sense of contraction and inner instability.

In Buddhist practice, the contraction of *dukkha* is not an abstract, philosophical concept but a real, palpable experience of the heart-mind that finds expression in the body. Surely we have all had those days when everything seems to go wrong, during which we might experience a throbbing headache, tension in the jaw, tightness in the neck and shoulders, clenched fists, or stomach cramps—all painfully obvious, physical manifestations of *dukkha*. According to the Buddha, such contraction is happening not only on stressful days but all the time, usually on a more subtle level, yet it is nonetheless detectable if one chooses to pay attention. Indeed one of the intentions behind meditation is to make the mind calm, steady, and ever more receptive to the subtler experiences of physical and emotional contraction.

On the other side of the spectrum is *sukkha,* often translated as "blissfulness." Again we have the root word *kha,* this time with a positive prefix, describing a vast, open, and harmonious space. One can imagine a blue summer sky with a few wispy white thought-clouds drifting by peacefully. Less metaphorically, most of us can probably recall at least one experience of being deeply relaxed yet highly alert, whether after a particularly effective session of massage, yoga, or meditation, or during a runner's high or other blissful, altered state.

A less common, more complete experience of *sukkha* is that of feeling completely at one with everything, free of all restrictions including the notion that "this experience is happening to me."

The Buddhist path can be understood quite simply as a movement from *dukkha* to *sukkha*—from relative restriction and dis-ease to greater spaciousness and bliss. On a smaller scale, this transition often occurs during a single session of meditation as the mind becomes more serene and open, more liberated from self-concepts and personal narratives of being a hero or a zero. Here the distinction must be made between *states* and *stages*, the former being temporary and the latter being more or less permanent. While progressing along the path, one may experience moments or even periods of *sukkha*, and the task is to learn how to strengthen and maintain such a state until it becomes established as a stage—the mind's new default setting. This is much easier said than done, given the tendency of the mind to grasp after what is pleasurable.

Herein lies a paradox and a great challenge. Blissful states of inner spaciousness provide valuable feedback that one is on the right track, yet clinging to them will surely cause further suffering, often in the form of storytelling: "Ahh, *sukkha* ... I must be a good meditator. Perhaps I will be enlightened soon!" or "Alas, more *dukkha* ... I am a bad practitioner and will never be liberated." As long as this kind of dynamic exists, one is certainly not enlightened, yet an awareness of this push-and-pull is itself enlightening. True liberation involves being free of even the desire to be free, yet one must possess this desire in order to make spiritual progress.

Right relationship to inner space, then, involves a skillful desire for *sukkha*, as well as an awareness of when the mind is in the grips of *dukkha*. Although the desire for liberation was allowed by the Buddha as the only wholesome sort, this desire itself must be free from selfishness, for as long as it is bound to a selfish urge, it is also attached to suffering. This detached-yet-engaged approach is what the Buddha meant by "right effort," what Lao Tzu meant by *wu wei* ("doing not doing"), and what the Dalai Lama calls "wise selfishness." In great people like these who have overcome the restrictions of the self, spaciousness of mind and heart arises naturally and is sustained without effort. Until one has reached such a state, skillful balance (or wise relation) between suffering and its cessation—between *dukkha* and *sukkha*—is key.

BUDDHIST COSMOLOGY

Greater spaciousness of the heart-mind or *citta*—inner spaciousness— brings about a sense of greater harmony in the outer world. This kind of *sukkha* is all the more important on an increasingly crowded planet, where expansive physical spaces are becoming harder to find. Even in affluent countries where personal space is valued and freedom of movement is feasible, the frequency of human interaction is historically high. At the same time, these interactions occur among a greater variety of ethnic and religious groups than in the past, when "the other" was typically viewed with immediate suspicion if not hostility. Our present circumstances thus demand greater tolerance and respect, not only towards our fellow (and female) earthlings but towards other forms of terrestrial life.

The apparent contraction of outer space, augmented by the speed of modern travel and communication, can be counteracted by the expansion of inner space to include the entire Earth community. As the world shrinks (virtually speaking), each of us can more easily wrap our heart-mind around it so that our sense of space extends beyond the personal and towards the universal. We can think less in terms of

This traditional Tibetan Buddhist painting or *thangka* depicts the *Bhavachakra* or wheel of life. Within the wheel are the six realms of existence: those of the gods (top), demigods (upper right), humans (upper left), animals (lower right), hungry ghosts (lower left), and hell beings (bottom). In the center of the wheel, desire, aversion, and delusion are depicted by a rooster, snake, and pig. The wheel itself is being held by Mara, the god of illusion.

me (and where on Earth I happen to be located) and more in terms of *we* (and where in space and time—in the cosmic adventure—that our planet happens to be); less in terms of individual welfare and more in terms of global survival and well-being. This increased spaciousness of the mind naturally elicits greater open-heartedness and compassion towards other beings with whom we share space-time.

In Tibetan Buddhist cosmology, ours is only one among six realms of space, the other five being those of the gods, the demi-gods, the animals, the hungry ghosts or *pretas,* and the hell beings. In the human realm, individuals suffer from clinging or grasping, while gods suffer from pride, demi-gods from jealousy, animals from ignorance and cruelty, *pretas* from insatiable hunger and thirst, and hell beings from anger and physical torment. Together these six realms constitute *samsara*—the realms of cyclical suffering, death, and rebirth, outside of which lie the countless realms of enlightened beings or Buddhas (the historical Buddha being merely one of these). Given that all individuals in *samsara* suffer, each one deserves compassion, including those who inhabit different realms of space and presumably cannot be seen.

This cosmic scheme not only expands the "bubble of compassion" beyond even the visible realm, it highlights the relationship between one's state of consciousness and one's conception of space, a correlation pointed out by Jean Gebser and emphasized throughout this book. In each of the realms of *samsara,* beings perceive their surroundings in a particular way depending upon their state of mind, whether prideful, jealous, desirous, unreflective, hungry, or angry. Although *samsara* is usually depicted as a wheel (called the *Bhavachakra*—the wheel of life or suffering), the six realms can also be imagined as being stacked on top of each other, with the god realm being quite spacious (a kind of "suffering lite" in which each individual gets his own cloud throne) and the hell realm being densely populated (with bodies stuffed into cauldrons and crammed between sheets of ice).

If taken metaphorically, the realms of *samsara* can be regarded as distinct types of earthly experience as determined by the *karma* of socioeconomic status: the upper-class "gods," the upper-middle-class "demi-gods" (who often envy the extremely wealthy), the working-class humans, the poor "animals," the homeless "hungry ghosts," and the psychologically disturbed "hell beings," all of whom experience varying degrees of mental and physical freedom (i.e., different senses of personal space, as reflected in sprawling mansions and crowded slums or prisons).

Finally, from a psychological perspective, the six realms can be understood as representing specific states of mind that all sentient beings experience at one time or another, each of which again influences one's sense of crowdedness or *dukkha*. In this metaphorical model, anger is a much more tight and contracted psychic space than pride, which is nevertheless a form of dis-ease.

ON EARTH AS IT IS IN HEAVEN

The close correspondence between inner space and outer space points to the fact that ultimately these two cannot be distinguished. Of course, on the relative level, each of us experiences a separation between our self and others—mentally, emotionally, and physically. We have different ideas and feelings about the world and occupy unique locations in space. But as we detach from these idiosyncrasies and begin to identify with the Earth and the entire Cosmos, such boundaries start to weaken and fade. Ultimately, all spatial limitations—distinctions between here and there, inner and outer, self and other—disappear completely. Not that one's normal perception of space ceases to function, but it is recognized and experienced as a kind of illusion or play.

One of the many practices of the Vajrayana path of Buddhism involves visualizing the material world, just as it is, as a perfect Buddha realm. In what could be considered extreme or full-contact optimism, the space in which you find yourself is seen to be suffused with divine radiance, with every object sacred and symbolic, every individual an enlightened Buddha, every action geared towards the happiness and liberation of all beings. Even unfortunate events are seen as precious opportunities, giving rise to feelings of joy, deep gratitude, and spaciousness. Form becomes emptiness; *samsara* becomes *nirvana*.

To perceive the world as an enlightened realm is surely a challenge, especially at a time when genuine suffering is so widespread. But this meditation may bring about temporary experiences of *sukkha* that could one day lead to a permanent shift of consciousness. As a practice, its function is to facilitate not an external change but an internal one, and therein lies its promise and its danger. If approached unskillfully, this Vajrayana meditation may lead to a sense of complacency, a false notion that since everything is perfect, no change is necessary and no action is required—why not just sit back and enjoy the scenery? Such an attitude is typical in the god realm, where the suffering of beings in other realms tends to go unheeded, and also occurs all too often among

The symbol of Vajrayana Buddhism is the *vajra,* a ritual object associated with a thunderbolt and symbolic of penetrating insight. Its feminine counterpart is the bell, symbolizing emptiness.

affluent humans and those who believe too strongly in the "secret law of attraction" and the idea that each of us creates our own reality. The truth is that we all face difficult trials and unforeseen losses and therefore deserve compassion. We don't have complete control over the circumstances of our lives, but we do have a fair—and ideally increasing—amount of control over how we react to them.

My point is that this world, whether perceived as absolutely perfect or hopelessly flawed, demands our active participation and compassionate engagement, our unconditional acceptance and love. Personal *karma* has brought us to a particular place on Earth, and our collective *karma* has brought our species to a particular point in history—a period of intensifying contraction and dis-ease that must be encountered and counteracted with an equally spacious mind and an open heart.

7.
WISE RELATION WITH TIME

Since the early part of the twentieth century, science has understood that space and time are not separate, fixed entities but are dynamically intertwined as space-time. This revolutionary insight is apparent on the intergalactic and subatomic levels but remains counterintuitive on the human level. In our daily experience, space and time do seem to be independent as described by classical physics, and for this reason they are treated separately here. Still, the hope is that the interpenetration of space and time will become clearer as we proceed.

Considered on its own, time is clearly a mysterious phenomenon that has inspired much philosophical debate and speculation over the centuries. Does time exist independent from thought? Does it exist independent of events that occur "over" time? How long is "the present" and when or how does it become the past? Does time flow in only one direction, and if so, why? If time does flow, is its movement regular or variable? What exactly *is* time? Mystics tend to assert that time is merely an illusion, while philosophers and scientists tend to agree that time does exist, but often disagree on what it is and how it functions.

Aristotle defined time as the "measure of change," implying that it is only perceived (or perhaps inferred) from the observation of processes. In this "relational" theory of time, there is no time apart from change. Later thinkers like the seventeenth-century physicist Isaac Barrow and his student Isaac Newton disagreed with Aristotle, asserting that time is absolute; it exists and has always existed on its own, apart from change and motion which occur "within" time. Notice that this dispute between physical time and psychological time is essentially a variation on the familiar feud between science and spirituality, between epistemology and ontology, between the immanent chicken and the transcendental egg. The question—also begged by the proverbial tree that falls in the forest—is what, if anything, exists independent of perception? In other words, is there an objective reality? Or, how much does mind matter?

Einstein's 1905 theory of special relativity demonstrated that time moves at different speeds for observers moving at different velocities, particularly when approaching the speed of light, at which time begins to slow down. This seems to support the psychological theory of time, except that Einstein's "observers" were never explicitly defined as sentient beings; they could just as well be mechanical clocks or simply abstract points of reference. The usual understanding, however, is that Einstein disproved the idea that time exists independently of observation, leaving open the question of whether time exists apart from events (a second form of absolutism).

To Einstein's contemporary Hermann Minkowski, the relativity of time indicated the existence of something more fundamental, an underlying reality not subject to variation from one frame of reference to the next. Indeed this substrate is space-time, defined by Einstein as a four-dimensional continuum, with time as a unique, one-dimensional sub-space of this continuum. Einstein's model has since gained nearly universal acceptance in the scientific community, although some of its kinks are still being worked out through string theory and quantum loop gravity, both of which are outside the scope of this discussion and, frankly, over my head.

The conventional Newtonian view of time has been dealt a serious uppercut by Einstein and a staggering left hook by subsequent physicists, who have observed instantaneous, non-local connections between subatomic particles. This and other quantum-level discoveries challenge the convictions of both Newton and Einstein that everything in the universe must move slower than the speed of light, and also defy traditional notions of cause and effect. Moreover, they once again emphasize the importance of the observer, thereby scoring another point for Aristotle and his relational theory of time.

THE SPIRAL OF EXISTENCE

Another proponent of relational time was Jean Gebser, who noted that one's experience of time, like one's perception of space, depends upon one's form of consciousness. Throughout evolution and history, humanity's relationship to time has undergone many changes and revolutions, as outlined earlier. Prehistoric cultures encountered and measured time through natural cycles of days and nights, lunar cycles, and seasons, and later through an increasingly sophisticated tracking of the movements of the planets and stars. During the mental structure of consciousness beginning with the ancient Greeks, time became increasingly linear, particularly during the Christian era, during which St. Augustine and later Thomas Aquinas conceived of time as a straightforward progression from Genesis to Judgment. This religious redefinition was made explicit by the abandonment of lunar calendars and the widespread adoption of the solar *Anno Domini* calendar.

In the time since Christ, the Western mind's conception of time has become further removed from organic cycles, with time's measurement becoming more mathematical and regular, more precise and incremental. Since the Industrial Revolution, time has become increasingly bound up with productivity and money, while circular clocks have been all but replaced by digital timepieces—a series of numbers now globally synchronized by satellite. With most humans now living in light-polluted cities, our collective connection with the stars has literally faded, and with it our relationship to the mystery and majesty of the Cosmos. Meanwhile, most of us have gotten so

The *ouroboros*, from an alchemical text.

accustomed to *doing*—moving, shaking, and multi-tasking—that we have forgotten how to *be*—how to abide comfortably in the present without fretting about the future or dwelling on the past.

Indeed, although modern humans—particularly those of us living in developed countries—undoubtedly enjoy more overall freedom and affluence than ever before, it could be argued that our peculiar relationship with time has made us more psychologically impoverished and imprisoned than any people who have ever lived. By and large, we have a poor understanding of both our historical and evolutionary past. Our fascination with novelty has made us forget—or at least take for granted—the remarkable achievements of our forebears, including those of the first living cell from which we all descend. Our obsession with progress has not only harmed the Earth but hindered our own happiness, which always seems to lie in the near future, just out of reach. We know little of eternity and have instead become ever more tightly bound by clock time, which, like our planet's resources, seems to be growing scarcer by the moment.

While the West has come to regard time as linear, many Eastern cultures continue to think in terms of circles or cycles, such as that of death and rebirth, often symbolized by a wheel. A variation on the theme of reincarnation is that of eternal recurrence, an idea with roots in ancient Egypt and branches in the Pythagorean and Stoic schools of ancient Greece. Also called "eternal return," this system of thought, which has been symbolized by the alchemical *ouroboros*, or snake biting its own tail, is based on the notion that the universe is infinite in duration and finite in matter, and therefore any given configuration is bound to repeat itself indefinitely. Some thinkers, like Nietzsche, have applied this idea to human existence, suggesting that each of us is fated to repeat our life, without variation, an infinite number of times. In true existentialist fashion, Nietzsche called the idea "horrifying and paralyzing," the "heaviest weight"[23] imaginable, unless one can somehow come to truly love one's life and fully embrace one's fate.

While the philosophy of eternal recurrence might inspire certain people to live in the best possible way, it regards free will as nothing more than an illusion. Still, if the illusion is thoroughly and eternally convincing, then making wise choices is nonetheless crucial and this incarnation is just as meaningful as any in the past or future. Similarly, the "identity of indiscernibles" put forward by Leibniz states that any number of things with the exact same characteristics (lives, in this case) are essentially the same, therefore living an infinite number of identical lives is just like living one life. Furthermore, the basic premise of eternal return—that time is infinite and matter finite—seems to be at odds with the current scientific understanding that the universe was born at a specific point in the past and will continue to expand until all of its energy dissipates. Our own Sun will fizzle out in about five billion years and eventually the entire universe will grow cold, dark, lifeless, and inert.*

Cosmologically speaking, many Eastern traditions also regard the universe as eternal, forever expanding and contracting, expanding and contracting like a divine diaphragm. But these traditions deviate considerably from the fatalism of eternal recurrence in that they allow for the possibility of change, purification of one's *karma*, and eventual liberation from the cycle of rebirth (alternatively, one may

---

*Alternatively, the universe contains enough mass to reach a point of maximum expansion and then begin contracting until it again becomes a singularity that may once again explode. Another theory suggests that continued expansion will indeed result in heat death, at which time another Big Bang will occur somewhere in the universe and the cycle will continue, *ad infinitum*. Yet another option is that our universe is just one of countless multiverses eternally popping in and out of existence in different dimensions.

choose to become a Bodhisattva and remain in *samsara* until all beings are liberated). The existence of free will and choice means that the future is always open-ended.

If the traditional Christian notion of time can be visualized as an arrow, and eternal return as a circle or ouroboros, then most spiritual paths can be seen as a spiral: cyclical yet different at each go-around. My suggestion is that this symbol could just as well represent integral thinking, as it fuses the linearity of left-brain, rational, analytical thinking with the circularity of right-brain, creative, intuitive thinking; the solar with the lunar, the masculine with the feminine. In two dimensions, the spiral connects inner and outer, while a 3-D spiral also connects upper and lower. Like the universe and a single human lifetime (or a series of lifetimes), the spiral is fractal in nature and goes through certain cycles or stages—ascending towards greater

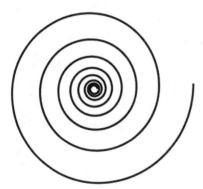

order, integration, and complexity or descending towards disorder, disintegration, and entropy (or going in both directions at once). As a line with both centrifugal and centripetal directionality, the spiral symbolizes the paradox of evolution and involution (or creativity and entropy).

TYPES OF TIME

From a purely subjective point of view, the movement of time is obviously not fixed and absolute. Time flies when you're having fun, drags during traffic jams or boring lectures, and for some reason seems to speed up over the course of a lifetime. When applied to individual awareness, Gebser's idea that one's perception of time is dependent

upon one's mindset is consistent with many mystical traditions including Buddhism, in which time may be transcended altogether during
certain states or at some eventual stage of spiritual evolution. To transcend time is to encounter eternity, understood not as "a very long
time" but as being beyond or outside temporality. Just as all spatial
limitations of here and there are overcome in *nirvana,* one no longer
experiences past, present, and future in the conventional sense but
inhabits what is often called "the eternal now."

Gebser wrote that "freedom from time is freedom *per se.*" Although
this phrase rings true, it could also be misinterpreted as escapist, as
could Buddhism and perhaps mysticism in general. While certain
schools of the so-called small vehicle (Hinayana) branch of Buddhism
do prioritize personal emancipation, the Mahayana (great vehicle)
schools recognize that individual liberation is bound up with collective liberation and therefore emphasize the Bodhisattva ideal. My
own viewpoint is that the world, particularly in its vulnerable and
dis-eased state, is better served by the wisdom, patience, selflessness,
and compassion of the Bodhisattva than by the aspirant who wishes
to leave the world and its cares behind.

Joanna Macy would surely agree, her claim being that what is
needed most direly is not a way to escape from time but to inhabit
time in a more thorough and holistic way. What we must overcome is
the modern tendency towards short-term thinking and instant gratification, learning instead to experience a "deep time" that honors
the work and wisdom of our ancestors while considering the welfare
of beings that will live many generations in the future. At the same
time, there must be a recognition of the undeniable poignancy of
the present and the transformative power of timelessness—a fuller
appreciation of the "four times" of past, present, future, and eternity.
To experience deep time, then, is to experience the present moment

as absolutely unique in cosmic history yet as eternal as any other—a precious opportunity to wake from the dreams of the past and create a better future.

In Greek mythology, the god of time was Kronos or Chronos, whose name inspired the English words "chronometer," "chronology," "chronicle," etc. Often depicted as an aged, bearded man (picture the more modern images of Father Time), Kronos presided over ordinary or linear time as measured by calendars and timepieces. A second god of time was Kairos, associated not with quantitative time but with qualitative or extraordinary time. Usually symbolized by a young man, Kairos represents the opportune or perfect moment in which something significant and decisive happens, the "now" in which action must be taken. Usually charged with emotion, Kairos moments are those that linger in our memory.

As Jung observed and many agree, we are currently living in a moment of *kairos*. Although industrial society has fallen deeper and deeper under the mesmerizing spell of Kronos, the spirit of his youthful counterpart still lives within us, inviting us to step through the doorway into a new and better world and worldview. Such a monumental transition must occur relatively quickly if we are to avert a large-scale, systemic collapse, yet it must happen organically; it cannot be rushed or forced. Our spiritual challenge, it seems, is to "make haste slowly," balancing *chronos* and *kairos*, doing and being, linear and circular time, history and the eternal now.

LOOKING BACK THROUGH TIME

The discoveries of astrophysicists and the insights of mystics invite speculation about time travel—is such a thing possible? In a physical sense, probably not, unless someone manages to build a device capable of moving at the speed of light, flying through a black hole, or squeezing through a wormhole in space-time. In another sense, however, time travel is always happening in our field of perception. Whenever we look at something, what we are seeing is that thing as it existed in the past, since the light it reflects (or radiates, according to Alfred North Whitehead) has taken a certain amount of time to reach our eyes. Granted, for earthly objects the time lag is small enough to be negligible, but the case is altogether different when we cast our gaze towards the heavens.

To look up at the stars (or down, if you prefer to imagine it as such) is to peer back through time, sometimes millions or even billions of years. Consider the Andromeda Galaxy, for example, our nearest galactic neighbor, which appears as a fuzzy dot located in the constellation of Andromeda. By the time the light from this sister galaxy reaches your retina, it has been traveling for 2.5 million years, since the very dawn of humanity. What a trip to consider the evolutionary journey that has taken place since those photons first began their own epic race through space at 186,000 miles per second.

Meanwhile, within the constellation of Sagittarius lies the center of our own galaxy, widely believed to be marked by a massive black hole. Stars closest to this sacred heart of the Milky Way lie almost 30,000 light-years away, meaning that their light has been streaking through space since the period of the first Paleolithic cave paintings and the last of the saber-toothed tigers.

With a little research, everyone older than four years should be able to find a star whose light has been traveling since the time of their birth. In my case, the star is 36 Ursae Majoris, located almost 42 light-years away, well within our cozy corner of the Milky Way. At the other extreme, the light from the furthest stars has been traveling for billions of years, since before the Earth and Sun existed, while the invisible background radiation hails from the very beginning of the universe and, theoretically, of time itself.

As Brian Swimme points out in *The Hidden Heart of the Cosmos*, light from the Andromeda Galaxy and from millions of other stars has been emanating throughout human history, reaching the eyes of Neanderthal hunters, Babylonian kings, Roman emperors, Renaissance artists, and Romantic poets. Only relatively recently, however, have we developed the technology and the intellectual capacity to decode the information carried in this light and translate it into a cohesive cosmology—a universe story that has actually been here all along. As star-stuff gazing up at starlight, we have been gradually coming to this story just as it has been literally streaming towards us; we have begun to wake up to our place in space and time. To quote Swimme: "The human is the space created in the universe process for hearing and celebrating the stories of the universe that fill the universe."[24]

8.
WISE RELATION WITH THE DIVINE

Having made it past space and time, we are now officially on shaky ground, for the question of whether there exists a metaphysical "ground of existence" is obviously the subject of much debate. Indeed it may be the most vexing question ever faced by humanity, which seems uniquely blessed/cursed with a deep and abiding desire to get to the bottom of it all. Stated simply, the fundamental question is whether or not there is a God, the basic complication being in defining what "God" might be. Theologians usually think in terms of an omnipotent creator or Supreme Being; the philosophically

In constructing this diagram of the "72 Names of God," the seventeenth-century religious scholar Athanasius Kircher drew mainly from esoteric Jewish writings.

inclined might imagine a more abstract force, essence, or guiding principle; mystics try to describe an indescribable state of pure bliss or a field of conscious energy; some folks equate god with love; and atheists believe that all of these believers—and the vast majority of the world's people—are fooling themselves.

The Abrahamic traditions have tended to personalize the Divine, assigning it a gender and human attributes like benevolence and anger as well as proper names—Yahweh or Jehovah or Allah—while to Christians, God can be named as well as recognized in physical human form as Jesus. Religiously minded Hindus worship Shiva, Vishnu, Krishna, Lakshmi, or any number of India's countless gods and goddesses, whereas mystically inclined Hindus conceive of these as universal forces rather than actual beings and generally favor a monism centered on Brahman or the Absolute, which does not have

283

human characteristics. Other Eastern traditions speak of the Divine in similarly abstract terms such as the Ultimate, the Unmanifest, the Ground, the Tao, Non-duality, Suchness, or Being.

Buddhism is essentially non-theist, meaning that it makes no claims about the actual, ontological existence of a divine creator. The Buddha himself was philosophically agnostic and literally silent on the subject, preferring to speak only about that which could be known, with knowledge based on direct experience. He demanded no deference to any religious authority, including his own, and often told his followers *"ehi-passiko,"* meaning "come see for yourself." Although one might consult respected teachers or sacred scriptures along the Buddhist path, the primary responsibility lies with the practitioner, who may eventually come to discover her own numinous Buddha nature.

As a mystical path, however, Buddhism does have something to say about the ground of existence, which is that there really is no *terra firma* upon which to stand. The ultimate reality or *Dharma*, according to the Buddha, is *shunyata* or emptiness, which does not mean that nothing exists, rather that nothing exists as wholly independent or self-sufficient. In a tangible way, all beings depend upon other beings and on the Earth and Sun, while in a more abstract way, forms depend upon space, space and time are interdependent, time could not exist without eternity, etc. Everything owes its existence to ever-changing and interdependent causes and conditions, and our habit of thinking of things—possessions, positions, friends, lovers, emotional and physical states—as unchanging and independent is the cause of our attachment and the source of our dis-ease.

Mystical traditions tend to be less concerned with *conceptions* of ultimate reality than with *experiences* of ultimate reality and hence usually prescribe some means of achieving higher states of consciousness, whether through meditation, breathing techniques, visualization, chanting, dance, the ingestion of sacred medicines, or some combination of the above. The Buddhist path, which values both knowledge and experience, combines study and practice to facilitate a deepening realization of emptiness, which is not an escape to some otherworldly paradise but a full comprehension of things as they really are. To an enlightened mind, the world appears just as it appears to an unenlightened mind, except that the former "sees through" conventional appearances; she becomes liberated from attachment, not from the world. To discourage escapism or attachment to non-attachment, certain Buddhist texts expound upon "the emptiness of emptiness," meaning that *shunyata* is not a conclusion at which to finally arrive but an ongoing process of non-arrival.

IMMANENCE AND TRANSCENDENCE

Somewhat separate from the question of God's existence is whether divinity is immanent or transcendent—an integral part of the material world or something wholly distinct from it. Many prehistoric peoples and indigenous cultures have tended towards the former orientation, conceiving of the natural world as populated and animated by spirits that may or may not be connected to a universal Great Mother or a Great Spirit. During the Axial Age, the elemental gods and goddesses began to give way to a single, transcendent, male God who was either loosely, occasionally, or mysteriously connected with the world, while Plato and Aristotle drew a line in the ether by arguing in favor of transcendence and immanence, respectively.

Some theistic traditions consider God to be both immanent and transcendent, simultaneously in the world and outside of it (a position called panentheism). Christianity, for example, regards Jesus the Son as the main manifestation of God the Father, with the Holy Spirit as

285

a sort of link between heaven and earth. By contrast, Deism, which was popular among Enlightenment-era Europeans, conceives of God as a totally transcendent being who created the universe as an intricate machine and then absconded—a watchmaker who watches but does not intervene. On the other philosophical extreme is pantheism, which regards divinity as entirely immanent, with no distinction between Nature and the Divine. To an atheist, meanwhile, God is neither here nor there.

Throughout this book I have been using the term "the Divine" instead of "God," as the latter usually refers to a masculine Supreme Being in general or the Judeo-Christian deity in particular. "The Divine" strikes me as more spiritual than religious—a fairly generic term that applies equally well to polytheism, monotheism, deism, pantheism, or panentheism. As you may have figured, my belief is that the Earth and the Cosmos are sacred and numinous, a pantheistic sentiment that allows room for polytheistic or animistic interpretations of the world. Thanks in part to Jung and his formulation of archetypes, I can relate to "the spirit of the mountain" or the Great Mother as psychologically real and relevant, while in regard to their ontological existence—and that of a Supreme Being—I follow the Buddha's lead by pleading the Fifth.

Of particular interest to me are the possible intersections of Buddhism and pantheism (of which deep/integral cosmology, it seems to me, is a variant) and how these two systems might relate to a new worldview that is more ecologically sensitive, more philosophically versatile, and especially more compassionate. If Buddhism and pantheism value Buddha nature and Nature respectively, then their integration—a recognition of the Buddha nature of Mother Nature—may help create a more sacred, sane, and hospitable world in which all lives are revered and all lifestyles respected. Although humans may never be able to create a heaven on Earth in the physical sense, Buddhism and pantheism acknowledge that the possibility does exist in a psychological sense. Both traditions recognize that heaven is not something far off in space and time, rather it is immanent and imminent; it exists here and now. As Jesus said, "the Kingdom of the Father is spread out upon the earth, and men do not see it."

Roughly two hundred years after Christ, the Indian philosopher Nagarjuna similarly taught that *"samsara is nirvana; nirvana is samsara."* Apart from the Buddha himself, Nagarjuna is perhaps the most respected figure in the Buddhist world, having expounded upon the concept of emptiness and proposed a "two-truths" doctrine that distinguishes between conventional reality or *dharma* and absolute reality or *Dharma*, which coexist harmoniously. Based partly on this important concept, Nagarjuna developed a system of logic similar to the Greek tetralemma in which all assertions about a given subject are ultimately rejected. In the following example, none of the individual statements below would be regarded as true, but taken together they reflect the most sublime truth:

> *God exists. God does not exist.*
> *God both exists and does not exist.*
> *God neither exists nor does not exist.*

NON-DUALITY, WONDER, AND MYSTERY

According to mystics, conventional and ultimate reality are resolved in non-duality, a form of consciousness in which all seeming opposites—existence and non-existence, time and eternity, self and other, good and bad, light and dark—are unified or transcended. In the

287

Hindu school of Advaita Vedanta, for example, the individual self ·or *atman* is said to be ultimately identical with Brahman or the Absolute, while in the Nyimgma school of Tibetan Buddhism (which disavows *atman*), the term "Dzogchen" refers to a method of achieving non-dual awareness and, in true non-dual fashion, non-duality itself. Also called "The Great Perfection," Dzogchen is regarded as the true nature of mind, likened to a flawless mirror that reflects form but is not affected in any way by its reflections. It is described as pure, primordial awareness: radiant, all-pervasive, indestructible, incorruptible, and complete.

While mystical traditions tend to agree that non-duality is the ultimate reality, there is a fair amount of disagreement in sacred literature about the characteristics of this reality, leading some philosophers to question its ultimateness. Are all spiritual traditions really just different paths to the same goal, as suggested by religious scholars like Joseph Campbell and Huston Smith, or do different descriptions of God indicate different destinations altogether? Is it just a question of terminology, or is Reality really just relative? To me, the obvious difficulty in answering this question and in describing the Divine underscores the fact that it can never be fully apprehended by the rational mind. It lies beyond reason, thought, and language, in the realm of mystery. My belief is that the very ground of existence is Mystery, the subjective experience of which is Wonder.

"Wonder" is a wonderful word, with a few distinct connotations. Usually people wonder about particular unknowns that can actually be known, given a little effort ("I wonder what time the movie starts") or a little patience ("I wonder if it will rain this evening"). This kind of wonder is not very gripping, at least relative to wondering about deeper questions such as the meaning of life, the origin and fate of the universe, the nature of suffering, or the existence of God. But even this type of wonder, being largely intellectual or conceptual in nature, is not the most powerful. In its most potent form, wonder is a type of awe that opens the heart to the sublime, ineffable, and paradoxical nature of existence.

The German philosopher Martin Heidegger described our period in history as the end of "the first beginning," an age that began with the ancient Greeks. In contrast to the early philosophers, who understood wonder *(thaumazein)* as the "beginning of philosophy," modern humans have lost much of their capacity for wonder and genuine thought, as indicated by Nietzsche's proclamation of God's demise. According to Heidegger, wonder has been replaced by "its thief," curiosity, which arises in the face of the unusual and presupposes existence as the usual order. Wonder, by contrast, sees the most usual as the most unusual; "in wonder, we stop taking for granted the fact that things are . . . The . . . extraordinary is right under our noses; what is wondrous is that beings be."[25] In other words, the most mysterious and wonderful thing is existence itself—the simple fact that there is something instead of nothing.

A full experience of wonder is both emotional and deeply spiritual. It may in fact be the most pure and genuine of spiritual experiences, available not only to mystics but to each of us in our everyday lives. Wonder involves surrender, letting go of the compulsion to know, to quantify, to control, to grasp. As a kind of radical unknowing, wonder is selfless and therefore liberating. It inspires quiet joy, true reverence, overwhelming gratitude, and deep humility. To quote Einstein:

> He to whom this emotion is a stranger, who can no longer wonder and stand rapt in awe, is as good as dead . . . To sense that behind anything that can be experienced there is something that our minds cannot grasp, whose beauty and sublimity reaches us only indirectly: this is religiousness.[26]

As an embodiment of *thaumazein,* Einstein is also alleged to have said: "There are only two ways to live your life. One is as though nothing is a miracle. The other is as though everything is a miracle."[27] For my part, I have tried to convey the idea that humanity is not the result of a single miracle that occurred a few thousand years ago; the much more unbelievable truth is that our existence is due to a continuous and unbroken chain of miracles stretching back almost 14 billion years, and receding into infinity.

Since we all desire and perhaps require a certain amount of psychological security, an open-ended, wonder-filled orientation to the Divine presents a spiritual challenge. To fully embrace Mystery is to practice an openness of the heart-mind, a spaciousness or *sukkha* that can accommodate and even celebrate uncertainty and paradox. An openness of *citta* also invites compassion, which in the end is the most valuable spiritual treasure. In this sense, I am at heart an ethical pragmatist who believes that the ultimate worth of any belief system lies less in its "truthiness" than in its ability to engender feelings of love and compassion. What matters most is not what you think, but how you feel and act, particularly in regard to other living beings. If your belief system fails to make you a more kind, tolerant, respectful, forgiving, patient, loving, and peaceful person, then it is essentially useless.

At the end of the day, we are all left squinting into the twilight of what Lao Tzu called "the Mystery of Mysteries," humbled to the core by the "ineffable beauty and fragility" described by astronauts and celebrated by artists and poets. Their words, songs, and images may be the deepest expressions of global truth that we have.

"MIRACLES" BY WALT WHITMAN

Why, who makes much of a miracle?

As to me, I know of nothing else but miracles,

Whether I walk the streets of Manhattan,

Or dart my sight over the roofs of houses toward the sky,

Or wade with naked feet along the beach just in the edge of the water,

Or stand under trees in the woods,

Or talk by day with anyone I love, or sleep in the bed at night
* with anyone I love,*

Or sit at table at dinner with the rest,

Or look at strangers opposite me riding in the car,

Or watch honey bees busy around the hive of a summer forenoon,

Or animals feeding in the fields,

Or birds, or the wonderfulness of insects in the air,

Or the wonderfulness of the sundown, or of stars shining so quiet
* and bright,*

Or the exquisite delicate thin curve of the new moon in spring;

These with the rest, one and all, are to me miracles,

The whole referring, yet each distinct and in its place.

To me every hour of the light and dark is a miracle,

Every cubic inch of space is a miracle,

Every square yard of the surface of the earth is spread with the same,

Every foot of the interior swarms with the same.

To me the sea is a continual miracle,

The fishes that swim—the rocks—the motion of the waves—the ships
* with the men in them,*

What stranger miracles are there?

EPILOGUE

To insist upon what you are and who you are and the meaning of your life, to insist that "this is it," is to condemn yourself to a partial story. It's only when you move into chaos that novelty can emerge . . . Because something new and precious has entered into our life; we don't know what it is, but we're certain of one thing: if we try to fit it into the structures of meaning that we already have, those structures will eliminate it. . . .

What's happening in our time is "geotherapy" . . . a therapeutic event of the whole earth. For self-awareness to understand its embeddedness in matter is for the whole earth to alter its functioning. We are in this tremendous moment of ordeal, but what happens in the midst of ordeal is that a new voice is heard . . . A story emerges from the very center of the ordeal; it's the gift in the middle of the despair.

—Brian Swimme[1]

A common Chinese saying goes: "May you live in interesting times." Depending on one's perspective, this can seem like either a benevolent blessing or a malevolent curse. These are certainly interesting times on planet Earth; on that point most of us would probably agree. But the question that seems to be on so many minds is whether being alive during this period—characterized by considerable suffering, irrevocable loss, and accelerating change during which one can take nothing for granted—is a stroke of good fortune or bad.

This dilemma reminds me of another Chinese export, a folk tale of Taoist origin: An old, poor farmer once owned a beautiful mare, until one day she ran away. When the neighbors heard the news, they all visited the farmer's house with long faces, saying, "Oh, how unfortunate you are!" to which the farmer calmly replied, "We shall see." A few weeks later, the mare returned, accompanied by a magnificent stallion. Again the neighbors all came to see the farmer, this time smiling and saying, "Oh, how fortunate you are!" to which the farmer again said, "We shall see." A few days later, the farmer's son was out riding the new stallion when he fell from the saddle and broke his leg. Upon hearing of this, the neighbors again dropped by to see the old farmer, this time saying with sadness, "Oh, how unfortunate you are!" to which the farmer again said, "We shall see." Soon thereafter, a war broke out in the region, and when the army came looking for recruits, the farmer's injured son was excused from fighting. Again the neighbors visited the old farmer, telling him, "Oh, how fortunate you are!" to which the farmer again replied, "We shall see." And on the story goes. . . .

The moral, it seems, is that any attitude towards one's personal circumstances is simply a temporary state of mind based on an inability to see the larger context and accept the reality of ongoing change. It's just the "feeling tone" that automatically arises in reaction to whatever might be happening. It's the voice of the ego always announcing its approval or disapproval, regardless of whether the object of consideration is a particular event (yay or nay), one's life in general (thumbs up or thumbs down), or the current global crisis (a cosmic coming-of-age or a karmic reckoning).

When surveying the bigger picture, such as that presented by photos of the Earth from space and by books like this one, it seems clear that we are all living in extraordinary times. Whether one regards this as fortunate or unfortunate would seem to hinge upon one's spiritual beliefs—is there a purpose to life? Is there a reason for being alive at this particular time? Do we each have a destiny to fulfill? Do we share a collective destiny? Perhaps this life was chosen for us. Or perhaps we ourselves chose to be born into this particular form and this particular family, at this particular time, in order to learn certain lessons, share certain talents, or communicate certain truths.

Whatever the case, here we are, smack in the middle of reality. We don't necessarily have to like it, but we do have to come to terms with it (even denial and escape are forms of engagement, albeit not the most skillful). From a Buddhist or Taoist perspective, whatever arises is simply the blossoming of seeds planted in the past, over which we have no control in the present. What we *can* control, however, is how we face the situation at hand, and our ability to respond skillfully depends upon the quality of our consciousness and the content of our character, the state of our heart and mind.

There is no denying that humanity currently faces enormous and unprecedented challenges. At the same time, these challenges are unique only in degree, not in essence. As the Buddha pointed out, life in any era is fraught with trials and tribulations, and all sentient beings are confronted with the same basic task: that of finding a way to deal with change, impermanence, and loss with grace, equanimity, and compassion.

We live at a time of increasing chaos, but out of chaos and disruption emerges great creativity, as conveyed by the quotation above.

295

We live at a time of rapid and accelerating change, but as we all know, change is the only constant in life, the only thing we can truly rely on.

We live at a time of great uncertainty, but then again everything in life is uncertain, except the inevitability of death. Paradoxically, to embrace mortality is to live fully and fearlessly.

In one sense, then, our situation is not completely unique. Yet during these extraordinary times, some of us may be called upon to do extraordinary things, of which we might never have dreamed we were capable. Just as the world may be radically transformed in the forthcoming decades, so might we who live through this period become completely different from the people we are today. Even more than usual, we are being asked to remain unattached to ego and expectation.

Apart from our individual talents, skills, knowledge, and wisdom, each of us shares one particularly remarkable trait: that of self-reflective awareness. From a subjective point of view, this too may seem at times like a spiritual blessing and at others an existential curse. But from a global perspective, humanity's unique form of consciousness clearly represents a great power, with which comes great responsibility.

Are we finally willing to accept our role as caretakers of the Earth, of other species, and of each other? Are we ready to become full global citizens? Will we accept "the present" as a precious and miraculous gift from eternity, not to be squandered or cast aside?

As the old Chinese farmer says, "We shall see."

APPENDIX: POEMS

We Are the Ones We've Been Waiting For

You have been telling the people that this is the Eleventh Hour.
Now you must go back and tell the people that this is The Hour.

And there are things to be considered:

Where are you living?
What are you doing?
What are your relationships?
Are you in right relation?
Where is your water?
Know your garden.
It is time to speak your Truth.

Create your community. Be good to each other. And do not look outside
yourself for the leader.

This could be a good time!

There is a river flowing now very fast. It is so great and swift that there are
those who will be afraid. They will try to hold on to the shore. They will feel
they are being torn apart, and they will suffer greatly.

Know the river has its destination. The elders say we must let go of the shore, push off into the middle of the river, keep our eyes open, and our heads above the water. See who is in there with you and celebrate.

At this time in history, we are to take nothing personally. Least of all, ourselves. For the moment that we do, our spiritual growth and journey comes to a halt.

The time of the lone wolf is over. Gather yourselves!

Banish the word "struggle" from your attitude and your vocabulary.

All that we do now must be done in a sacred manner and in celebration.

We are the ones we've been waiting for.

— The Elders Oraibi, Arizona Hopi Nation
http://www.spiritofmaat.com/messages/oct28/hopi.htm

The Metta Sutta

This is what should be done
By one who is skilled in goodness,
And who knows the path of peace:
Let them be able and upright,
Straightforward and gentle in speech.
Humble and not conceited,
Contented and easily satisfied.
Unburdened with duties and frugal in their ways.
Peaceful and calm, and wise and skillful,
Not proud and demanding in nature.
Let them not do the slightest thing
That the wise would later reprove.
Wishing in gladness and in safety:
May all beings be at ease.

Whatever living beings there may be,
Whether they are weak or strong, omitting none,
The great or the mighty, medium, short or small,
The seen and the unseen,
Those living near and far away,
Those born and to-be-born,
May all beings be at ease.
Let none deceive another,
Or despise any being in any state.
Let none through anger or ill-will
Wish harm upon another.
Even as a mother protects with her life
Her child, her only child,
So with a boundless heart
Should one cherish all living beings,
Radiating kindness over the entire world.
Spreading upwards to the skies,
And downwards to the depths;
Outwards and unbounded,
Free from hatred and ill will.
Whether standing or walking, seated or lying down,
Free from drowsiness,
One should sustain this recollection.
This is said to be the sublime abiding.
By not holding to fixed views,
The pure-hearted one, having clarity of vision,
Being freed from all sense desires,
Is not born again into this world.

NOTES

Introduction

1. From www.solarviews.com/eng/earthsp.htm.

ONE: The Reality of Global Suffering

1. Wikiquote, http://en.wikiquote.org/wiki/Marcus_Aurelius.
2. Jung, Carl. *Alchemical Studies, Vol. 13,* paragraph 335, page 265.
3. Suess, Eduard. *Die Entstehung Der Alpen* (The Origin of the Alps). Vienna: W. Braunmuller, 1857.
4. Wikipedia, http://en.wikipedia.org/wiki/IPCC_Fourth_Assessment_Report.
5. Hansen, Sato, Kharecha, Beerling, Berner, Masson-Delmotte, Pagani, Raymo, Royer, and Zachos. "Target Atmospheric CO_2: Where Should We Aim?"; http://arxiv.org/pdf/0804.1126v3.
6. "CO_2 Levels Up 40% since Industrial Revolution: Study." *Financial Times,* May 14, 2008; http://www.financialexpress.com/news/co2-levels-up-40-since-industrial-revolution-study/309160/.
7. "Global Warming Basics." National Resources Defense Council; www.nrdc.org/globalwarming/f101.asp.
8. "An Accurate Picture of Ice Loss in Greenland." *ScienceDaily,* October 10, 2008; www.sciencedaily.com/releases/2008/09/080930081355.htm.
9. Adam, David. "Meltdown Feared as Arctic Ice Cover Falls to Record Winter Low." *Guardian,* May 15, 2006; www.guardian.co.uk/world/2006/may/15/antarctica.environment.
10. Brown, Lester R. *Plan B 3.0: Mobilizing to Save Civilization.* New York: W.W. Norton, Inc., 2008, page 49.

11. Brahic, Catherine. "Sea Level Rises Could Far Exceed IPCC Estimates." *New Scientist,* September 1, 2008; www.newscientist.com/ article/dn14634-sea-level-rises-could-far-exceed-ipcc-estimates.html.

12. Hansen, James. "Huge Sea Level Rises Are Coming Unless We Act Now." *New Scientist,* July 25, 2007; www.newscientist.com/article/ mg19526141.600.

13. International Union for the Conservation of Nature; www.planetwork.net/climate.

14. "Half of Mammals 'in Decline', Says Extinction Red List." Agence France Press, October 6, 2008; http://afp.google.com/article/ ALeqM5hpftiFBrckhaI_mtTA15UzqTfubg.

15. "Rainforest Alliance." CopperWiki; www.copperwiki.org/index.php/ Rainforest_Alliance.

16. "Forest Holocaust." *National Geographic Online;* www.nationalgeographic.com/eye/deforestation/effect.html.

17. "UN Issues Desertification Warning." BBC News; http://news.bbc.co.uk/2/hi/africa/6247802.stm.

18. Cornell University. "Soil Erosion Threatens Environment and Human Health, Study Reports." *ScienceDaily,* March 23, 2006; http://www .sciencedaily.com/releases/2006/03/060322141021.htm.

19. "Loss of Topsoil." Center for Earth Leadership; http://earthleaders .org/publications/stress_topsoil.

20. "WHO Challenges World to Improve Air Quality." World Health Organization; www.who.int/mediacentre/news/releases/2006/ pr52/en/print.html.

21. "Indoor Air Facts No. 4 (revised), Sick Building Syndrome." U.S. Environmental Protection Agency; www.epa.gov/iaq/pubs/sbs.html.

22. "Oil Pollution." Smithsonian Institution; http://seawifs.gsfc.nasa .gov/OCEAN_PLANET/HTML/peril_oil_pollution.html.

23. Dumas, Daisy. "Landfill-on-Sea." *The Ecologist Online,* February 7, 2009; www.theecologist.org/pages/archive_detail.asp?content_ id=1169.

24. "Review of the State of the World Fishery Resources: Marine Fisheries." Food and Agriculture Organization (Rome, Italy); www.fao.org/docrep/003/w4248e/w4248e35.htm.

25. "Coral Triangle: Protecting the Most Diverse Reefs on Earth." The Nature Conservancy; www.nature.org/wherewework/asiapacific/coraltriangle/about/.

26. Mackay, Neil. "U.S. Forces' Use of Depleted Uranium Weapons Is 'Illegal.'" *Common Dreams,* March 30, 2003; www.commondreams.org/headlines03/0330-02.htm.

27. U.S. Department of Energy Five-Year Plan FY 2007-2011, Volume II, March 15, 2006.

28. "Nuclear Waste." Marathon Resources; www.marathonresources.com.au/nuclearwaste.asp.

29. Brown, page 49.

30. Diamond, Jared. "What's Your Consumption Factor?" *New York Times online,* January 2, 2008; www.nytimes.com/2008/01/02/opinion/02diamond.html.

31. "Planet's Tougher Problems Persist, UN Report Warns." UNEP; www.unep.org/Documents.Multilingual/Default.asp?l=en&ArticleID=5688&DocumentID=519.

32. Brown, page 27.

33. Bush, Jason. "China and India: A Rage for Oil." *Business Week,* September 25, 2005; www.businessweek.com/magazine/content/05_36/b3949086_mz015.htm.

34. "State of World Cities Report 2008/9." UN-Habitat; www.unhabitat.org/content.asp?cid=6040&catid=7&typeid=5&subMenuId=0.

35. Machel, Graça. "Impact of Armed Conflict on Children." UNICEF; www.un.org/rights/introduc.htm.

36. Wikipedia, <http://en.wikipedia.org/wiki/Casualties_of_the_Iraq_War#cite_note-tribune-19.

37. Orszag, Peter. "Estimated Costs of U.S. Operations in Iraq and Afghanistan and of Other Activities Related to the War on Terrorism." U.S. Congressional Budget Office, October 24, 2007.

38. "The Cost of War." American Friends Service Committee; www.afsc.org/Iraq/ht/display/ContentDetails/i/19245.

39. "Sunburn, Smoking, Alcohol and Obesity Fuelling Rising Cancer Rates." *Cancer Research UK*, August 8, 2007; http://info.cancerresearchuk.org/news/archive/pressreleases/2007/august/348735.

40. "Obesity and Overweight." World Health Organization; www.who.int/dietphysicalactivity/publications/facts/obesity/en/.

41. "Childhood Overweight and Obesity." WHO; www.who.int/dietphysicalactivity/childhood/en/.

42. "Depression." WHO; www.who.int/mental_health/management/depression/definition/en/.

43. "Heart Disease." Centers for Disease Control; www.cdc.gov/heartdisease/.

44. "Cardiovascular disease: prevention and control." WHO; www.who.int/dietphysicalactivity/publications/facts/cvd/en/.

45. "2008 Report on the Global AIDS Epidemic." UNAIDS; www.unaids.org/en/KnowledgeCentre/HIVData/GlobalReport/2008/2008_Global_report.asp>.

46. Gallup-Healthways Well-Being Index; www.well-beingindex.com/.

47. Macy, Joanna. *World as Lover, World as Self: Courage for Global Justice and Ecological Renewal.* Berkeley, CA: Parallax Press, 2007, page 18.

TWO: The Roots of Global Suffering

1. Nietzsche, Friedrich. *The Gay Science.* Vintage: New York, 1974, pages 181–182.

2. Macy, Joanna. *World as Lover, World as Self: Courage for Global Justice and Ecological Renewal.* Berkeley, CA: Parallax Press, 2007, pages 44–45.

3. Gebser, Jean. *The Ever-Present Origin.* Athens, OH: Ohio University Press, 1953, page 43.

4. Ibid., page 46.

5. Ibid., page 67.

6. Ibid., page 71.

7. Wikipedia, http://en.wikipedia.org/wiki/Ishmael_(novel).

8. Wikipedia, http://en.wikipedia.org/wiki/Ishmael_(novel).

9. Gebser, page 77.

10. Tarnas, Richard. *The Passion of the Western Mind: Understanding the Ideas That Have Shaped Our World View.* New York: Ballantine Books, 1991, page 19.

11. Kirk, G.S., and Raven, J.E. *The Presocratic Philosophers.* Cambridge: University Press, 1957.

12. McEvilley, Thomas. *The Shape of Ancient Thought: Comparative Studies in Greek and Indian Philosophies.* New York: Alworth Press, 2002.

13. Tarnas, page 114.

14. Ibid., page 189.

15. Ibid., pages 274–275.

16. Ibid., page 280.

17. Ibid., page 302.

18. Ibid., page 301.

19. Ibid., page 317.

20. Ibid., page 338.

21. Ibid., page 343.

22. Ibid., page 356.

23. Ibid., page 389.

24. Kirkegaard quotes, www.goodreads.com/author/quotes/6172.S_ren_Kierkegaard?page=2.

25. Tarnas, page 400.

26. Ellis, David. "Exxon Shatters Profit Records." CNN Money.com; http://money.cnn.com/2008/02/01/news/companies/exxon_earnings/.

27. Madslien, Jorn. "Military Spending Sets New Record." BBC News, June 8, 2009.

28. Nietzsche, Friedrich. *Thus Spoke Zarathustra.* Third Part, 45, "The Wanderer." New York: Penguin, 1969.

THREE: The Relief of Global Suffering

1. Jung, Carl. "The Undiscovered Self," in *Collected Works of Carl Gustav Jung*, vol. 10. Princeton: Princeton University Press, 1970, paragraphs 585–586.
2. Wikiquote, <http://en.wikiquote.org/wiki/Albert_Einstein.
3. TED talks, www.ted.com/talks/stephen_petranek_counts_down_to_armageddon.html.
4. Bache, Christopher. *Dark Night, Early Dawn.* Albany, NY: State University of New York Press, 2000, page 220.
5. Ibid., page 231.
6. Ibid., page 240.
7. Ibid., page 241.
8. Ibid., page 242.
9. Ibid., page 243.
10. Ibid., page 245.
11. From www.thomasberry.org.
12. Gebser, Jean. *The Ever-Present Origin.* Athens, OH: Ohio University Press, 1953, page 6.
13. Jeans, James. *The Mysterious Universe.* Cambridge: Cambridge University Press, 1930, Chapter 5.
14. Einstein, Albert. "Mein Weltbild" (My Worldview), published as "The World as I See It" in *Forum and Century*, 1930, and in *Living Philosophies*, New York: Simon and Schuster, 1931.
15. Swimme, Brian. *Canticle to the Cosmos* (video series). Center for the Story of the Universe, www.brianswimme.org.
16. Swimme, Brian. *The Hidden Heart of the Cosmos: Humanity and the New Story.* Maryknoll, NY: Orbis Books, 1996, page 100.
17. Bohr, Neils. *Atomic Theory and the Description of Nature.* Cambridge: Cambridge University Press, 1934, page 54.
18. From http://thankgodforevolution.com/endorsements.
19. Owen, Richard. "Vatican Adds Seven Deadly Sins Including Damaging Environment and Drug Dealing." Fox News; www.foxnews.com/story/0,2933,336330,00.html.

20. Wilson, Edward O. *The Future of Life*. New York: Vintage Books, 2002, page 158.

21. Ibid.

22. Hawken, Paul. *Blessed Unrest: How the World's Largest Movement Came into Being and Why Nobody Saw It Coming*. New York: Penguin, 2008, pages 188–189.

23. "15 Greenest Cities." *Grist*, July 19, 2007; www.grist.org/article/cities3/.

24. O'Carrol, Eoin. "Ecuador constitution would grant unalienable rights to nature." *Christian Science Monitor*, September 3, 2008; www.csmonitor.com/Environment/Bright-Green/2008/0903/ecuador-constitution-would-grant-inalienable-rights-to-nature.

25. The Earth Charter Initiative website, www.earthcharterinaction.org/content/.

26. Layard, Richard. "Happiness: Has Social Science a Clue?" March 2003; http://cep.lse.ac.uk/events/lectures/layard/RL030303.pdf.

27. Pinchbeck, Daniel. "How the Snake Sheds Its Skin" in *The Mystery of 2012: Predictions, Prophecies and Possibilities*. Boulder, CO: Sounds True, 2007, page 330.

FOUR: The Road to Recovery

1. Calaprice, Alice. *The New Quotable Einstein*. Princeton: Princeton University Press, 2005, page 206.

2. Obama's "Chorus of Millions" Speech, February 5, 2008. The line "we are the ones we have been waiting for" was first penned by poet June Jordan in a piece entitled "Poem for South African Women." It was also used by Alice Walker as the title of a book of essays published in 2006. The line appears in a widely circulated poem attributed to the Arizona Hopi Nation (see page 235).

3. Global World Economy, http://en.wikipedia.org/wiki/World_economy.

4. Wilber, Ken. "Monumentally, Gloriously, Divinely Big Egos." *One Taste, The Journals of Ken Wilber*, http://wilber.shambhala.com/html/books/ontast_mogobi.cfm/.

5. Jung, Carl Gustav. *Memories, Dreams, Reflections.* New York: Vintage Books, 1965, page 325.

6. His Holiness the Dalai Lama. *The Universe in a Single Atom.* New York: Broadway Books, 2005, page 199.

7. From www.novaroma.org/via_romana/stoicism.html.

8. Pinchbeck, Daniel. "How the Snake Sheds Its Skin" in *The Mystery of 2012: Predictions, Prophecies and Possibilities.* Boulder, CO: Sounds True, 2007, page 332.

9. Smith, Wesley J. "The Silent Scream of the Asparagus." *The Weekly Standard,* May 12, 2008, Volume 013, Issue 33; www.weeklystandard .com/Content/Public/Articles/000/000/015/065njdoe.asp.

10. (Swiss) Federal Ethics Committee on Non-Human Biotechnology (ECNH). "The Dignity of Living Beings with Regard to Plants," page 10.

11. Steinfeld, Gerber, Wassenaar, et al. "Livestock's Long Shadow: Environmental Issues and Options." Food and Agriculture Organization of the United Nations, page 22 (in PDF).

12. Ibid., page 23 (in PDF).

13. Goodland, Robert, and Anhang, Jeff. "Livestock and Climate Change"; www.worldwatch.org/files/pdf/Livestock%20and%20 Climate%20Change.pdf.

14. Alanne, Mikko. "Meat the Truth." September 24, 2009; www. huffingtonpost.com/mikko-alanne/meat-the-truth_b_299187.html.

15. (Swiss) Federal Ethics Committee on Non-Human Biotechnology (ECNH), page 11.

16. His Holiness the Dalai Lama, page 199.

17. Wikipedia, http://en.wikipedia.org/wiki/Anima_mundi_(spirit).

18. Swimme, Brian. *Canticle to the Cosmos* (video lecture series). Center for the Story of the Universe; www.brianswimme.org.

19. Tarnas, Richard. *Cosmos and Psyche: Intimations of a New World View.* New York: Plume, 2007, page 482.

20. Ibid., page 480.

21. Tarnas, Richard. *The Passion of the Western Mind: Understanding the Ideas That Have Shaped Our World View.* New York: Ballantine Books, 1991, pages 443–445.

22. Wikipedia, http://en.wikipedia.org/wiki/Home_births.

23. Wikipedia, http://en.wikipedia.org/wiki/Eternal_return.

24. Swimme, Brian. *The Hidden Heart of the Cosmos: Humanity and the New Story.* Maryknoll, NY: Orbis Books, 1996, page 66.

25. Stone, Brad Elliott. "Curiosity as the Thief of Wonder: An Essay on Heidegger's Critique of the Ordinary Conception of Time." *Kronoscope* 6.2, 2006, page 9.

26. Einstein, Albert. "Mein Weltbild" (My Worldview), published as "The World as I See It" in *Forum and Century*, 1930, and in *Living Philosophies*, New York: Simon and Schuster, 1931.

27. From http://www.goodreads.com/quotes/show/987.

Epilogue

1. Swimme, Brian. *Canticle to the Cosmos* (video series). Center for the Story of the Universe; www.brianswimme.org.

PRIMARY SOURCES

Bache, Christopher. *Dark Night, Early Dawn*. Albany, NY: State University of New York Press, 2000.

Brown, Lester R. *Plan B 3.0: Mobilizing to Save Civilization*. New York: W.W. Norton, Inc., 2008.

Gebser, Jean. *The Ever-Present Origin*. Athens, OH: Ohio University Press, 1953.

Ghose, Sri Aurobindo. *The Future Evolution of Man: The Divine Life Upon Earth*. Twin Lakes, WI: Lotus Press, 1974.

Grof, Stanislav. *Psychology of the Future*. Albany, NY: State University of New York Press, 2000.

Harding, Stephan. *Animate Earth: Science, Intuition and Gaia*. White River Junction, VT: Chelsea Green Publishing Company, 2006.

Hawken, Paul. *Blessed Unrest: How the World's Largest Movement Came into Being and Why Nobody Saw It Coming*. New York: Penguin, 2008.

His Holiness the Dalai Lama. *The Universe in a Single Atom*. New York: Broadway Books, 2005.

Hopkins, Rob. *The Transition Handbook: From Oil Dependency to Local Resilience*. Devon, UK: Green Books Ltd., 2008.

Jung, Carl Gustav. *Memories, Dreams, Reflections*. New York: Vintage Books, 1965.

Macy, Joanna. *World as Lover, World as Self: Courage for Global Justice and Ecological Renewal*. Berkeley, CA: Parallax Press, 2007.

Mathews, Freya. *For Love of Matter: A Contemporary Panpsychism*. Albany, NY: State University of New York Press, 2003.

Mitchell, Donald W. *Buddhism: Introducing the Buddhist Experience*. New York: Oxford University Press, 2002.

Pinchbeck, Daniel. *2012: The Return of Quetzalcoatl.* New York: Penguin Books, 2006.

Primack, Joel, and Abrams, Nancy. *The View from the Center of the Universe: Discovering Our Extraordinary Place in the Cosmos.* New York: Riverhead Books, 2006.

Simon, Tami (publisher). *The Mystery of 2012: Predictions, Prophecies and Possibilities.* Boulder, CO: Sounds True, 2007.

Swimme, Brian, and Berry, Thomas. *The Universe Story: From the Primordial Flaring Forth to the Ecozoic Era, A Celebration of the Unfolding of the Cosmos.* New York: Harper Collins, 1992.

Swimme, Brian. *The Hidden Heart of the Cosmos: Humanity and the New Story.* Maryknoll, NY: Orbis Books, 1996.

Swimme, Brian. *Canticle to the Cosmos* (video lecture series). Center for the Story of the Universe.

Tarnas, Richard. *Cosmos and Psyche: Intimations of a New World View.* New York: Plume, 2007.

Tarnas, Richard. *The Passion of the Western Mind: Understanding the Ideas That Have Shaped Our World View.* New York: Ballantine Books, 1991.

Wilber, Ken. *Integral Psychology.* Boston: Shambhala Publications, 2000.

Wilson, Edward O. *The Future of Life.* New York: Vintage Books, 2002.

INDEX

Sentience, 233, 235–36
Sextiles, 248, 249–50, 251
Shadow
  concept of, 19
  confronting, 17–20
Shamanism, 194–95
Shamanism: Archaic Techniques of Ecstasy (Eliade), 194–95
Sheldrake, Rupert, 243
Shelley, Mary, 123–24
Shunyata, 173, 284–85
Sick building syndrome, 37
Sierra Club, 184
Simplicity, voluntary, 44
Smith, Huston, 288
Smog, 36
The Social Contract (Rousseau), 122
Socrates, 10, 95–96, 115, 126
Solar system
  in astrology, 244–48
  diameter of, 169
  formation of, 75–76
  location of, 170
  models of, 108–11
Sophia, 261
Space
  integral consciousness and, 165–67
  perspective and, 104
  structures of consciousness and, 101–2
  time and, 272
  wise relation with, 264, 265–72

Species
  extinctions of, 27, 29–33
  wise relation with other, 233–42
Speech, right, 200, 202
Spinoza, Baruch, 112
Spiral, as symbol, 278
Spiritual emergencies, 160
Spirituality
  renaissance of, 191–93
  transformational vs. translational approaches to, 204–6
Sprawl, 49–51
Squares (astrological), 248, 249, 251
Stars
  formation of, 75
  light from, 281–82
  nearest, 169
Stoics, 60, 97–99, 225–26
Strong, Maurice, 189
Strong anthropic principle (SAP), 179
Subjectivity, 119–21
Sudan, war in, 51–52
Suess, Eduard, 20
Suffering. *See also Dukkha*
  cause of, 65, 144
  The Four Noble Truths, 11, 15, 143–44
  reactions to, 18
Sufism, 205
Sukkha, 265–67, 271, 290

ABOUT THE AUTHOR

D arrin Drda is a writer, artist, and musician who has traveled widely and worked under the auspices of the Dalai Lama. He is a longtime practitioner and occasional instructor of Insight meditation, and a facilitator for the Awakening the Dreamer symposium, which promotes ecological sustainability, social justice, and spiritual fulfillment. Drda holds a Master of Arts degree in Philosophy, Cosmology, and Consciousness from the California Institute of Integral Studies in San Francisco.

ABOUT EVOLVER EDITIONS

EVOLVER EDITIONS promotes a new counterculture that recognizes humanity's visionary potential and takes tangible, pragmatic steps to realize it. EVOLVER EDITIONS explores the dynamics of personal, collective, and global change from a wide range of perspectives.

EVOLVER EDITIONS is an imprint of the nonprofit publishing house North Atlantic Books and is produced in collaboration with Evolver LLC, a company founded in 2007 that publishes the web magazine Reality Sandwich (www.realitysandwich.com), runs the social network Evolver.net (www.evolver.net), and recently launched a new series of live video seminars, Evolver Intensives (www.evolverintensives.com). Evolver also supports the Evolver Social Movement, which is building a global network of communities who collaborate, share knowledge, and engage in transformative practices.

For more information, please visit www.evolvereditions.com.